REFORMING THE CHICAGO TEAMSTERS

Reforming the
CHICAGO
TEAMSTERS

The Story of Local 705

ROBERT BRUNO

Northern

Illinois

University

Press

Library of Congress Cataloging-in-Publication Data

Bruno, Robert, 1955–

Reforming the Chicago Teamsters : the story of Local 705 / Robert Bruno.

   p.   cm.

Includes bibliographical references and index.

ISBN 0-87580-596-5 (alk. paper)

1. International Brotherhood of Teamsters, Chauffeurs, Warehousemen, and Helpers

of America—History. 2. Teamsters Local 705 (Chicago, Ill.)—History. 3. International

Brotherhood of Teamsters, Chauffeurs, Warehousemen, and Helpers of America—

Corrupt practices—History. 4. Teamsters—Labor unions—United States—History.

5. Truck drivers—Labor unions—United States—History. 6. Labor unions—United

States—History. I. Title.

HD6515.T22I583 2003

331.88'11388324'0977311—dc21

2002044917

Cover photo courtesy of Jeff Weiss, Director of Communications,

Chicago Federation of Labor, AFL-CIO

Union buttons courtesy of Katina Skoufis Barnett

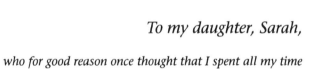

To my daughter, Sarah,

who for good reason once thought that I spent all my time

away from home at "the Teamsters."

Contents

Acknowledgments

I never set out to write a book about Teamster democracy. My initial idea was a research paper about the relationship between union democracy and effective unionism. It struck me that, while the idea was likely to produce some interesting research findings, given the legendary difficulty "outsiders" have had in accessing union records, the project would at best assume a modest level of inquiry. I was wrong. In short order a brief research paper had grown into a full-blown analysis of how one unique union—Chicago Teamster Local 705—had transformed itself from corrupt and inefficient to democratic and high-powered. First to recognize the potential depth of my original idea was fellow labor studies educator Bruce Nissen. Bruce has made a career of giving good advice to more junior colleagues. I consider this suggestion to be one of his best.

The work would never have developed, of course, without the extraordinary cooperation of Local 705 officers and members. When I first suggested the study to Gerald Zero, Local 705 secretary-treasurer, I was hoping for at best a little interview time and access to some records. Months later I was still talking to union members and culling through dust-laden files boxed away in the basement of the Teamster Auditorium. I was allowed to set up a small workstation at Teamster City, and Zero gave me full access to union records. Along with his willingness to set aside considerable time to answer my questions, Zero's commitment to a scholarly approach to the local's history was critical to the work's credibility.

I was very fortunate to have the cooperation of many other 705 Teamsters. Each of the people interviewed for this book gave of their time, and I am deeply appreciative of their willingness to help me tell the local's important story. Some members, like union representatives Dan Campbell, Mark Postilion, Paul Waterhouse, and Katina Barnett, despite being repeatedly contacted, never grew impatient or tired of my queries. There were plenty of opportunities for these folks simply to brush me aside or to refuse to return a call or accept a request, but instead they offered answers and provided documented information. To a labor educator in search of a compelling and genuine union story, access to data and people was the project's lifeline.

In addition to the representatives mentioned above, I am grateful to the local's executive board attorney Michael Holland for not finding some reason to eject me from the union's offices. It was his desk that became my temporary workstation and his legal papers that were displaced by my research notes and files. If anyone had a reason to be uncooperative it was Holland. Instead, he was the most informative source on the democratic change unfolding at Local 705. Holland has a genuine respect for intellectual activity and extensive experience with union democratization projects. The work that follows greatly benefits from his academic curiosity and real-world trade union expertise.

I also had the full cooperation of Local 705 members who were not always allied with the local leadership and who during the course of this work competed for political control of the union. I am indebted to John McCormick, Archie Cook, Michael Dean, Michel Husar, and Eugene Phillips for permitting me to cover their local officer campaigns for union leadership. Each man had a critique of the local's political history that was important to telling the story of 705's transformation to democracy. It would have been a far less substantive and honest book without their contributions.

Along with union personnel, I was privileged to work with Martin Johnson, acquisitions editor at Northern Illinois University Press. Martin regularly offered sound suggestions for improving early drafts of the work and for helping me to craft out productive responses to outside reviewers. In addition, the press's managing editor, Susan Bean, constructively shepherded the manuscript through the final copyediting stages. I was fortunate to have both Martin's and Susan's help in bringing this work to the public and for making this writing experience a pleasurable exercise.

As my union democracy paper developed into a book-length manuscript, I became dependent on the quiet assistance of two extremely competent and professional office colleagues. Linda Ellis and Cathy Kwiatkowski, two staff employees who work in the Chicago Labor Education Program office, have both been instrumental in helping me to manage my time and university assignments. If not for their ability to coordinate the office's work, it is unlikely that I could have written even a brief abstract about the Teamsters and union democracy, let alone a book. No university professor could have had better support, and I owe Linda and Cathy a big thank-you.

While I wait to the end of the acknowledgments to thank my wife, Lynn, it is not out of sentimentality. She took an interest in my union democracy writing—as she does in everything I write—and by way of critical questions, helped me to generate new thoughts about the subject. For her loving help I will forgive her initial jovial musing that "a book about Teamster democracy shouldn't be that long." As it turns out, the subject of Teamster democracy in Chicago is worthy of a good read, and one hopes what follows will not be too arduous.

REFORMING THE CHICAGO TEAMSTERS

Introduction

On 7 February 1991, a boisterous crowd of Chicago Teamsters gathered at the union hall to nominate delegates to the Teamsters international convention in the spring. As usual in such meetings, opposition to endorsed union candidates met with a deluge of abuse from members loyal to the leadership. During the heated debate, Local 705 truck driver Leroy Ellis rose to declare his intentions to run as a delegate on a slate opposed to the incumbent officeholders. Before Ellis could finish, he was assaulted with a heavy glass ashtray, which shattered his collarbone. The attack unleashed a brawl that left dozens of union members dazed, battered, and bloodied. In the ensuing election, the dissidents failed to win a single spot.[1]

To union members alienated by the local's history of illegal practices, fraudulent and irrelevant elections, autocratic behavior, and thuggish treatment of rank-and-filers, the union hall brawl epitomized the corrupting influences of absolute power. In the eyes of most rank-and-filers, Local 705 was more an unassailable feudal monarchy than a labor organization. But on 2 December 2000, less than ten years after the assault on Ellis, members of Local 705 participated in a full-fledged political campaign featuring five slates of candidates. Power was no longer the exclusive property of an elite few. In the dawn of another Chicago winter, rank-and-file union members had their votes peacefully and fairly counted, without the threat of physical harm. It was an act of democratic promise that earlier union reformers could hardly have imagined.

To make the journey from bloody brawls to peaceful elections, the members of Local 705 were forced to undergo a wrenching process of democratization. Supported by a newly elected reform international union president during the 1990s, a resident body of experienced, battle-hardened dissidents transformed the nation's second largest Teamster local. Local 705's story is a detailed and intimate account, drawn from public and union records, of how a one-time national leader in the unionized trucking industry became a corrupt, inefficient, and despotic labor organization and then dramatically transformed itself, by a process that the *Wall Street Journal* hailed as "a model of reform."[2] On at least two counts, however, it is more than a case study of union reform.

First, industrial-relations commentators have consistently noted the absence of any industrial-relations studies that compare a democratically run union with one autocratically governed. Local 705 is a single case, of course, but it nonetheless provides just such a comprehensive comparison. In addition, Local 705's democratization is especially relevant now because many researchers have been considering the various models and forms of union transformation.[3] The Local 705 story demonstrates that when unions institute democratic reforms, they are better able to represent member interests. In contrast to corrupt union practices or the actions of a hierarchically bound union apparatus, only democratic processes and rank-and-file activism can create a worker organization that fulfills the highest ideals of trade unionism. In the special case of the Teamsters, it took a combination of legal actions and worker agitation to rid the union of its sordid history of corrupt and antidemocratic behavior.

Teamster Corruption

Although the international union was once a powerful source for dramatically improving the working lives of truck drivers, it was also intricately connected to organized crime. From 1956 to 1959, the sensational McClellan Congressional Committee Hearings revealed to the public a union notorious—among those who were closer to it—for threatening employers and union members alike. Televised proceedings featured union and underworld connections, ghost locals, racketeering practices, sweetheart contracts, stolen union funds, uncontested local officer elections, the failure to hold membership meetings, nepotism and favoritism in assigning desirable work, bombings, and assorted forms of employer and worker harassments. In this condition the union was a fertile field in which corruption could flourish and union dues could be converted into a high-paying investment for organized crime. For instance, Salvatore Gravano, a former Gambino mob family underboss, stated that the Gambino family "earned" at least $1.5 million a year through the control of just one New York City International Brotherhood of Teamsters (IBT) local.[4]

One of the most notorious Chicago examples of Teamster corruption was Joseph Glimco, a trustee of Teamsters Taxicab Local 777. Glimco had been arrested thirty-six times and twice charged with murder. In addition, merchants in the Chicago Fulton Street Market had testified before a federal grand jury that they had been forced to pay kickbacks to the Teamster boss under the threat of physical violence. Along with the kickback scheme, Glimco was also found to have stolen $124,000 from the taxicab local's treasury.[5] Glimco's role in Chicago Teamster corruption, though sizable, was overshadowed by that of a local insurance company executive and mob henchman, Paul "Red" Dorfman. By the late 1940s Dorfman was a major figure in the Chicago "Outfit"[6] with close ties to syndicate head Tony

Accardo. It was Dorfman who introduced James Riddle Hoffa to the Chicago mafia, and in return, the Teamster chief turned over to Dorfman control of the union's enormous Central States Health Fund. Dorfman then enriched both himself and his family by awarding most of the funds' insurance business to a company run by his son Allen. In a little more than two years (1952–1954), the younger Dorfman proceeded to drain more than $1.6 million from the Health fund in excessive commissions and service fees. Dorfman's extraction operation was further bolstered with the creation in 1955 of the Central States pension fund. The Teamster fund was once considered "the most abused pension fund in America" and was not-so-jokingly referred to as the "mob's bank."[7] In the late 1970s, it was estimated that the fund lost $385 million because of loans to organized crime figures—loans that either were never repaid or were underpaid. Allen Dorfman's financial looting of the union's funds, however, met a dramatic end in 1983 when he was shot eight times in the head while walking to his car, parked near an area hotel.

By the time two rounds of hearings were completed, in 1957, the McClellan Committee had already amassed eighty-two charges against Teamster officials, and more than half of the fifty-eight volumes of written testimony were exclusively focused on the IBT. Despite the damaging evidence unearthed during the McClellan Committee proceedings, genuine democratization of the Teamsters proved elusive. An initial attempt was made in 1958 with the creation of the court-mediated three-member Board of Monitors. The board was to function as a Teamster watchdog and to recommend some limited union reforms. However, the monitorship quickly and steadily disintegrated, and by 1961 the board was dissolved. It had managed to achieve some minor changes but failed to bring about any significant reform in the union.[8]

For another thirty years, union corruption and autocracy were endemic. The union's underside was again displayed in 1979 when reputed Chicago crime lord Joey "The Clown" Lombardo was caught on tape discussing a method for securing the international union's presidency for mob favorite Roy Williams. On the tape Chicago Teamster officials are heard arranging votes for Williams with Lombardo and Allen Dorfman. The embarrassment of fixing union elections aside, IBT corruption continued unabated. George Meany, president of the American Federation of Labor–Congress of Industrial Organizations (AFL-CIO), had once shockingly portrayed the IBT as organized labor's "number one enemy," and that infamous ranking seemed impervious to challenge.[9] In 1986 the President's Commission on Crime called the IBT the "union most controlled by the mob," and shortly thereafter another investigative government body identified 214 Teamster officials guilty of corrupt acts, including 66 related to organized crime. One legal commentator, musing on the union's 1950s reputation for corruption, wrote in 1989 that the earlier characterization of the IBT "remains as accurate today as it was in Hoffa's day."[10]

RICO and Teamster Reform

But in 1989, spurred on by nearly two decades of courageous rank-and-file Teamster reform movements doggedly attacking the union's undemocratic leadership, the federal government finally took meaningful action against the Teamsters. Using a weapon previously reserved for winning indictment against organized crime, the Justice Department filed a Racketeer Influenced Corrupt Organization (RICO) civil lawsuit against the Teamsters. After nearly four months of contentious evasions, the union capitulated to an unprecedented government-dictated and -enforced Consent Order. Relief for the rank and file was widespread. A trio of court-appointed officers would monitor everything from union appointments to cashing checks, connections with criminal elements, and conducting elections.

Although it is certain that the various rank-and-file movements publicly agitating for union reform contributed to the federal government's decision to move against the Teamsters, there are a number of theories as to why a Republican administration in 1989 decided to act decisively. It had been conventional wisdom that the Teamsters' friendly relationship with past Republican presidents had earned the union a special prosecutorial exemption from the Justice Department. So what had changed by the late 1980s? Observers have separately noted the role of politically ambitious government prosecutors, such as Rudolph Giuliani, in pushing the lawsuit. Others have stressed industrial executives' business concerns about the Mafia's influence on rising shipping costs. The government also had accumulated data revealing the drain on the economy that resulted from labor racketeering. Commentators further pointed out that the combination of mob influence and rank-and-file rebellion had created a volatile situation in the critical transportation industry. Still others argued that the sizable attrition of Teamster members since the 1979 deregulation of the trucking industry had undermined the need for an implicit deal between the Republican Party and the union. Each of these explanations offers cause for the government's overdue intervention, but in any case it seems certain that, as Dan La Botz has stated, "the Republican-Teamsters alliance had entered an era of diminishing returns."[11]

As part of the negotiated settlement of the RICO suit, in 1991 the union held its first referendum election for international officers. The historic vote made possible the election of reform candidate Ron Carey to the general presidency and heralded the beginning of a long combative process of restoring democratic rights to rank-and-file members. With the assistance of a three-person Independent Review Board, empowered to monitor the union's behavior, the agreement represented the end of union mob-boss tyranny and ushered in a period of dramatic internal changes.

Since the 1991 election, the union membership has withstood forty-one trusteeships, 217 permanent member expulsions, charges against nine international officers or appointees, the criminal conviction of an international director of governmental affairs, and the expenditure of $20 million in taxpayer funds in attempts to get the union to act democratically. In addition, an international election for union president was overturned, and in 1997 the union's reform president, Ron Carey, was banned from the union for misusing the membership's dues money. In Chicago alone, the Review Board disciplined twenty-five IBT officials, and eleven were expelled for their organized crime activity. And Carey placed five Chicago Teamsters locals into trusteeship for various kinds of improper conduct. As one observer commented, the Teamsters were a union that "inspired the institutional equivalent of a foreign invasion" to begin respecting worker rights.[12]

But the RICO suit, along with the rank-and-file-led reform presidency of Ron Carey and the agitation of local "democrats," dramatically altered the governance and performance of Chicago Local 705. In 1993 Carey and the Review Board imposed a trusteeship on Local 705. Under amendments made to national labor laws in 1959, all international unions were given the authority and the duty to remove policymaking power from a local executive board in order to correct corruption or financial malpractice, to assure the performance of collective bargaining agreements, and to restore democratic procedures.[13] Control of Local 705 was temporarily shifted to a trustee, who, operating under federal court supervision and the approval of the Review Board, began to rid the local of corrupt influences.

Acting also under federal oversight, the International Executive Board removed Daniel Ligurotis, Local 705 secretary-treasurer, from office for improper actions, and the union's Ethical Practices Committee subsequently expelled other corrupt officials for mob ties and violations of the union constitution.[14] The international board also filed lawsuits against people who had stolen from the membership, and a number of large settlements were won. According to the terms of the RICO settlement, the trusteeship of Local 705 proved devastatingly effective. But as important as it was to cleanse the union of corrupt figures, something equally vital if less glamorous was occurring. As the trusteeship unfolded, 705 workers, for the first time, were finding that as union members they had legal rights and that the union really did belong to the rank and file.

Along with numerous procedural changes that connected the rank and file to the business of the union, the reformers brought to a halt the long-standing practice of interference in Local 705 elections by Teamster employers. In a pernicious undermining of democratic unionism, Chicago employers had regularly influenced the outcome of Local 705 political struggles by punishing dissenters. Preferring a more cooperative labor leadership and a less democratically oriented union organizational structure, employers often colluded with Local 705 chieftains to discharge troublesome rank-and-file political activists. But the reforms initiated in 1993 wrenched the local's democratic temper out of corporate managers' clutches and delivered it into the multiple hands of dues-paying Teamsters.

Most remarkable of all, after the trusteeship was lifted, the union's governance and culture was dramatically altered by three historic competitive and honest elections. By the winter of 2000, fresh paint, progressive leadership, and membership involvement "down at the union hall" had replaced the bloodstains of a decade earlier.

The Importance of Democratic Unions

The case for democratic unions is not a difficult one to make. Union responsiveness to the expressed needs of workers is essential to building a civil society, because work is hard. Hard work is punishment if you cannot determine how much your labor is worth or if you have no voice in how you are treated. No matter the level of difficulty, work is the life activity that most consumes our time. It is also where we Americans acquire the means to live as functional and meaningful citizens. The Bill of Rights guarantees political liberties, but it does not put bread on the table. Government laws, regulations, taxing and subsidy policies, and entitlement programs offer various degrees of material support, but in America people sell their labor power because it is the most efficient way to get what they need to prosper.

If working is the activity that offers the best promise of democratic citizenship, then working as a member of a union is the most empowering way for millions of wage earners to live as citizens. Unionization in America has proved to be an unquestionable economic and political good for working-class people who exchange their sweat equity for dollars and cents.[15] But signing a union card or a bargaining agreement does not automatically fulfill the promise of today's workplace organization. The power of a union to remain vital and relevant to the rank and file is closely linked to its internal governance. Unions governed by officials undeterred by democratic procedures and rank-and-file demands for input too often decay into little more than family fiefdoms, disinterested in and incapable of promoting workers' interests. Simply put, if worker benefits are to be maximized, union members must have the right to determine how the union will operate. Without a democratically inspired collective representative, a worker's opportunities to pursue life, liberty, and happiness are determined autocratically by a single person or a handful of disinterested strangers. But effective representation by a democratically governed union can provide workers a mechanism to fashion a better future.

Driving a Truck for a Living

The "teaming" and trucking business has changed dramatically in the last three decades. As the industry developed from one that at one time featured mostly short-haul shipments made under a chaotic hodgepodge of locally derived rules into a national business dramatically expanded in the 1950s by a federally funded Interstate Highway System, working conditions have altered significantly. Once highly regulated by government agencies and a powerful union, the trucking industry now is characterized by thousands of nonunion drivers and a minimalist regulatory state. As detailed in Mike Belzer's *Sweatshops on Wheels*, "truck drivers have ridden a roller coaster over the last few decades."[16] Much of that topsy-turvy ride can be explained by the federal deregulation of the industry in the late 1970s and the 1980s.

Recoiling from the inflationary impact of a crude oil shortage, in 1980 a Democratic Congress and a Republican president joined in unraveling what a progressive Congress had begun to stitch together nearly fifty years earlier. In 1935 Congress passed the Motor Carrier Act, requiring that all trucking companies comply with the rules established by the Interstate Commerce Commission (ICC). The ICC's reach included restricting entry into the over-the-road transportation business, authorizing rate bureaus to set collective nonpredatory operating rates, and requiring that firms adopt safety-related limits on driving practices.

As intercity trucking rapidly grew throughout the second and third decades of the century, in part because of the Depression-era connection between highway construction and employment, the influx of a large number of general freight drivers, moving materials across state borders, signaled a change in industry composition. No longer was the industry characterized solely by "local draymen and drivers delivering coal, beer, laundry, bread and other items" to nearby businesses. By 1940 the trucking industry was already segmented into separate markets for heavy truckload carriers (TL) and smaller less-than-truckload shippers (LTL).[17]

The passage of a series of Federal-Aid Highway Acts in the 1950s catapulted the trucking industry over the railroads as America's principal transportation medium. Bolstered by powerful highway advocates, the federal government left unaided the antiquated railroad system. Between 1933 and 1955, the numbers of freight cars, locomotives, and miles of track all declined. Although rail freight still hauled a great deal of material, the way the nation made use of trucks permanently changed from a secondary railroad "feeder" system to direct, point-to-point hauling. As a result, between 1940 and 1968, trucking's share of total ton-miles shipped increased from 10 percent to 22 percent, while railroads' share fell from 61 percent to 41 percent. At the same time, the share of gross operating revenue going to trucking increased from 17 percent to 50 percent, while that of railroads fell from 75 percent to 41 percent. Tom Lewis portrayed the trucking industry's growth and the diminishing importance of rail freight by noting, "Railroads were withering like a great and noble but diseased oak tree."[18] Even the oil shocks and soaring gas prices of the late 1970s did not alter the trend to move more and more freight over the road.

But in 1980 deregulation changed the rules of the road. Entry into the transportation market was opened up that year by the Motor Carrier Act, after which competition became much more intense. The ranks of nonunion carriers had nearly doubled between 1981 and 1983, and 183 shippers had gone out of business. Carriers were now permitted to offer discounted and discriminatory prices, ushering in a wild race to become the low-cost shipper. As proponents of deregulation had expected, dismantling the "regulatory environment governing the economics of the interstate trucking industry" put enormous pressure on unionized carriers to cut the wages of their employees in order to match the lower shipping costs now being offered by largely nonunionized carriers.[19] The Teamsters did permit considerable cost-saving changes in work practices and agreed to freeze wages, postpone cost-of-living adjustments, and accept a lower starting wage for new hires, but they could not put the brakes on the devastating loss of unionized drivers.

Within ten years of the transportation law's enactment, most of the top thirty pre-deregulatory-period trucking firms either had folded or had been merged. Union density had fallen from a peak of 65 percent in 1973 to fewer than 25 percent of all drivers on the road two decades later. As union density tumbled, so did drivers' earnings. Belzer notes that drivers experienced an average annual loss of income of 30 percent between 1977 and 1995. Dramatizing the steep income loss, Belzer states: "Had real wages remained constant for truckers during this period, the average worker in the trucking industry would have earned a total of $140,658 more than he did."[20]

The free-market race to become the low-cost provider also produced dangerous road conditions. As Belzer reports, a 1997 trucking industry study revealed that many TL drivers were working five hours a week beyond the legal limit of sixty. Based on these drive times, he identifies an "extensive effort by firms and drivers themselves to sweat their labor to reach target earnings levels."[21] Longer hours on the road have meant more tired union, nonunion, and owner-operator drivers working under tighter deadlines and narrow piecework compensation plans. It was not always this way.

Driving a truck used to be a job paying well above the national average. Teamsters were the "knights of the road" and unqualified pacesetters in postwar bargained pay and benefits. As chapter 1 explains, the union not only had the ability to choke off the nation's economic commerce, but it also sidled up close to presidents and understood the art of political hardball. But deregulation, union corruption, and an inept, tepid response to the deregulatory assault degraded much of the union's well-earned bravado. Paradoxically, the physical and psychological "sweating" of truck drivers contributed strongly toward stimulating both a rank-and-file democratic movement and a nostalgic, "Old Guard–like" backlash against reform in locals across the country.

However incomplete or difficult the process of democratization has proved to be, after backpedaling through the turbulent deregulatory period, the Teamsters emerged near the end of the century as labor's shock troops against seemingly unassailable new economic forces. In the summer of 1997, when few commentators thought it possible, the Teamsters stunned the nation by shutting down the United Parcel Service Company. The national strike lasted seventeen days and ended in a win for the union. It was hailed at the time as one of labor's biggest victories in forty years. The strike was a creative mobilization of thousands of rank-and-file members and was fought against the contemporary shift of labor markets away from well-paying, full-time union jobs and toward poorly paying, part-time nonunion work. In Chicago, Local 705 fought its own victorious battle with UPS and kept the firm's package cars garaged one week longer than anywhere else in the nation.

The IBT's clout is not limited to the nation's economy or politics. In 1995 the labor movement experienced its own version of revolution, and the Teamsters was one of the unions turning the axis. Inspired in part by the political failures of the previous twenty years, an insurgency slate led by John Sweeney was elevated to the AFL-CIO leadership. Sweeney's New Voice Team represented a split within the 16-million-member federation. Incumbent president Tom Donohue had the support of nearly 40 percent of the proportioned union votes required to stay in office. Although Sweeney was backed by a number of large unions (e.g., Service Employees International Union, United Steelworkers, United Autoworkers), the math revealed that the vote of the designated Teamster delegates would determine who would govern the national labor body. In the end Carey's commitment to a reinvigorated labor movement threw the race to Sweeney and ushered in the promise of a more activist national union organization. Importantly, the new leadership committed the national federation's political strategy to a singular focus on encouraging members to vote on the bases of workplace issues. This renewed mobilization around political action has continued to benefit the Democrats, as evidenced by the Teamsters' endorsement—though it was late—of Al Gore in the 2000 presidential election.

Defining and Measuring Union Democracy

Before we begin to discuss the ways union democracy has been analytically approached, it needs to be stated that the overwhelming number of local union officials are not corrupt and are not participating in illegal behavior. As revealed by Freeman and Medoff in *What Do Unions Do?* less than 1 percent of approximately sixty-five thousand union locals have been found guilty of harboring individuals who have violated criminal laws.[22] If every corrupt official were purged from the labor movement (an unquestionable good, to be sure), little would have been done collectively to revitalize it as a workplace and social institution. The absence of criminal behavior does not mean that unions are sufficiently mobilizing the power that rank-and-file democracy can bring to bear on the production relationship. Democracy in labor unions requires that unions be more than free of corrupt leaders; they must be pluralistic institutions responsive to membership demands.

Whether unions are democratic institutions has been deemed an important post–World War II social science question because unions act upon society as political agents. As Karl Marx recognized in 1871, when workers negotiate with their employers for a reduction of working hours, they are economic actors, but when they lobby "to force through an eight hour [a day] etc., *law*," they are acting as part of a "political movement."[23] No longer just about voluntary private relationships with cooperative free-market employers, unions figure into the calculus of a country's policymaking machinery. Research, consequently, has been driven by questions concerning the arenas in which democracy is possible within a labor organization (i.e., the role of leadership and elections and the status of oppositional groups, normative culture, and conflict).

The concept of union democracy has not been an easy one to authoritatively address and communicate to the general public. It was not the first work of its kind, but ever since Lipset, Trow, and Coleman's *Union Democracy* was published in 1956, the mechanics of democratic trade unionism have been a beguiling subject for students of labor unions. Questions about how democracy is defined, how it should be measured, what its prerequisites and component parts are, and under what conditions it can exist have characterized the relevant literature. Much of the work has focused on and applied competing versions of organizational theory.[24] Grant McConnell went so far as to theorize that interest organizations—like unions—were examples of "private governments" and likely to be undemocratic in character. Samuel Estreicher even argued that it was immaterial whether collective bargaining agents were democratic or autocratic, as long as covered employees had "low cost" opportunities to "cast secret ballot votes" on important economic issues. In short, for a majority of people inside and outside the union movement, the closest they appear to come to a consensus on the positive contributions that democratic behavior makes to the lives of working people is to assert that "it may be said to do so."[25]

Approaches to Union Democracy

In their efforts to define and assess union democracy, researchers and practitioners have principally relied on two approaches. The more prevalent and conventional of the perspectives is the "legalistic" one, which focuses on formal constitutional measures. This approach imports the civil and political rights guaranteed to the citizens of a democratic nation-state into the intraunion relationship. It is predicated on majority-minority rights provisions and is primarily a structural analysis.[26]

A second popular approach is built upon the "behavioral" existence of internal parties competing for the support of the rank and file by projecting differing political-economic ideologies. According to this view, democracy is to be found where effective opposition groups can contest elections, organize caucuses, promote "back-bench" policy positions, and otherwise keep leaders accountable to the members. Consistent with the idea of organized internal parties is a strong commitment to rank-and-file participation.[27] To the behaviorists, democracy is visible in the political competition that necessarily arises when union members are consciously and collectively determining their fortunes.

There is a third, less common conceptualization—the one principally relied on in this book—which identifies union democracy as the "substantive outcome" of a labor-management struggle to define the rules that govern shop-floor life. The focus here is on the relationship between union democratic procedures and collective bargaining achievements.[28] This outcome-oriented perspective establishes a different set of criteria for judging an institution's democratic temper. Instead of a strict focus on electoral procedures and the character of political parties, attention shifts to the results of membership debates and policymaking. In other words, democracy should be judged as much by the benefits it bestows upon its practitioners as on the fairness of its operating procedures.

This perspective also introduces interparty power struggles, such as the labor-management relationship, into the environment in which intraparty struggles, such as union political competition, evolve. Overlaid across the often Byzantine intricacies of union politics are the command and control structure and the labor relations philosophy of corporate employers. Businesses in America have historically operated as top-down institutions concentrating employment decisions within a narrow band of personnel relations officials. Likewise, unions in America have been forced to adopt a mirrorlike structure in order to negotiate eye-to-eye with their corporate partners. In other words, negotiating with the business boss required identifying and putting forward a union boss. Although media use of the term *boss* too often unjustly demonized union leaders as thugs, it is correct that a majority of rank-and-file members ceded most decision making to a handful of elected and nonelected officials. Certainly the average union worker should have demanded a greater role in his or her union, but it was not just the incredible material advancements won by union leaders after World War II that conditioned individual dues-payers to accept the status quo. Of equal, if unexamined, importance was that the business boss wanted it that way.

Undemocratic corporate entities have little interest in promoting democratically run labor organizations, particularly for their own workers. As protectors and maximizers of shareholder interests, managers typically interpret a widening of employee involvement in employment matters as bad for business. Nonetheless, corporate America learned to tolerate unionism, at least for a brief period, but in doing so they insisted on and won the right to deal exclusively with the "union leadership." As honest and capable as it may have been, the leadership could only be a fraction of the membership. Although corporate structures and practices never determined a union's democratic temper, there was little in modern capitalism that encouraged workplace-related activism. In the case of a dishonest union leadership, like the one that reigned at Local 705, managerial behavior protected an elite dictatorial approach to union control.

As is evident throughout part 1 of the following narrative, management at Local 705 companies preferred the shenanigans of old guard union officials. The payoff was obvious: fewer disputes with the workers, customary sweetheart contracts, and a compliant workforce. But after the local trusteeship, all that changed, and Local 705 began to resist managerial power. In turn, management at United Parcel Service, for example, decided to treat the union like a dangerous intruder. Whereas union business agents had previously quietly resolved problems behind closed doors, and contracts were signed repeatedly without issue, after the reform movement every labor-management issue became a very public battle for control over the workplace. And democratic unionism was now, for the first time, producing triumphant unionism.

Union democracy, then, is a mechanism for shaping the "relations of production." In this sense the power that workers attain to govern their shop-floor relations and define "the limits of capital's power" is a measure of the union's democratic quality. The relationship between union democratic procedures and collective bargaining achievements is more often assumed than proved, however. To be sure, studies of union governance structures and behavioral regulation have proliferated. So, too, have works on corruption and rank-and-file commitment. Even the formation of dissenting caucuses has been the subject of published material.[29] What is far less common is an empirical study of the relationship between internal democratic union political behavior and the defense of rank-and-file interests.

Academic observers have theorized about such relationships, but few have attempted to empirically answer the critical question that underlies all queries into internal union politics: what difference would (does) democracy make? The answer would appear to be obvious. It seems intuitive that the more voice workers have in determining how their union is run, the more likely they will be to support the institution. The abundant scholarship on rank-and-file union commitment and satisfaction bears out a positive relationship between individual opportunities for input and union loyalty.[30]

What is less clear is whether the opportunity for employee input makes a difference in how the union leadership conducts business with the employer. In other words, does majority rule shape a material output different from the one a more centralized top-down approach would generate? In the case of Local 705, the answer was affirmative. Democratic practice mattered because the destructive effects of a deregulated trucking market and the union structural realignment made possible through civil litigation served to redistribute the resources available to reformers at Chicago Local 705 and at other IBT shops around the country. Autocratic rule and the lack of rank-and-file democracy were tolerated when wages were rising, benefits were good, and jobs were plentiful. But when the quality of representation seriously deteriorated and the union card was no longer worth the paper it was printed on, governance issues became critical to organizational performance. With every contractual concession and each additional nonunionized truck driver at the wheel, the opportunities for reform widened. Not that the pain meted out by economic and political events was sufficient to create a new governing philosophy. International and local Teamster leadership resisted to the bitter end, and most workers were too confused, alienated, or afraid to mount a political challenge against "the way things were." But one after another, new groups formed and re-formed and reformed yet again to put forth a new agenda for the union. That agenda always required more membership freedom and union involvement, but its overt message was for better contracts, fewer concessions, and more militant opposition to the trucking companies.

Organization of the Book

The story of Local 705's democratic transformation began with the trusteeship imposed in 1993 and reached a milestone with the officer elections of December 2000. This book covers the period from 1993 until the fall of 2000 and considers the formal aspects of internal governance as well as how the relationship between the leadership and the rank and file became more egalitarian and participatory. Although dramatic changes began at the time of the 1993 trusteeship, in the winter of 2000 Local 705 rank-and-file members were given the responsibility to elect new union officers. This was an ideal opportunity to observe how union democracy influences union politics. The election and accompanying campaign became an unprecedented political struggle for control of the Chicago local. But more importantly, it also represented a battle over the concept of democratic unionism. For that reason the 2000 campaign and officer elections serve as the final event in this book's analysis of Local 705's dramatic transformation.

My analysis extensively utilizes the local's general executive board (GEB) monthly membership records; steward and craft meeting minutes; bargaining agreements; grievance, arbitration, and labor board records; organizing files; and union political campaign material, as well as miscellaneous correspondence. In appropriate cases, where records permit, a comparison is made between the pre- and posttrusteeship periods. In addition, interviews with local officers and staff who have worked under both the old regime and the new, and with political opponents of the incumbent leadership, are cited to supplement union records. Finally, I draw on my own participant-observer impressions of union membership, craft, and steward meetings and campaign meetings and events to lend greater depth to my conclusions.

As I conducted this research, I had unfettered access to all documents and records relevant to the questions under examination. Written data was drawn from multiple sources, including the local union's archives. Every officer, staff member, and steward was encouraged to speak on the record and to cooperate with the study. In a number of cases, initial and follow-up interviews were conducted with officers, representatives, and union counsel. In addition to the interviews with the local leadership, the heads of all contesting political slates openly and consistently answered questions and, with some limitations, offered a close examination of their campaign strategies.

It may seem odd to many informed and merely curious readers that a case study of a Chicago Teamster union is used to draw conclusions about democratic unionism. By any comparisons there are few other large international union histories that can match the Teamsters in degrees and forms of corruption and undemocratic behavior. But it is precisely the IBT's long, arduous, ongoing escape from dictatorial control that provides students of unionism with a critical opportunity to examine how democratic theory is transformed into democratic practice.

▲ PART ONE ▲

The Corruption and Redemption of Local 705

CHAPTER ONE

Teamsters' Power and Politics

To even the most remote observer of the labor movement, equating democracy with the Teamsters seems outrageous. This is, after all, the same international union that has seen six of its ten presidents either indicted or convicted of a federal crime or removed from office for serious violations of union rules. For most of its history, the IBT has been synonymous in the public's mind with corruption. But that view is incomplete. Labor historian Robert Ziegler has noted the duality of the union's legacy, stating that the "union was as dynamic as it was crime ridden."[1] This effective yet corrupt organization had great influence over the nation's economic and political fortunes, and Local 705 was one of the union's most powerful and independent locals in the country.

Organizing the Road

In 1898 a small number of Detroit wagon-drivers, seeking a measure of protection against the social costs of industrialization, organized the Team Drivers International Union and received an AFL charter. But in 1902 a much larger number of drivers in Chicago rebelled and formed the independent Teamster National Union. One year later, AFL president Samuel Gompers brought the two rival unions together at a national team driver's convention in Niagara Falls, New York. At the close of the proceedings, both groups agreed to form the International Brotherhood of Teamsters, Chauffeurs, Warehousemen, Stablemen, and Helpers of America. The new union would be headquartered in Indianapolis, and its first president was Cornelius Shea.

Shea's only term of office was clouded by a charge of extortion. Although he was not convicted, he was voted out of office in 1907, and the teaming reins were passed on to Daniel Tobin. For the next forty-five years, which included the early days of motorization and the trucking industry's achievement of dominance, Tobin governed a loose association of growing and relatively scandal-free local unions. Beginning as a craft-based, intracity mover of goods, the Teamsters adopted an industrial organizing structure as technology made the transportation of material over longer distances both possible and economical.

The union's early growth and transformation was aided by the brilliant organizing efforts of its Minneapolis-based Trotskyite leader, Farrell Dobbs. By the early 1940s, Dobbs had help the union develop a battle plan to tie the movement and handling of local, regional, and national commodities into a unified campaign for rationalizing the trucking industry. As Michael Belzer explains, "Road drivers carried their message from city to city, telling dockworkers and drivers region wide that unionization could bring them far better wages and conditions than they experienced to date."[2]

The union's industrial character was further advanced during the international presidency of Dave Beck. Nicknamed "His Majesty the Wheel," as president from 1952 to 1957, Beck restructured the union into separate crafts, trades, or divisions. Membership increased steadily, and by the end of World War II the union had become a national bargaining power. Unfortunately, Beck also practiced the art of self-aggrandizement that would be copied by other Teamster presidents. The Teamster chief, who was derisively referred to as "Beck the Strikebreaker," benefited financially at the expense of dues-payers, and in 1957 he was convicted of tax evasion.[3]

The organizing successes of the 1930s and 1940s also helped to elevate a young organizer named James R. Hoffa to national prominence. Under Beck's rule, the Detroit-based Hoffa ran the union's organizing efforts with an imaginative and effective approach. By the late 1950s, Hoffa had emerged as the president of the Teamsters, and the results for truck drivers and the labor movement were breathtaking. Despite being expelled in 1957 from the AFL-CIO for corruption, between 1958 and 1967 Teamster truckers earned wage increases of 40 percent, well above the gains in most other industries. The ability to win wage and benefit increases was boosted by the union's 1964 pattern-bargained National Master Freight Agreement (NMFA). The NMFA was historic because, as Belzer points out, it nullified the trucking employers' ability to whipsaw "one terminal, city or region against another."[4]

Hoffa's control of the drivers' union was brought to a screeching halt when he was imprisoned in 1967 for jury tampering. In his absence the union was run by a Hoffa protégé, Frank Fitzsimmons. A close associate of Hoffa's from the early organizing days in Detroit, "Fritz" had few of his predecessor's capabilities, and a string of bargaining failures characterized his days as union president (1967–1981). The union's ineptitude and disdain for rank-and-file problems continued unabated with the short-lived presidency of Roy Williams. Head of the Teamsters for only eighteen months, Williams was convicted in 1982 for attempting to bribe a U.S. senator. His replacement, Jackie Presser, fared no better. In 1986 Presser was indicted by a federal grand jury on embezzlement charges.[5] The unbroken line of discredited union leaders finally closed with the brief, do-nothing reigns in 1988 of Walter Mathis and William McCarthy.

In 1991, under federal supervision, Ron Carey took a plurality of the vote and won the IBT presidency in the union's first referendum vote. Under Carey's reform leadership, the international union rejuvenated its organizing efforts, utilized creative, proactive corporate fight-back strategies, increased membership involvement, and cleansed the union of many corrupt and ineffective local officers. But his tenure was shockingly cut short. In 1996 Carey ran for reelection against James Hoffa Jr. and was declared the winner by a very narrow margin. But because improper contributions to his campaign "may have affected the outcome of the election," the results were set aside, a rerun election was called, and Carey was disqualified from running as a candidate in the rerun election.[6] In the 1998 contest, Hoffa defeated a badly underfinanced but surprisingly competitive Tom Leedham, who was endorsed by the Teamsters for a Democratic Union. Three years later Hoffa won reelection by once again drubbing the decidedly less challenging Leedham by a nearly three-to-one margin.

Governing the Road

Along with possessing, for most of their history, the blitzkrieglike capacity to economically immobilize the nation's economy, the Teamsters have been a national political force. Their partisan commitments have, however, undergone shifting allegiances. In the late 1930s and throughout World War II, the union was one of the strongest supporters of the Franklin Delano Roosevelt–led Democratic Party. For instance, it was the Teamsters who, along with CIO founder John L. Lewis, persuaded the American Federation of Labor (AFL) to support a national unemployment bill and a host of related New Deal legislation. One of those New Deal measures allocated $1.8 billion between 1933 and 1940 for road construction. The Teamsters' central role in the political fortunes of the New Deal was also evident when in 1944 FDR announced, from Teamster headquarters in Washington, his unprecedented plan to run for a fourth presidential term.

But beginning with the Truman-signed and Teamster-targeted Hobbs Anti-Racketeering Act in 1946, the union began to chart a less certain Democratic Party trajectory.[7] By 1956 the union had severed its relationship with the junior party and decided to endorse Republican president Dwight D. Eisenhower's reelection campaign. The endorsement of Eisenhower was facilitated by his 1954 recommendation that Teamster president Dave Beck be appointed to the newly formed Advisory Committee on a National Highway Program. Beck's placement put him in a critical position to help advance the development of a heavily subsidized road-building program, known popularly as the Interstate Highway System. With nearly three thousand miles of road to be built, the new highway project would be a boon for Teamsters.

The support for Republican administrations increased as the union and Hoffa became the targets of John and Robert Kennedy's public investigations into allegations of Teamster mob connections. The investigations had revealed that the heads of the mob families in New York and Chicago had been influential in choosing national and local Teamster leaders. In response, in 1959 Congress passed the Landrum-Griffin Act, largely to tame the power of the drivers' union. Hoffa was so angry about the actions of the Kennedy brothers that he began a new national political action campaign, DRIVE (Democratic, Republican, Independent Voter Education), primarily to defeat "President Kennedy and other anti-union politicians."[8]

Hoffa was unable to defeat the Kennedys or stay out of prison, but the union's Republican endorsements continued throughout the Nixon and Ford years. International preferences for the Grand Old Party did not, however, always square with the political influence wielded by local Teamster unions. Chicago Local 705 long-term and strong-willed head Louis Peick was a Jimmy Carter confidant. The president and Peick had a two-minute phone conversation on 2 December 1979. No record of what the two men talked about could be found, but the president placed the call.[9] Even when the AFL-CIO Executive Council voted to readmit the IBT in 1987, the renegade union decided to remain loyal to the most anti-union president since Herbert Hoover. One year into his first term, Ronald Reagan sent a surreal videotape message to the delegates attending the Teamsters national convention, expressing his desire to work "together with my union brothers toward a shared goal."[10] The Teamsters had been the lone prominent national union to endorse Reagan's campaign. And when George Bush won the presidency in 1988, Teamster president and lifelong friend William McCarthy appeared proudly at his side before a number of union audiences.

Despite their long fealty to Republican presidential candidates, in 1992 the union switched allegiances. Aided by court-enforced orders and the nearly twenty years of trench warfare fought by courageous rank-and-file union dissidents, a new form of internal governance was brought to the Teamsters. In addition, Carey began to build bridges to the Democratic Party. He endorsed Bill Clinton and "pledged $4 million on the most intense effort by the Teamsters to turn out the membership to vote for the chosen candidate."[11] When one year later Clinton returned a Democratic president to the White House, he did so as the political choice of the 1.7-million-member Teamsters.

But, true to the union's past political fickleness, during the 2000 presidential campaign, newly elected union president James Hoffa Jr. flirted with a George W. Bush presidency. Hoffa was the lone AFL-CIO leader to attend the Republican Party convention in Philadelphia, and the Teamsters were the last major union to endorse Gore's candidacy. Publicly allying themselves with the Tennessean did not mean, however, that the Teamster union would be a partisan partner of the Democrats. When Bush put together a White House administration transition team, it included a representative from only one labor union, the Teamsters. In addition, since Bush's tainted Electoral College victory, Hoffa is one of only a few national industrial union leaders to endorse any part of the Bush White House agenda. Bush showed his appreciation by referring to Hoffa as a "good man" who is "running a good union in an aboveboard way."[12]

As colorful as the history of the International Brotherhood of Teamsters is, the story of the Teamsters in Chicago is critical to understanding the special standing that Local 705 holds in the reform movement. Chicago over the twentieth century became an autonomous union fortress against both the hegemonic desires of the national trucking companies and a centralized international union.[13]

What's the Matter, Chicago?

At the dawn of the twentieth century, Chicago's commercial needs were daily fulfilled by the regular rounds of team drivers leading four thousand horses and mules throughout the city. But if work was plentiful for a driver, it was undeniably life-shortening. In an article titled "What's the Matter with Chicago?" Socialist Party and labor leader Eugene Debs wrote that the city was "the product of modern capitalism, and like all other great commercial centers, is unfit for human habitation." A horse-team driver could not have missed the de-humanizing irony that the city "had more laws to protect horses than the men who drove, curried, and fed them."[14]

In the post–Civil War period, city streets were the perfect embodiments of an unrestrained, progress-at-all-costs urbanism. In 1880 Chicago had only 1 mile of stone pavement and 140 miles of streets covered with wood planks, gravel, and macadam. As a result, heavy rain and snow made travel by wagon or rail nearly impossible. During the city's spring "reign of mud," caused by a rapid thaw of snow and ice, travel in Chicago was a test of human and animal endurance. Weather and paving aside, streets were also used for more than getting around. Because there were insufficient waste-treatment facilities, streets also served as the repository for garbage and sewage. Streets in some areas were so cluttered with waste that settlement movement pioneer Jane Addams once discovered "a pavement eighteen inches under the surface of rotting fruit and filthy rags."[15]

Along with human-generated deposits, the streets also became a dumping ground for the routine disposal of a variety of livestock. Chicago's commercial and livery needs were served daily by four thousand horses and mules and far too few garbage collectors. And despite ordinances to protect these animals, in 1897 public health officials hauled away the carcasses of fifteen hundred horses. The combination of dirt, waste, dying animals, and bad air contributed to a tuberculosis epidemic that accounted for one-third of the adult deaths and one-half of the infant deaths reported in the city between 1908 and 1909. Although driving was dangerous to the health and safety of both teamster and occupant, it was no walk in the park for pedestrians. One of the most pressing public and political issues of the late nineteenth and early twentieth centuries was the control over and the safety of city streets. Rail companies, teaming employers, nascent car manufacturers, city dwellers, and storefront retailers all lobbied for regulatory protection. The street was the first urban space to become a contested terrain between large and small capitalists, on one hand, and the working-class drivers and residents who collided daily in the urban environment, on the other.

Conditions were equally bad for teamsters throughout the Midwest. In response to the harsh working conditions faced by drivers, in 1903 Chicago teamsters took out an IBT charter as Truck Drivers Union Local 705. Chicago was home to a rapidly growing number of drivers collecting garbage, chauffeuring wealthy patrons from downtown hotels to train depots, and carrying materials from rail yards and manufacturing centers to retail establishments throughout the city. Working conditions and pay were ripe for unionization. But driving a team of horses as a union member was nearly as hazardous as navigating the city's busy, littered, and filthy streets. Severe employer and police resistance met most organizing efforts. The violent opposition of employers, however, was typically answered by a remarkably courageous show of worker defiance. Unionization would come to Chicago teamsters, but not without a cost in human life.

Chicago employers understood the significance of a drivers' union that could control the movement of people and materials in and out of the city. At the turn of the century, commercial development boomed in Chicago, and its rapid modernization since the Columbian World Exposition in 1893 was built on the transportation industry. Whether traveling by barge, train, wagon, or motorized truck, Chicago drivers were the linchpins of the city's financial success. Keeping the cost of transportation low precipitated the city's first violent police riot in 1902, when the Midwest Beef Trust went to war against striking drivers at south side meatpacking houses.[16] One year later, 1,200 livery drivers and 900 garbage collectors went on strike to raise their weekly pay from $11 to $14 for a twelve-hour workday.

Their act of defiance was met by the formation of the Associated Teaming Interests, an association of employers opposed to signing union agreements. The employers demanded that drivers climb aboard their wagons and meet their regular rounds. The police and the company owners threatened firings and worse. But with scattered violence shaking the upscale public spaces in front of downtown hotels and theaters, striking teamsters kept their horses unsaddled for over ten months before reaching an agreement with the employers. There was, however, a tragic event that provided a short pause to the work stoppage. Drivers led their wagons and carriages for approximately one week, following the enormous fire at the Iroquois Theater that killed 602 people, mostly women and children. In an effort to assist public safety volunteers in removing the corpses from the destroyed theater, the union offered to temporarily halt the strike. When the last body was removed, the wagons were put back into their barns.[17]

Looking for every opportunity to destroy the organized drivers, the united employers got another chance one year later. In 1904 the Teamsters attempted to persuade nonunion drivers to honor a strike line set up at a furniture company. Their efforts were met with "squads of police . . . using clubs" to break up the union blockades "made by plunging horses and heavy trucks driven by friends of the strikers." The union's ability to stage a forceful street battle and to meet police sticks with their own homemade weapons dragged the numerous "hand-to-hand clashes" on for hours. The *Chicago American* newspaper reported that the employers' association, headed by F. W. Job, was "running the fight and using the company only as an entering wedge in their efforts to crush the union."[18] When the fighting finally ended, a large number of men were badly injured and arrested for rioting.

The teaming association's union opposition was regularly bankrolled and directed by the anti-union "open shop" Chicago Employers' Association (CEA), which hosted in 1903 the "greatest contest between capital and organized labor this country has ever seen." Under the chilling headline "War on Union Believed Near," the *Chicago Daily Tribune* detailed a planned national convention of the anti-union National Association of Employers. As part of the effort to eradicate unionism in the city, in 1905 the CEA responded to a Teamsters' strike against Montgomery Ward by announcing that "guns will be carried" by a special force of inspectors to protect nonunion livery drivers who agreed to move people around the city. The strike escalated into a violent confrontation that took the lives of 21 people and seriously wounded another 415. In the midst of the upheaval, Debs came to the Chicago Coliseum and, before ten thousand people, rallied the workers; but despite his oratory skills, the employers crushed the strike.[19]

In the aftermath of the Montgomery Ward fiasco, the union regrouped and over the next ten years began to successfully organize. With the Teamsters signing up a growing portion of the city's ninety-five thousand transportation workers, agents of the employers' association renewed their call for a union-free Chicago. In April of 1919, the Illinois Manufacturers Association sponsored a lecture at the Chicago Congress Hotel by John Kirby, the president of the Lumberman's Association. Kirby's speech included a positive reference and linkage to the Ku Klux Klan's "running carpetbaggers out of the south" and a recommendation that the country's "labor problem" be handled in the same way. The *New Majority* newspaper, an organ of the Chicago Federation of Labor (CFL), claimed that Kirby had "proposed a KKK to assault and murder officers and members of the AFL."[20] Less than a month later, a well-known Teamster official was treated like a carpetbagger.

During a strike of hotel wait staff at the Lincoln Hotel, Asmus Jessen, a business agent for the Teamsters, approached a man who was directing another worker to move a clothing trunk from the lobby of the hotel. The Teamsters had agreed not to make deliveries to the hotel during the strike, and Asmus was there that day because he had heard that scab teamsters had been brought into the Lincoln. As Asmus approached the man, he yelled out, "What are you doing?" His question was answered when the man pulled a revolver from inside his coat pocket and fatally shot the Teamster agent twice through the stomach. Asmus remained conscious only long enough to identify his assailant. His funeral was attended by four thousand mourners and shut down a long stretch of the city's busy south side traffic for hours.[21] Asmus's death underscored the macabre reality that "teamster membership buttons were reversible, with one side to be used at parades and a black side to be worn at members' funerals."[22]

In addition to the buttons, Local 705 members carried written proof of their union affiliation. By 1911 the local was printing its first dues book. Joseph Rasch was one of roughly 1,000 members paying monthly dues, which started at 25 cents and then slowly increased to 50 cents by 1919. Dues money went to administering the union, organizing new members, providing strike support, and mobilizing for political action. In 1919 Otto Rhein, an ex-member of Local 705, ran as a Chicago Cook County Labor Party candidate for the state assembly from the fourth district.[23] The local had also put its growing membership and treasury to use in securing a prominent place on the executive boards of both the Chicago Federation of Labor and the State Federation of Labor. Beginning in 1904 Local 705 sent no fewer than ten members to the annual state labor convention. At gatherings of the city and state federations, the union quickly became a leading opponent of child labor and an advocate for health benefits and worker compensation.

Despite employer resistance, throughout the first quarter of the twentieth century, Local 705 teamsters made steady economic progress. In 1919 the weekly wage scale of drivers was raised by a healthy $3.00, and their earnings were pegged to the size and weight of the loads they were pulling.[24] A single-horse wagon, for example, guaranteed $15.50 a week, whereas a four-horse team brought home $19.50. In 1941, with gasoline engine vehicles taking over as the dominant form of city transportation, chauffeurs or truck drivers were earning $23.00 per week for one-ton trucks and $34.00 for seven-ton carriers. What the driver was sitting on may have changed, but the formula for being paid had not.

In addition, by the mid-1920s most contracts included a formula for overtime payments and provided for holiday time off. Agreements detailed a daily work schedule that included travel time to and from the barn. Early 705 Teamster contracts also contained a joint labor-management dispute resolution process and provisions for electing or appointing stewards to enforce the agreements. They defined in fine detail exactly what the drivers were required to do and what they could not be ordered to do. For example, drivers were expected to "soap their harness" or "clean their motors" once a week, "but under no circumstances were wagon haulers allowed to handle manure."[25]

By 1940 Local 705 had contracts with oil drivers, dock and platform workers, and service station attendants. The union's 1956 master agreement with tanker companies included shift differential pay, seniority protections, guaranteed daily and weekly pay, a paid vacation schedule, a union security (assuring that members remain in the union for the life of the agreement), and a check-off clause (a company deduction of dues from workers' paychecks). These items had become standard fare for labor contracts, but some pre–World War II agreements prefigured later changing labor markets. A 1939 deal with service station owners stipulated "no more than one part-time employee per week for each five regular employees at each filling station." In 1945 the local also negotiated a work pact with the city's largest cartage companies that required the trucking firms to exclusively use union teamsters to operate new equipment. And five years later the agreement added a "Movement of Garage" section that stated that if an employer relocated his garage, the union drivers would be maintained and paid at union scale.[26]

The 1945 and 1950 contracts incrementally built upon a memorable agreement of 1943. In that year, after five months of fruitless negotiations, the union and the employers' bargaining representatives (the Cartage Exchange of Chicago and the Illinois Motor Truck Operators Association) submitted their deadlocked contract proposals to the National War Labor Board (NWLB). The NWLB was created to settle labor disputes during World War II. Local 705 provided the federal dispute panel with a ninety-two-page brief, which included forty-four exhibits comparing, among other things, the wages of truck drivers in thirteen comparable major cities. At the hourly wage rate offered by the Chicago employers, Local 705's would be the lowest in the nation. As the case was being considered by the NWLB, the union continued to work at the lower pay scale. Ultimately, the weight and gravity of the union's evidence was substantial, and the board awarded nearly fourteen thousand Chicago drivers a wage increase of $5.00 a week, retroactive to the beginning of the year. The decision cost about two thousand unionized employers $1.5 million in back pay.[27]

By 1941 the local had arranged to provide medical coverage for all of its members. The program was financed through a $1.00-a-month dues contribution, and health care was provided by a Danish American hospital. The local eventually came to own and operate its own health clinic and pharmacy, which it continued to do until the late 1980s. In addition to health and welfare benefits, contracts included employer contributions to a retirement fund. The first pension checks were distributed in 1956, and by the mid-1980s, Local 705 was making monthly payments to 3,231 regular pensioners. The local's ability to provide retirement pay was bolstered in 1958 when the local used its formidable muscle to win a $.39 hourly pay boost for 27,000 freight drivers and a $4.00 weekly pay increase for more than four thousand gas and oil drivers.[28]

As the Teamsters became one of the most feared unions in post–World War II America, some Chicago truck drivers held a proud distinction. Elected in 1957, James Riddle Hoffa ruled over the nearly 2-million-member international union until he was removed from office in 1967. During his reign he achieved a considerable amount of influence over the union's governance and bargaining behavior by consolidating control over the numerous locals in the Midwest. But despite Hoffa's network of union, mob, and political contacts, he was never able to win over the complete allegiance of Local 705.

In 1959 Hoffa made a Chicago appearance before a standing-room-only audience of Local 705 members to ask the local to cede to him the power to negotiate a master agreement with the large trucking companies. Hoffa had been successful in convincing most locals around the country to allow him to centralize bargaining, and he came to Chicago with the purpose of reining in Local 705. He failed miserably. At a special meeting called shortly after Hoffa's fist-pounding appeal, the membership overwhelmingly voted to reject the powerful Teamster boss's power grab.[29]

With a membership steadily climbing well over twenty thousand workers, the local was big enough and, as a result of operating in one of the most important industrial hubs in the country, powerful enough to command real influence over the fortunes of the nation's freight drivers. Evidence of the local's special standing was displayed in 1970, when IBT general president Frank Fitzsimmons negotiated a National Master Freight Agreement with the country's largest freight haulers. But along with two other Chicago unions, Local 705 rejected the agreement and found itself as the lead party in a national Teamster "wildcat" strike (i.e., one unauthorized by the international union) against both the freight companies and the international union.[30]

In Chicago the drivers were holding out for a $3.00 per hour raise plus improvements in fringe benefits. Area trucking firms were offering only the nationally agreed rate of $1.10 with no benefit gains. Fitzsimmons came to Chicago to try to mollify the local leaders, but he was sent home disappointed and ranting, "Most of the strikers have been intimidated by a few militants." In an effort to break the strike, Illinois Republican senator Charles Percy came to Chicago and charged that the local strike was a threat to community well-being. Even the New York Times felt compelled to editorialize against 705's secretary-treasurer and highest ranking officer, Louis Peick, and other Chicago officials for bringing back the "dog-eat-dog practices that prevailed when local barons dominated the Teamsters."[31]

On March 25, after a number of unproductive meetings at the Conrad Hilton Hotel, Peick called the employers' latest offer "laughable." The trucking management negotiators fired back that the offer was actually a 6.36 percent wage increase over three years. Peick derisively responded, "Percentages won't buy bread."[32] One week later, after an embarrassing six-minute negotiation session, Peick announced that "something was about to pop." On April 7 the popping began, as select strikes hit a handful of companies. Although Local 705's stance was courageous and likely to determine the balance of power nationally between the IBT and the freight companies, it was a monumental task. The local had 650 separate contracts to settle with more than 1,200 firms, who were represented by six separate trucking associations. But the local demonstrated undaunted staying power and brought the employers to heel. By July the work stoppage was over.

The "Chicago Settlement" increased hourly pay 50 cents more than the national deal and improved benefits, whereas the Fitzsimmons "compromise" had included no benefit improvement. Just as he had done three years earlier, the IBT president was forced to reopen the national agreement, and as a result he upped the wage increase by another 20 cents.[33] To everyone following bargaining between the trucking industry and the Teamsters, it was very obvious where the standard was being set. When during the strike Peick commented that "they didn't learn their lesson," he was talking as much about the international union as the companies.[34]

Peick's prominence and the local's strength were displayed time and again throughout the 1970s. But regardless of the load being hauled, it was the freight industry upon which Local 705 built its beefy reputation. For most of the postwar years, the local's dominant employers were large freight and intracity (i.e., cartage) haulers. But as the 1970s deregulatory movement kicked into high gear, Peick was faced with a new bargaining challenge. Changes in federal law had expanded the market for small package delivery, and by the early 1980s, United Parcel Service (UPS) had emerged as the local's largest single employer. UPS's Chicago operation began modestly on July 22, 1940, as a private contract service to two large retail department stores. Recognizing the limitations of this market, in 1956 the company expanded its services by acquiring "common carrier" rights to deliver packages between all addresses for any customers. In 1960 UPS opened three new Chicago area facilities and by the end of the decade had added another three, bringing its total workforce to approximately four thousand.[35]

Growing operations in the Midwest meant dealing with the Teamsters. From UPS's early days in Chicago, UPS and the Teamsters had constructed a cooperative relationship. In the 1940s, Chicago Local 725 represented the firm's retail drivers. But as the company prepared to ramp up its operations in the late 1950s, workers at Local 725 voted to merge with the much larger Local 705. From the merger forward, Local 705 peacefully negotiated a separate agreement with the delivery service.[36] During Peick's and Danny Ligurotis's administrations, with the exception of a brief dispute in 1961, consecutive three-year contracts were routinely negotiated and signed without any work stoppages. In most cases the contracts were little more than extensions of the previous agreements.

Steady growth characterized UPS's business development, until the package delivery firm constructed a colossal central sorting facility immediately outside the Chicago city limits. Opened in 1994, the Chicago Area Consolidated Hub (CACH) came to employ roughly 400 package car drivers and approximately 8,000 "inside" sorters. CACH brought the number of Chicago metro area UPS facilities to eleven and increased union employment levels at the company by the late 1990s to nearly 15,000. Local 705 represented over 95 percent of those workers, and the UPS division amounted to 61 percent of the union's membership.[37]

Despite the enlarged bargaining relationship, Peick's response to the change was minimalist at best and dismissive at worst. His inattention to the needs of a rapidly multiplying UPS workforce would prove to have enormous political consequences for the local's internal governance. Since the mid-1970s, the UPS division had been the source of most democratic agitation within the local. Stewards and business agents underserved UPS, and the local executive board was closed to package delivery members. As a result, UPS workers were treated as second-class union members, and long-simmering grievances moved a small number of them to strategize about ways to win local office. In a strange twist of fate, the capital expansion of an employer notorious for "sweating" its workers pumped up the one-time "stepsisters" of the local into the brawny, favored child of an emergent reform movement.

The lesson for most of the twentieth century was that Local 705 was independent, militant, powerful, and, though not democratic, certainly effective. Drivers and platform workers benefited from well-paying jobs and negotiated employer-funded health, welfare, and pension plans. Members also enjoyed a degree of social interaction that only a large and financially secure local could provide. Every Labor Day after World War II until the CFL ceased holding its citywide parade, Local 705 imaginatively dressed up a long flatbed truck in flowers and papier-mâché, and proudly took their place in the procession of Chicago unions. In the 1960s a highlight of each year was the annual Local 705 summer event held at Four Lakes Picnic Area. Approximately 10,000 workers and their families came to the large, resortlike setting to feast on 20,000 hot dogs, 10,000 ice cream bars, 15,000 cans of soda, and 60 barrels of beer. Each year Snappy the Clown and his seven associates entertained the children by performing magic tricks and supervising games throughout the day. The annual extravaganza cost the local about $28,000.[38] Times were indeed good.

Unfortunately, as the national economic and regulatory conditions under which tractor-trailer drivers operated became more hostile in the 1980s, the local grew less meaningful in the lives of its members. Its leadership also became more disconnected with reality. In a 1976 Labor Day piece in the CFL's newspaper, Peick wrote that despite popular criticism of organized labor's ability to honestly represent its members, "the overwhelming majority of the membership and others helped by the labor movement are satisfied with what is being done by the union." Peick acknowledged that for union officials, "the rewards [of leadership] are the quiet words of gratitude from the members."[39] When the Local 705 chief penned his holiday greetings, he knew not only that there was considerable rank-and-file dissatisfaction within the union but also that something much louder was lurking beneath the quiet words.

In 1987, after serving for nearly three decades as a local officer and ten years as an international vice president, Peick was forced to retire from union office because of his deteriorating health; his second in command, Daniel Ligurotis, assumed control over the local. Upon his ascension at Local 705, Ligurotis was appointed an international vice president, and one year later he became director of the powerful Central States Conference.

IBT president William McCarthy may have signaled Ligurotis's career trajectory by customarily introducing the Chicago boss as "a real smart guy and the future of the union."[40] In the 1991 Teamster election won by Ron Carey, Ligurotis ran from the number-two spot behind Walter Shea and finished third in a three-man contest, collecting a paltry 71,735 votes.

The economics and politics of the transportation market had changed. The Teamster local that Ligurotis had inherited was still large, autonomous, and autocratic, but it was now a more dangerous organization to govern. Reform caucuses in Chicago and around the country had proved remarkably resilient. While there would soon be word from the Southern District of New York of a pending massive lawsuit against the international union, this was Chicago, and Ligurotis knew firsthand that things were always different here. He was about to be proved right in unexpected ways.

CHAPTER TWO

Fighting Corruption

Chicago had always been a "big, brawling play-for-keeps world" for Teamsters, and sometimes the price of playing was very high. Assorted national investigations in the late 1950s had revealed that an array of organized crime figures were intricately involved with Chicago Teamster officials. Local 705 business agent Sam Canino found out just how brawling the city was when in the late 1960s he nonchalantly lifted his garage door and was greeted with a gunshot blast that blew away part of his face. 705 Teamster chief Louis Peick was also allegedly the victim of a 1950 mob attack. While walking from a third-floor flat on Fullerton Avenue, Peick was ambushed by two men who left him bloody from a bullet wound. Union-related violence was also at the center of a 1973 National Labor Relations Board (NLRB) ruling against Local 705 officials who were found guilty of fifteen years of "sheer racketeering" in a scheme to coerce service station employers to sign union contracts. Owners who resisted were threatened that their stations would be "dried up" and workers reluctant to accept union representation would be "taken care of."[1]

Using heavy-handed methods against enemies had been a standard practice in Chicago and within Teamsters Local 705. No group of union members felt the sting of official oppression more than those who dared to organize on behalf of a change in leadership and policies. At the beginning of the 1970s, a small group of workers came together to form Teamsters Ranks United to Help (T.R.U.T.H.). They peppered job sites with a four-page newsletter that regularly attacked "King Looey Peick" (Louis Peick) and the union leadership for their concessionary contract deals with employers. The newsletter also criticized "King Looey" for his imperial and undemocratic ways. Workers accused "Dictator Peick" of using threats of reprisals against members who dared speak up about the terms under which they labored. In 1973 a group of T.R.U.T.H. members, angry over pension plan inequities, rallied outside the union leader's "castle" (the union office) and threatened to come back with "many more of our fellow members again and again and again."[2]

At most they seem to have been deemed a nuisance by the leadership. But a nuisance, if left undisturbed, could become a threat. Consequently, the regime attacked the legitimacy of the group by pointing out that "T.R.U.T.H. dissidents members [actions] were disruptive."[3] The leadership also appears to have orchestrated an endless number of flyers, letters, resolutions, and petitions allegedly representing the majority views of the membership against the efforts of vocal "dissident groups." These dues-paying members of the union were denigrated as a third-column "element" and redefined as "so-called merchants of doom," "uniformed critics," and "communists."

As the local chieftains publicly harangued their detractors, unhappy workers formed, unformed, and reformed themselves into new protest groups. One particularly dynamic association took the name UPSurge. Stitched together by part-time workers at the Jefferson Street UPS package center, UPSurge members were, according to Bob Persak, "very radical."[4] Persak had worked at UPS for more than thirty years and recalls that the people involved with the Jefferson Street crowd were the "icebreakers" in the reform movement. UPSurge workers, like their fellow dissidents, were as active in combating workplace abuse as they were in challenging union governance "down at the hall."

UPSurge and other dissidents typically targeted the old guard's long, disgraceful record of selectively providing workers with the benefits they had earned. One case, which became a national issue for the reform movement, involved Local 705 member John Daniel. Daniel was a twenty-three-year local driver who, because of failing eyesight, had to retire. Upon his involuntary retirement in 1973, the 705 trustees notified Daniel that he was not entitled to a pension because of a single three-month layoff. Daniel then unsuccessfully sued the local's pension trustees for embezzlement of funds.[5] Despite losing, Daniel's efforts signaled to the Teamster bureaucracy that the reform movement was acquiring the organizational means to be effective.

The dissidents' threat to the local leadership gathered steam when the grassroots opposition gelled into the more formidable PROD. As a Chicago area chapter of the national Professional Drivers' Council, local PROD members aggressively pushed for improvements in driver safety and internal democratic reforms. PROD's efforts received immediate attention from Local 705's executive board. In the winter of 1978, PROD held an open Chicago area meeting attended by approximately 135 drivers, including a "large contingent" from Local 705. Among the crowd were two undercover Local 705 business agents. The agents subsequently filed a two-and-a-half-page report with Peick that itemized each speaker's comments and concluded by noting that at the group's next meeting local officers and bylaws would be voted on. The firsthand account also informed Peick that attendance "[would be] restricted to card (i.e., PROD) carrying members." Despite the need for credentials, Peick not only managed to place, "through various devices," three agents at the next meeting, but also found a way for them to vote.[6]

At both national and local levels, old guard disdain was also mounting against Teamsters for a Democratic Union (TDU), the rank-and-file dissident organization dedicated to reforming the union. TDU and PROD had merged nationally in 1979, and as reform pressure solidified, the actions of the regime became more reactionary. In October of 1983, a profane and boisterous crowd of Peick supporters boarded a bus headed for the Hilton Hotel in Romulus, Michigan. The agitated riders carried signs that read "TDU—They Destroy Unions." Romulus was the site of TDU's annual convention, and Teamsters from various cities, organized into an antidemocratic faction called the Brotherhood of Loyal American and Strong Teamsters (BLAST), converged on the Hilton with a lesson of brute force to impart. BLAST members damaged the meeting room and chased the assembled union dissidents out into the street.[7]

Back in Chicago, publications from TDU were labeled "socialist" and "slanderous." Anyone affiliated with TDU or PROD was accused of disloyalty and fermenting discord within the local. As internal union charges were filed for the first time against local officers, the executive board claimed that TDU provisions to democratize the local would cost the members an additional "$1,000,000 per year."[8] The leadership was now facing a well-organized national movement of rank-and-file reformers, and instead of preserving the mechanisms that would have processed the divergent interests of the membership, they circled the wagons.

Peick had also associated with followers of a right-wing national group calling itself the U.S. Labor Party. Headed by Lyndon LaRouche, the U.S. Labor Party had been characterized by other unions as possessing "the making of a fascist movement."[9] But for all the unsavory qualities of the party, Peick and other Teamster leaders relied on the group to produce scurrilous literature attacking the credibility of the reformers. The anti-TDU barrage had its intended effect. Prior to the trusteeship, no more than a hundred workers joined any of the protest configurations, and the numbers at 705 actually went down with the PROD-TDU merger. "A lot of people felt that PROD was a good organization protecting driver safety," Persak explained. "But with TDU, people weren't so sure." No doubt handicapped by the local leadership's propaganda, the TDU chapter nonetheless formed a steering committee and met in the basements of different members' homes. One of the basements belonged to Local 705 member Gerry Zero, and chapter officer John McCormick (also a 705 member) chaired a number of those meetings.

Trying to create a grassroots movement "was very helter-skelter," Persak recalled. Mike Belzer remembers it more ominously. In 1978 Belzer was a Local 705 member, driving a truck for Transport Services. His opposition to Teamster old guard rule led him to the presidency of the Chicago PROD chapter. Throughout the 1970s and 1980s, reformers like Belzer put themselves forward as candidates for convention delegate and local officer positions. During this period, electing officers was little more than a triennial coronation. Often during a nomination meeting, a floor resolution would be offered "recognizing the efforts and results of the leadership" or recommending that the secretary-treasurer be given an award for "distinguished service." Just getting on the ballot was an act of heroism. John McCormick recalled that "during nomination meetings the regime would bring in 'gang bangers' with vote Ligurotis signs and surround opposition candidates to intimidate them from putting their name into nomination."[10]

When intimidation failed, more persuasive approaches were used. During the local's nomination meeting for convention delegates in 1991, thugs beat up 705 member Leroy Ellis. An African American Chicago truck driver, Ellis had been a top-ten-ranked World Boxing Association heavyweight prizefighter in the 1970s and a sparring partner of Muhammad Ali. Ellis also happened to be a TDU member who had the distinction of being the union's first African American elected as an international vice president. The end result of these strong-arm tactics was most often to elect an unopposed slate of candidates by casting a "white ballot" to signify "unanimous consent."[11]

Longtime local rank-and-filers remembered that companies like UPS took a keen interest in union politics. Nothing, of course, was more political or a more certain determinant of the tenor of labor relations than a union election. Bedford Park package-car driver Bill Kelly painfully recalled the cozy relationship that UPS management forged with union business agents and elected leaders during the pretrusteeship years. In 1983 Kelly was dismissed from the company after allegedly failing a required Department of Transportation eye exam. He was reported to have a "lazy eye" and, despite a flawless driving record, was discharged; the union did not even request a hearing. When Kelly inquired about the union's inaction, his business agent subtly informed him that he "was not one of the in-guys." Being "in" meant working closely with the Peick-appointed staff. Kelly was mystified by the comment. At the time he was "just one of those guys that pays his dues and keeps a low profile." But after he was forced to file a lawsuit against the company and the union to get his job back, Kelly began to publicly agitate for changes in the local. "Now the threats became more aggressive," he noted. On a regular basis he fended off comments from his Peick-friendly business agent such as "Planning to work next week?" Although he did not recall ever being threatened by a UPS supervisor, Kelly understood that "going against the union" was bad for job security.[12]

The message was not lost on John McCormick. In 1979 the future local president was discharged for "driving off route" and forced to accept a two-week suspension without pay as a condition for returning to work. This was a punishment rarely applied, and in McCormick's case it was very severe considering that his actual misdeed amounted to double-parking on a quiet street at five in the morning to pick up a paper and a cup of coffee.[13] Nonetheless, after eighteen years of driving and with Christmas less than a month away, McCormick found himself out of a job. As he struggled with the emotional stress of being unemployed, McCormick was certain he knew the cause of his unsavory predicament. Three years earlier he had run for local office against the incumbents and ever since had been branded an enemy of the union regime. McCormick's political activism against the union was subsequently ramped up, but he never lost sight of his conviction that the regime often included the management of UPS.

UPS employee Robert Maziarka was no friend of union officials either. Like McCormick, he ran unsuccessfully in the 1976 local election against the "Peick guys." Taking a whipping at the polls was only the beginning of his mistreatment at the hands of UPS and the union. As nasty as he found the electoral campaign, Maziarka learned that he had lost more than an election. Once back on the job, he was shadowed by UPS management. It became common for a supervisor to ride along with Maziarka on his daily routes. Soon he was being disciplined for a host of trumped-up minor violations. "It was aggravating to the point where you wanted to punch somebody," he admitted. Finally, after being subjected to countless irritations, Maziarka was informed that he was fired. The charge, "over staying the lunch hour," was supported by the union business agent, who accused Maziarka of "stealing time." Despite having multiple witnesses to counter the company's claim, Maziarka was never reinstated. His brief political experience taught him what every rank-and-filer tired of abuse eventually learned: "Attempting to try any kind of reform would lead to getting buried."[14]

The importance of union elections to company fortunes was so great that sometimes UPS saw fit to act proactively. On one occasion the firm helped a "friendly" union candidate get on the ballot. On 4 September 1990, Elizabeth Kinney, National Labor Relations Board regional director, officially informed Daniel Ligurotis that United Parcel Service had filed an unusual charge. The package delivery giant alleged that Local 705 had "restrained and coerced employees . . . in the exercise of the rights guaranteed in Section 7 of the Act . . . [by] coercively persuading people not to sign a Union election accreditation petition for a candidate" to office.[15] In this case UPS was not promoting the political fortunes of a union dissident but saw an opportunity to improve its bargaining power by challenging the old leadership. The board charge underscored the tense political environment, which often suffocated any signs of rank-and-file leadership.

When oppositional candidates did fight their way onto the ballot, they were usually not candidates for principal officer positions. As a rule, union dissidents challenged only for the four elected business agent slots, and in many elections the incumbent slate ran unopposed. The one significant exception to this pattern occurred in 1984. That year Belzer challenged Peick for the secretary-treasurer post and put together a slate that included the four principal officers. As was customary, local officer elections were conducted as "walk-in" votes at the union hall. Belzer recalled that Peick "goons" terrorized any member who enter the hall wearing a button or anything else indicating support for the opposition slate. In an election marred by violence and vote-buying, Belzer, the local PROD-TDU activist, managed to secure a quarter of the vote.[16]

In addition to elections, reformers regularly pushed procedural changes onto the local's agenda. In 1978 the Local 705 Reform Committee submitted to the membership a comprehensive, detailed list of bylaw amendments. Prominent among the proposals was one demanding that stewards, business agents, and fund trustees be elected, not appointed. Collectively, the bylaw amendments amounted to an unprecedented attempt to radically shift power in the local away from the appointed bureaucracy and toward the membership. On each proposal only a small minority of members voted against the status quo. The leadership routinely opposed such motions and rallied their soldiers to orchestrate a loud, crushing rejection of any limitations on the prerogatives of power. One-time recording secretary Bennie Jackson vividly remembers being "attacked in the [union] hall and beaten with a metal chair" for simply advocating that meeting dates be changed.[17]

The lack of any discernible successes in winning bylaw amendments or electing candidates eventually took its toll. Although Persak was still committed to democratic unionism, he represented a fair number of members in thinking that change would never come through the political process functioning at Local 705. Belzer agreed that because of a combination of fear, uncertainty, confusion, and a rigged set of rules, local reformers could "not debate, educate, motion, propose or vote" reform into the union. They never let up on the criticism of the local leadership, but dissidents were adamant about the need for a more forceful means to take the Teamsters back from the bad guys. "Only way change will come," Persak remembers predicting, "is by shoving it down their throat." By "their" he meant both the local leadership and the membership.

The RICO suit, Carey's election, and the local trusteeship were necessary devices that forced change from above. Mass membership support alone, before the trusteeship, would never have been enough to dislodge nearly ninety years of institutional control "against democracy, against militant grass-roots unionism." But reform of the Teamsters would not have happened without a rank-and-file movement. And it is certain that Carey would not have moved against the 705 cabal if he had not had a local army of dissidents who would fight to radically realign how the leadership and the ranks interacted. As Persak colorfully noted, "Once the trusteeship shoved democracy down, the people learned to like the taste."[18] The teaching came from what the reformers did after the trusteeship.

The Trusteeship of Local 705

Following Carey's 1991 election, an IRB investigation of Local 705 revealed a number of serious internal violations. The board produced a set of findings that "warrant[ed] the imposition of Trusteeship and the filing of charges against officers of Local 705." Union board members were charged with embezzling nearly $70,000 by making illegal severance payments to retiring local business agents, and Ligurotis (the local's secretary-treasurer from 1987 to 1992) was found guilty of taking an improper loan from the union treasury of approximately $77,000. The investigative report ruefully referred to Ligurotis's borrowing habits as treating the local treasury as if it were "his personal piggy bank."[19]

The executive board also had a bad habit of paying for work that was never done. The worst case was of Louis Esposito, the local's eighty-one-year-old vice president. He was paid his annual salary of $85,000 despite attending no meetings in 1993, and the evidence further suggested "that he has been inactive for some time." It was further confirmed that executive board members had repeatedly participated "in a pattern of corruption" designed to fleece the union's benefit plans. One particularly outrageous theft was the embezzling of $13.5 million from the union's health and welfare and pension funds. Under a intricate payola scheme, previous fund attorneys, doctors, insurance companies, and administrators had breached their "fiduciary duties, [and committed] malpractice, fraud, and various other unlawful actions."[20]

Corruption was principally, but not exclusively, financial. Also included in the corrupt-acts category was condoning illegal activity. Ligurotis's hiring practices were particularly questionable. For example, he hired Richard Bravieri as a "maintenance employee" despite his "conviction for extorting money from an employer" and then promoted him to a business agent post. The Local 705 chief then put Richard Green on the payroll despite his extortion conviction. Ligurotis completed the hiring trifecta by employing Edward Fickett as a business agent. Fickett's qualification for representing workers was that he was a convicted arsonist. The IRB's investigating officer also found that Richard Volkmar, Eugene Spizzirri, and Sam Canino were guilty of "dealing with organized crime"; they were forced to resign. Despite previous chest-thumping protestations from local union officials that there were "no hoodlums running our union," the hiring practices and personal associations of 705 officials strongly suggested otherwise.[21]

To address the mounting accumulation of wrongdoings, Carey appointed Harold "Eddie" Burke as temporary trustee of Local 705. Fresh from his critical involvement with the United Mine Workers of America's successful battle with the Pittston Mine Company, Burke had agreed to work as Carey's campaign manager in the union's first national referendum election. Burke quickly moved to inform local members about the trusteeship and to further investigate the executive board's practices.[22] He met almost immediate opposition from both the board and a faction within the rank and file.

Anticipating a rough welcome, Burke took extreme precautions in scheduling a trusteeship-hearing meeting for the membership. As part of his arrangements, he sent a detailed, penciled floor plan of the local's auditorium to the hearing examiners, assuring them that order could be maintained. The meeting turned into a riot, however, and defiance of the trusteeship forced Burke to request a temporary restraining order to compel the board to cease in their resistance. Along with opposition from the local hierarchy, Carey's appointee had to respond to handbills anonymously passed out by the Committee to Defend Local 705. The authors alleged an organized crime connection to the trustee under the headline "Is Eddie Burke an Errand Boy for the Mob?"[23]

Burke had little reason to expect cooperation. Despite the IBT's pledge of compliance with the 1989 Consent Decree, 705's leaders chose to "advise the International Union that the local union will not comply" with any investigation. Despite the tortured claims of sovereignty and other desperate attempts to derail a full airing of the local's misdeeds, punitive actions were taken against all charged parties, including a decision by the IRB to ban secretary-treasurer Ligurotis "for life from the union."[24] Burke was acting aggressively and doing his job well, but he had never intended to keep the Chicago post very long. Both he and the local reformers understood that it was important that the trusteeship provide for a transition to an elected democratic leadership. With the goal of returning governing authority to the local, Carey made a fateful decision to replace Burke with a 705 member.

Electing Reform, 1995 and 1997

On 18 July 1994, Gerald Zero was appointed "Trustee over the affairs of Teamsters Local Union 705." Zero was a Cicero-born, twenty-five-year truck-driving member of Local 705 and had served as Burke's assistant. Along with Local 705 UPS member John McCormick, Zero had also been appointed as an international representative shortly after Carey's 1991 election. Within six months of his trustee appointment, Zero requested from the IBT the authority to conduct an independently monitored officer election.[25] The 1995 election would be the first substantive test of the trusteeship's lasting impact. The uncertainties surrounding the first posttrusteeship vote challenged the reformers to put forward a slate of candidates that could inspire the ranks to stand up against the old guard elite. The question of who would lead the ticket was paramount.

As Zero remembers it, Burke asked the six-million-dollar question, "Who wants to run for the head of this local?" By contemporary accounts, it was not a plum assignment. Despite the local trusteeship, the reform agenda was not widely popular within 705. The odds of a reform slate winning a local election were considered slim at best. Zero, Burke, and John McCormick agreed that to elect a "new teamster," it was going to take an accommodation among the dissidents. Reaching an agreed-upon course turned out to be simpler than expected. Zero first informed Burke that he had no interest in running for office. McCormick, however, indicated his eagerness for the opportunity, and so a historic bargain was struck to run the long-term UPSer for the secretary-treasurer office. Until, according to Zero, Carey intervened.

"He called me to meet him at the O'Hare Airport Hilton," Zero remembers. It was just one month before the 1995 local nomination meeting for officers, and Carey wanted to talk about the slate. The two men had not been sitting together in Carey's hotel room for more than a few minutes when the international union president blurted out, "Everybody tells me you're the guy to head the slate." Zero respected Carey's judgment and expressed a willingness to run for office, but he worried about how McCormick would react to the change of plans. To rectify the problem, a special meeting was arranged where both men debated the slate for nearly five hours. The next day Zero surprisingly announced that he would "step aside" and support McCormick. For a second time the two men had reached an agreement. And once again Carey stepped in. When the IBT president heard of the decision, he phoned the local and made it clear that he wanted Zero to head the ticket and McCormick to hold the number-two slot (i.e., president). It was now definite; Zero would lead a union reform party into the asphalt jungle of Chicago Teamster politics.[26]

The 1995 Election

The leading figure opposing the Carey-picked team was 705 driver Dane Passo. A Chicago-born son and grandson of Teamster drivers, Passo had served as a steward, an organizer and a business agent under Ligurotis. He was an intense admirer of the legendary James R. Hoffa and well known for his ferocious support of Hoffa junior's attempt to win the Teamsters presidency. Married at eighteen, Passo left his job as a meat cutter in the early 1970s to drive a truck for Gertsen Cartage. His job included hauling steel to the mills spread out along the eastern edge of Lake Michigan in northwest Indiana. During his downtime he read a lot of books about James R. Hoffa.

The tough-talking Hoffa fascinated Passo. From the books and his attendance at Local 705 membership meetings, he developed a craving for more union involvement. His repeated pleas to Peick to be made a steward were always swiftly rebuffed. Then Danny Ligurotis became Local 705 chieftain. Ligurotis appointed him as Local sergeant of arms. It was a humble beginning, but Passo felt that he had been given a golden opportunity. In short order Ligurotis began to promote him into more important leadership positions.

He got a chance to demonstrate his dedication to the senior Hoffa legacy when in 1991 the son of the disappeared president announced his intentions to run in the union's first referendum election. Friends in Detroit told Passo about James P. Hoffa's plans, and he quickly signed on to help. But Hoffa was ruled ineligible by Michael Holland, election officer and soon-to-be Local 705 board attorney. Passo then shifted his political energies and openly went to work trying to relocate his immediate boss to Washington. Ligurotis ran unsuccessfully in the 1991 international election as a vice-presidential candidate with Daniel Shea. Passo admits that although he "did what [he] had to do for the ticket," he was really just biding time, "waiting for Jim to run again."[27]

Consistent with his pro-Hoffa sentiment, Passo declared war on the 705 trusteeship; "I spoke out big time against the trusteeship and accused Zero and the rest of being TDU pieces of shit." From the moment Burke arrived, Passo was consumed with one burning objective: "to destroy these guys, no matter what it takes." He plotted with others to "disrupt" the trusteeship in whatever way he could. His first chance came with the initial meeting of the membership called by Burke to explain the trusteeship.

More than fifteen hundred people attended the meeting, and Passo had stirred up a large majority of them to a feverish anti-Burke pitch. "We threw pop cans, coffee, fruit and stuff at Burke and raised so much hell that he had to adjourn the meeting." Passo went from that meeting triumphant and, with the 1995 election in mind, "began to work people." Shortly after the wild meeting, Passo agreed to run, with holdovers from the Ligurotis team, as a trustee on the Real Teamster Slate (RTS). With his now-trademark "take no prisoners" approach to political organizing, Passo began to campaign ferociously against the trusteeship candidates. His high-strung temper was about to cost him politically, however, and no one was more grateful than the reformers.

In 1995 Zero and McCormick were hard at work forming the Reform Pride Movement (RPM) slate, and Zero recalled the unsettling feelings he and his campaign staff experienced as they prepared to run for office. Jo Pressler was a Local 705 staffer and the RPM's campaign director, and she thought the reformers' chance of winning, if everything turned out right, was at best fifty-fifty. The campaign's modest expectations were shaped by the reality that the RTS had a good-sized bloc of support among the freight stewards and drivers. Passo and Ralph Mancini, the RTS candidate for secretary-treasurer, were among a group of experienced high-profile staff that had built up strong relationships within the freight barns. Despite the IRB's charges against the previous executive board, the trusteeship had not made the familiar old guard figures less popular. Members were confused, more than anything else, about the chain of events that convulsed their local. Zero feared that in an advanced state of uncertainty, the rank and file would, by default, trust the union leaders they knew. Then Passo and the RTS imploded.

At a membership meeting, Passo and others began to speak out against the trusteeship, calling it an "evil of the Teamsters." Although they were called out of order repeatedly, they refused to cease their tirade. As a result of Passo's orchestrated antics, Carey suspended him and other RTS supporters from the union for six months and declared them ineligible to run for local office. "They knew they couldn't win," Passo proudly claimed, implying that that was the reason he and the others were suspended.[28] With the slate's strongest vote-getters now on the sideline, the RPM suddenly found the path to political power a little easier to navigate. When the electioneering dust had settled, Zero and John McCormick led a sweep of RPM candidates into office over three challenging parties. "Passo's ineligibility was the most important incident during the trusteeship," Zero revealed. If "not for his knucklehead behavior we would have gotten beat." With the election results verified, the local was officially "released from trusteeship," and what many 705 members thought was impossible had come to pass: the installation of reform-minded officers.[29]

The 1997 Election

The new administration took office with an exhausting list of institutional repairs to complete and an active oppositional group critical of every reconstructive step.[30] Among the first actions taken by the new executive board was to continue the practice, begun under the trusteeship, of replacing those business agents and stewards who had failed to perform their job responsibilities. From December of 1993 until the days immediately following the installation of new officers, twenty-six agents were dismissed. But Zero and McCormick had barely scratched the local's corroded surface when in the fall of 1997 a timetable for a new mail-ballot election was posted. Union members would be mailed a ballot in early November, and ballots would be opened and counted on 6 December at 10:00 A.M.

The RPM forces approached the 1997 contest believing that they had a solid record of achievement to promote. They would campaign from the lofty perch of improved health and welfare and pension plans, better contracts, openness to the rank and file, and honest administration. Zero acknowledged that "we didn't want to go negative, after all we had been there for a while and members knew what we had done."[31] The party expected to win, but the opposition this time would not be fractured, and it had a secret plan that would in the end nearly sweep the reformers out of office.

Running this time as the United Slate candidate for secretary-treasurer, Passo gathered 120 key people to form a single opposition party. United Slate supporters held "talk sessions" with freight drivers and, unlike their practice in the previous election, also with UPS part-time workers. In the 1995 race, no one competed for part-timers' loyalty because they were considered unlikely voters. Election rules required that an eligible voter be a local union member for at least six months before the date of the election and have fully paid his or her dues. The requirement was a harsh one for part-timers at UPS. Turnover among part-time workers was nearly 60 percent every six months, and estimates were that no more than half of the part-time UPS membership would ever be eligible to vote. There was, of course, still the remaining eligible half, but they displayed little interest in the union, and consequently, Zero's team put together a very weak part-timers' campaign at UPS.

Passo knew, however, that in unifying the opposition, he had created a strong base of support among freight handlers and that "no one was thinking about the part-timers." But external events had raised the profile of the part-time workers. During the previous summer, the local had waged a strike against the company to create full-time jobs for workers who were cobbling together two four-hour shifts into one full day of work.[32] Passo believed that if part-time workers could be persuaded to vote, the party that won their support would have the key to victory. The United Slate chief decided to spend the last two weeks prior to the vote working UPS sites exclusively. He set up a camper trailer at the CACH facility and, over the loud sounds of popular music, gave out United T-shirts, hats, and buttons. The day the mail ballots were finally counted, Passo thought he had pulled off an upset.

As the count neared completion, Zero was holding on to a razor-thin lead over Passo.[33] With such a small margin separating the two, attention in the union hall now shifted to the pile of open but challenged ballots temporarily put aside during the count. Upon request from any of the slate's election observers, a ballot submitted by an eligible member can be challenged and temporarily set aside. These ballots are examined only when their number is equal to or greater than the vote differential separating the top two candidates. Given the margin dividing Zero and Passo, the unopened pile was ominously large. When the election officer began counting the challenged ballots, Zero led by 272 votes. Passo quickly picked up 60 votes. But then the election officer realized that the remaining uncounted and valid challenged ballots were fewer than 212. He stopped counting. Even if Passo had been awarded all of the challenged ballots, he could not have overtaken Zero.

After governing for two years within a cauldron of dissent and beating back a unified opposition, the RPM had been returned to office. Kenneth Paff, national director of TDU, declared that the results of the local election proved that "the reform forces have increased in Chicago and the Hoffa forces have gone." With two consecutive election victories, the reformers now set out to create what labor attorney Michael Holland called the "kind of democracy that yields better trade unionism."[34] Holland's point was a pragmatic reminder that a union is not the "Elks club" and that the institutional objective of any union was to improve the working lives of the membership; consequently, union democracy's substantive claims must be judged by the actual good it does.

As people associated with union transformation projects knew, Local 705's task was formidable. It was, to quote Teamster attorney Peggy Hillman, "like trying to teach elephants to dance."[35] The next steps would require using rank-and-file involvement to build a more potent workplace counterbalance to the power of freight haulers and package delivery firms.

CHAPTER THREE

Democratic Governance

Secretary-treasurer Dan Ligurotis and the executive board had committed serious violations, but for many years Local 705 officers had also stifled dissenting voices and had run the union like feudal lords. In the end, the trusteeship was simply the necessary means to end a long line of serial offenses against rank-and-file union citizenship. Fixing the offenses chronicled in the trusteeship report, however, was not enough to transform the union into a democratic and effective defender of worker rights. To become a democratic union, Local 705 would have to conduct a root-and-branch excision of the procedures that had been used to keep members acquiescent and invisible. To accommodate and implement the vast changes necessary to democratize Local 705, reform union leader Gerald Zero made a controversial and effective decision to hire a number of non-705 Teamsters. These "outsiders" would, in the 2000 election, become a source of political debate, but at the dawn of the posttrusteeship local, they proved invaluable to reshaping the union's political culture.

Local 705's Labor Intellectuals

As a result of the 1995 and 1997 elections, the personnel portfolios at Local 705 had changed dramatically. Zero had hired a large number of people from outside the union's workforce pool who were unattached to local union constituencies. Some new hires, like Tom Nightwine, Charlie Teas, and Dan Campbell, were career Teamsters. Others, such as Mike Lass, Jo Pressler, Jim Lyons, Richard DeVries, and Don Barnett, were either experienced members of other unions or, like Paul Waterhouse, talent from outside the labor movement. Although fully appreciating the union norm of hiring from within, Zero also knew that each non–Local 705 staff member was incredibly well educated and had taken seriously the power of progressive ideas. Without consciously setting out to develop a union brain trust, Zero managed to recruit a team of "labor intellectuals" dedicated to democratic unionism.

These recruits were capable of bringing energy and a radical critique to a union local badly in need of organizational change. For example, Teas had been an Ohio TDU member since 1979, and Campbell sat on the organization's national steering committee. Jim Lyons had attended the rank-and-file-oriented Wisconsin School of Workers, had been an officer in the food and commercial union, and had even run for a state senate position in North Dakota. Nightwine held an associate's degree in labor relations and was a longtime Teamster from Ohio. Lass was a revered, legendary, militant ex-leader of the Illinois firefighters' efforts to organize in the 1960s and 1970s. Among his numerous claims to fame was that Chicago mayor Michael Bilandic had once called Lass a "gunslinger" and a "carpetbagger."[1] DeVries, however, may have best represented the "ideal-typical outsider" that longtime 705ers despised so intensely. He was certainly the most ideologically radical of all the people Zero recruited.

In 1967 DeVries had been arrested and sentenced to serve three to five years for refusing to be inducted into the army. As a Vietnam War resister, he also sledge-hammered down the doors of a Selective Service office in Evanston, Indiana. But his true commitment to social justice came to the fore in 1971 while he was visiting a friend who worked for the Mennonite Society in Honduras. On the day after Christmas, DeVries hitched a ride from a truck driver who turned out to be an activist for the Frente de Sandinista in Nicaragua. The Sandinista Front was involved in a civil war with a brutal, American-backed military dictatorship. For nearly ten years, DeVries was part of a North American network supplying the Frente with assorted supplies.

When he came to Local 705 from a brief stint as the first Hispanic organizer hired by the Chicagoland Northeast Council of Carpenters, DeVries brought with him a taste for political activism and a guerilla-warfare approach to unionism. DeVries was appointed a union representative and did a brilliant job of rebuilding the local's moving division by using creative forms of employer annoyances to win a number of battles. In 1998 he handled Tom Leedham's Chicago-based phone banking operation and provided the underdog reform candidate with a soft couch to bed down in while campaigning in the area. Taken together, DeVries and the other non-705 and non-Teamster members represented a leadership committed first and foremost to democratic unionism.

The group that gathered in Chicago also had well-developed administrative and policymaking skills. Campbell and Nightwine, for example, had been part of the national UPS negotiations and grievance committees. Lyons had been president of a local meat cutters' union, and Teas had served as an IBT local secretary-treasurer for twelve years, as well as a joint council officer in Cleveland, Ohio. Pressler had worked for a public-sector union and, according to Zero, was "so smart and hardworking that she would always be scribbling ideas on restaurant napkins, pieces of scrap paper, the back of matchsticks—anything she could write on."[2] He was proud to point out that after a few years with the local, she went to work for AFL-CIO president John Sweeney.

The chain of events that brought reformers to power at Local 705 was undoubtedly made stronger by the introduction of a cadre of outsiders.

Unlike the situation in previous administrations, posttrusteeship union representatives were not tied to organized crime or nepotistic hirers. Nor did they have criminal records or a legacy of Chicago Teamster politics. Their presence was a reminder that democracy at Local 705 came not only from above and below, but also from outside.

Practicing Union Pluralism

One of the initial problems the new administration addressed was the holding of membership meetings. To be sure, the prereform leadership of Local 705 met its constitutional and legal duty to hold meetings. But in Machiavellian fashion, the very act of scheduling a meeting was an exercise in elite control and became the subject of a court case. Membership meetings had always been held at 7:00 P.M. on Thursday evenings. Yet throughout the 1970–1980 period, UPS members offered numerous union petitions requesting that the meeting date be moved to Sunday. Although there were occasions when the officers formally addressed the requests, none of the appeals were ever granted.[3]

The weekday evening, according to an IBT Chicago Joint Council 25 ruling, appeared to permit nearly 90 percent of the membership to attend; however, the UPS employees argued otherwise. They contended that the date "constituted a systematic attempt to deprive [them] of their equal right to attend membership meetings and to vote," in violation of the Labor-Management Reporting and Disclosure Act (LMRDA). The court for the Northern District of Illinois, Eastern Division, gave credence to the plaintiffs' complaint by noting that the "opinion of the Joint Council [was], strictly speaking, hearsay." However, the court did not grant the petitioning members' request for preliminary injunctive relief, holding that it would "be inappropriate at this time."[4]

Despite the court's ruling, members continued to advocate for a schedule change. Under democratic rules of order, such a nominal demand should have been easy enough for the union to accommodate. But Local 705's officers were not about to have their power limited by something as incidental as how they responded to membership requests. Members offered sworn court testimony that officers and business agents were "implacably opposed to their participation in union affairs" and asked that the defendants be enjoined from "striking or beating the plaintiffs or threatening plaintiffs with physical harm." UPS employees further contended that for their inquisitive efforts they "received various contusions, abrasions and lacerations of their arms, hands, legs, faces, backs and bodies."[5]

The resolve of the UPS members was buttressed by their having to endure a second-tier status within the local. As part of a package delivery division, UPS members were outside the conventional, almost mythical domain of the over-the-road, big-rig Teamster drivers. Drivers in short brown pants hardly fit with the romantic image of a rough and tough Teamster.

Nor did such members ever hold positions of authority in IBT locals in the region. Since the expansion of over-the-road travel, elected and appointed slots had been the exclusive property of freight drivers. The claim to control had been well protected for thirty years, and the changing local membership demographics and transportation landscape had not persuaded anyone in power that there was a need to gracefully adapt.

Before the trusteeship, local union meetings were primarily used by the regime to orchestrate membership endorsements. There is little in the record to disavow an observer from the notion that meetings were used as a mechanism to sanction the actions of the leadership. Although membership crowds were often boisterous, the leadership rarely permitted the floor squabbling to become a public debate on the union's governance and performance. Despite monthly attendance figures that averaged 548, it was a rare moment when someone other than an officer, steward, or agent verbally expressed a thought from the floor of the assembly. From 1972 until the imposition of the trusteeship, 159 regular membership meetings were held.[6] The total number of recorded comments from the assembly addressed to the executive board was a deafening 49. Remarkably, in 74 percent of the meetings, not a single voice was heard from the rank-and-file congregated body.

In some years democratic expression was completely absent. Even allowing for some sloppy record-keeping, the period from 1974 through the first two months of 1978 stands as an astonishing example of membership disengagement from the union's policymaking process. During this time only four workers commented from the floor, and in 1974 and 1976 no nonelected or nonappointed member used his or her free speech rights at a union meeting. Since it is highly unlikely that in these two years no one in the entire membership had reason or desire to be heard, it seems reasonable to assume that workers' voices were muzzled beyond comprehension.

Worker silence is even more puzzling throughout the 1980s. Membership and executive board meetings are awash in comments from the officers about federal deregulation of the transportation industry and the subsequent dramatic increase in threats to unionized operators' jobs from nonunion, "gypsy" drivers. In addition, by 1983, every major employer association in the city had requested a reopening of its labor agreement for the purpose of reducing "burdensome [union] driver costs." In 1982 the leadership had been forced to admit that a referendum vote on the master cartage agreement represented the "first time in the history of the union that it has gone to the membership for a cut back in wages."[7] Nonetheless, despite dire warnings of job loss, Local 705 members remained at best stoic and at worst paralyzed by the messages sent to them by their union leaders.

But with UPS representatives elected to the executive board in 1995, one of the first acts of the new reform leadership was to survey the members about a preferred meeting date. Based on the responses, Local 705's monthly member assembly would now take place on Sunday mornings. After the meeting-day change, the leadership shifted its attention to how the sessions were governed. One obnoxious practice demanded immediate relief. Prior to the trusteeship, if a person wished to address the membership, he or she had to get permission from the secretary-treasurer before the meeting began. Not only is such a requirement intimidating and easily thwarted; it is inherently servile. In addition, the power of the meeting chair to influence debate was enhanced by the use of only one microphone, which was stationed at the foot of the chair. A member who gained access to the microphone was best advised to censor her or his comments, since to speak in an unauthorized manner was to invite the ultimate act of tyranny: the chair would shut off the microphone.[8]

Proving that democratic revolutions often start from humble beginnings, the new reform leadership instituted a radical change. First, they did away with the permission-to-speak meeting with the secretary-treasurer. Then they opened up a channel for democratic expression by placing a second microphone on the floor of the assembly. Now, instead of having to ask permission to speak, rank-and-filers had only to step into the aisle and address their issues. Unlike the podium mike, wielded like an electronic Excalibur, the accessible placement of the second microphone had the effect of plugging in worker voices. Union members who had previously had nothing to say now often found two or more topics to talk and debate about. In the posttrusteeship period, an average of 10.13 ($N = 159$) workers have spoken out at each membership meeting. In stark contrast to the prereform era, there were no meetings conducted without membership input, and on most occasions, worker comments elicited information from the leadership.[9]

The exchange of rank-and-file ideas reconceptualized the way that membership meetings were used. In the pretrusteeship period, the congregating of local drivers was little more than farce. Yet it had both practical and ideological objectives. Meetings appeared designed to thwart the development of new ideas, informed critiques, and rank-and-file challenges to institutional control. Ideologically, they served to showcase and reinforce the power and righteousness of the regime. Prior to the trusteeship, no time or expense was spared in persuading the local membership that the union was under competent stewardship. On at least one occasion that effort took on an extreme, glamorous pose.

In the summer of 1987, the executive board entered into a contract with Charles Fuller Voices to produce a twenty-eight-minute promotional video of Local 705. When the film premiered at a local union meeting, members watched as a "clean-cut, nicely dressed" over-the-road eighteen-wheel truck driver approached "an attractive young woman . . . looking disconsolately at a very flat tire." Immediately recognizing the woman's forlorn disposition, the "driver gallantly offers to change the tire and goes straight to work on it." As this scene of stereotypical manly Good Samaritanism flittered by, viewers were reminded "that from top to bottom, this is a hard-hitting, tough, fair and honorable union local run by capable people."

What members thought of the film was not reported, but for the privilege of being part of the Hollywood-like show, workers forked over $89,581.18 in dues money.[10]

Although meetings under the RPM leadership did not dispense with announcements of celebratory news, membership discussions were elevated to genuine information sharing. The change was not immediate, though. Labor attorney Michael Holland recalled that when he began to supervise union meetings for the local, "they were the ugliest things I'd ever seen." The picture was not unexpected. Holland had developed his reform credentials by working with dissidents within the United Mine Workers in the 1970s. Upon arriving at the Teamsters, he knew well how tenuous the idea of democracy was to the union, still deeply divided. Meetings held shortly after the trusteeship was imposed were emblematic of all the anxieties, angers, passions, and hopes that lived deep within the belly of the local body. "Not even a pretense of substance to the proceedings," was how Holland described membership meetings at the dawn of the reform project. However, just five years later, he was thrilled to point out that "people are actually addressing and discussing the union's business."[11]

Holland's explanation for the assembled union's greater capacity for eliciting and respecting democratic debate is as practical as it is profound. First, in January 1996, the local began to prepare and then publish an agenda for all meetings. This move was unprecedented. A review of all pretrusteeship executive board meeting minutes (1963–1993) revealed little discussion dedicated to upcoming membership meetings. It is impossible even to identify a nexus between board topics and the membership meetings. But under the framework of the trusteeship, the principal reason for the board meetings was to prepare for a gathering of the assembly. Board sessions now included discussion and formulation of a "draft agenda" for the membership meetings.[12] The agenda, once approved, was then printed and passed out to members attending the monthly gatherings.

The text of the agenda was brief, but it preserved one fundamental principle of democratic discourse: it gave members a common understanding of what elements constituted the union's business. For the first time, members were made aware of what they had a right to know. Prior to the trusteeship, it was nearly impossible for a local member to know—let alone participate in— what the union was doing. Knowing the issues and obligations that defined the union's parameters made it possible for individual members to perform three democratic functions. First, they could develop at least a rudimentary expertise on matters relevant to the health and welfare of the union. Second, once informed of the affairs of the institution, members could better keep an informed vigilance over the actions of the leadership. Finally, by becoming more critical observers of the organization's behavior, dues-payers were able to legitimately agitate for changes in policy and leadership.

The published agenda also brought a consistent, dependable order to the proceedings. Unlike the days of discretionary governance, union meetings now exhibited a regular form and flow. With procedural order came more civility and, consequently, less member-to-member intimidation. A crude division of the house characterized union meetings before the trusteeship. Discussions were always poisoned by personal suspicion and posturing. Not surprisingly, meetings were usually adjourned in approximately forty-eight minutes. But, as Holland has observed, the substance and tone of member-ship interactions since the first supervised election have become decidedly more "sophisticated." This, he claims, has had a very salutary influence on the democratic character of the meetings. "As the debate became more so-phisticated there is less place for politics." Meetings now typically ran be-tween sixty and ninety minutes.

By creating a rational process for dispensing with the business at hand, the agenda also established a platform from which individual members could rightfully act. The agenda, according to Holland, helped the mem-bers to be able to "rise and speak with impunity," so that they "could leave each meeting feeling they were part of the process." Members knew that a set of officer reports on particular subjects would always be followed by an opportunity to address an array of items during the "Good and Welfare" section. "Good and Welfare" was the name given to that portion of the proceedings in which the meeting's locus of control shifted to the assem-bly. In the 1970s and 1980s, members had only occasionally known a for-mal, set-aside opportunity to exercise their right of expression.

Further evidence of a newfound respect for pluralistic representation is evident in the hiring practices of the present leadership. Upon taking ad-ministrative control in 1993, the reform leadership discharged twenty-six agents, citing their failure to represent the members. Not unexpectedly, in 1995 six of those agents ran unsuccessfully for office on opposition slates. But contrary to the formerly typical "new broom sweeps clean" approach to winning elections, the reform leadership retained half a dozen staffers who had either run as opposition candidates or actively campaigned for the challengers. Included in this group was Mike Colgan. Colgan was appointed a representative in the fall of 1998, after running against the incumbents in 1995 on the Real Teamster Slate. Individuals affiliated with the main opposition faction approached him again in 1997 about repeating his candidacy. Despite the fact that Colgan re-tained some unhappiness about his father's being fired as a representa-tive by the present leadership, he refused to oppose the reform slate. "Zero and McCormick were doing a good job," was reason enough for his continued support.[13]

Colgan admitted to a gradual and guarded endorsement of the changes implemented at the local, but Mark Postilion experienced a more thorough transformation. Before going on staff with the union, Postilion held strong "allegiances to the old guard." He was part of a small circle of local mem-bers who actively campaigned for the RTS, and as a kid he had attended a BLAST rally. Despite his past affiliations, Postilion voted in 1996 for Ron

Carey. His embrace of the reform effort was a sometimes testy process of education, stretching over a year and a half. Postilion explained, "I began fighting over myself, because I couldn't be wrong about what I believed for so long." After a lot of reading and talking about IBT history, he "basically realized that [he] had made a big mistake." Postilion's conversion would ultimately elevate him to the forefront of the local's reform politics.[14]

According to Gerald Zero, latecomers to the cause of reform were appointed because "they put the interests of the members first."[15] Even if other more pragmatic objectives were involved, the appointment of long-standing political opponents to staff positions suggests that the leadership has not been hostile to pluralism.

The Education of Local 705

If democracy was going to produce effective trade union representation at Local 705, it would need to be more than procedures for voting and holding meetings. It must also provide the staff and the members with the resources and skills necessary to actively participate in the union's business. According to union representative Charlie Teas, the key to building the local's capacity to protect the interests of the members was "reaching out to members to become involved."[16]

They became involved by way of a collection of structured educational and communication opportunities. Beginning in early 1994, the local initiated quarterly craft training courses. Under Jim Lyons's direction, approximately five hundred rank-and-file members attended various Sunday morning craft classes. Over the next year and half, the classes were expanded into eight different divisions. Sessions for each craft are run twice a year and, importantly, are specifically designed for the rank and file. Along with craft-specific material, agenda items included "Organizing for Better Contracts," "Family Medical Leave Act," "Contractual Discussions," "A Political Party for Workers," "Building a Stronger Union," "Your Rights on the Job," "Solving Workplace Problems," and "Unions vs. Corporate Power." Lyons noted that by transcending official contractual obligations, the training enables the "union [to] play a bigger role in the [members'] lives." Two key questions underscore every craft session and contribute to a better-educated membership: "How did this [economic and political state of the union movement] happen to us?" and "How do we change this?"[17]

The capacity of the rank-and-filers to understand the political, economic, and industrial context of their union identity is further buttressed by their ability to enroll in university labor education courses. Tuition is always reimbursed, and members are encouraged to take multiple classes. The local has also sent staff to the AFL-CIO George Meany Center for specialized instruction, and stewards have attended classes taught at the local hall by IBT Education Department officials.[18] Such diverse and targeted educational training was unheard of in the pretrusteeship era.[19]

Members were also given informational resources to help them understand the labor movement and to participate in the operations of the union. Prior to 1995 the local leadership disseminated information as if through an eyedropper. Communication with the membership was limited to officer reports and an occasional memorandum from the leadership announcing some contract settlement. When the reform officers were elected, the local embraced a much freer approach to disseminating information. In order to provide a regular vehicle for informing members, a motion to start a local newspaper was proffered in 1993, and one year later, in January 1994, *Teamsters Local 705 News* became a reality. Later called the *705 Update,* the premiere issue boldly declared, "This [is] your newsletter, so get involved, we want your input!"

Mundane items, such as office hours and local phone numbers, comingled with contract negotiation summaries and news about legislative issues. Although these articles represented the beginning of a dialogue between the leadership and the members, it was the black-bordered three-column listing on page 3 that really set a higher level of expectation for internal communications. Under the bold heading "Your Stewards . . ." appeared, for the first time in a form accessible to the membership in the local's history, the names and locations of all the union stewards. A later issue of the paper announced the operation of a voice mail system and printed the phone extensions of all officers and representatives.[20]

Under the editorship of Paul Waterhouse, the paper has since expanded into a twelve-page publication. It is mailed to every local member six times a year and regularly features communications from principal officers; updates on major contract, grievance, arbitration, legal, and organizing achievements; stories on individual members; and announcements about educational and special meetings. Waterhouse views the paper principally as a way to "trigger discussion." *705 Update* is, in its editor's words, "a call to action." The role of a messenger is only as good as the receptiveness of the receiver, however. Do members read the paper? According to a survey done in 1998, 81 percent of the full-time membership "always" or "most of the time" reads the paper.[21]

Individual representatives took it upon themselves to communicate with their barns through a combination of means. To prepare the part-timers to "walk and talk" union, the local published five issues of the *705 CACH-Update* and distributed them at the facility during shift changes. The newsletter informed workers of their employment and contractual rights and printed a full list of "CACH Stewards & Union Reps."[22] In a move that further symbolizes the leadership's intentions, the local also sent officers to the two plant entrances to pass out local labor agreements.

Recognizing that hundreds of CACH grievances were being filed and that members were unable or reluctant to attend union meetings, the local asked the international union for help. Assistance came in the form of a satellite union office set up near the CACH facility. All of these measures provided some opportunity for high-risk members to gain a greater owner-ship of their union. The CACH training underscored the importance of de-veloping capable and dedicated stewards and representatives. It is not coin-cidental that one of the first affirmative acts of the local trustee was to radically reform and expand the steward system. At the nadir of the pretrusteeship period, the role of the union steward had been perverted into what Jim Lyons called a "company conspiracy." Lyons was amazed at how little shop-floor representation existed. "Stewards couldn't do things, they had no idea of *Weingarten* [court-granted legal rights of a steward] and members would not file grievances because once they did they were pun-ished by the company." Lyons's assessment is strongly supported by a mountain of worker complaints filed during the 1970s and the 1980s about the lack of representation in the barns.

No record is available of how many stewards the local employed before the trusteeship, but there is indirect data from 1974 to 1993 that strongly suggests that the local did not utilize more than 150 stewards annually.[23] Fortunately, a comparison between the different regimes is possible because the local now keeps a written record of stewards. As of 1 April 1998, Local 705 deployed 342 union stewards. In other words, in a mere three years since the trusteeship, member representation more than doubled.

The growth of on-site union appointees is even more impressive in light of the 1980s drop in membership. With a membership only slightly higher than it was in the immediate pretrusteeship days, Local 705 has greatly decreased the ratio of stewards to rank-and-filers. Using a membership base of 18,000, the reform leadership brought the ratio down from roughly 1:120 in the late 1980s to 1:53 one decade later. Not only has representation increased, but it has also become dramatically more representative. In the pretrustee period, minority workplace leaders were practically nonexistent. Now, black, His-panic, and female members account for nearly 30 percent of all the stewards.

Before the trusteeship the critical rationale for appointing a new steward appeared to be the person's ability to provide electoral protection for the leadership. Not surprisingly, what made for effective politicking resulted in very bad caretaking. Understanding the way in which the role of the stew-ard was minimalized requires a description of the pretrusteeship grievance process. If a worker had a complaint, he or she was not expected to find a steward. Instead, the worker was given the phone number of a union of-fice secretary, who would, on occasion, type a word-for-word transcript of the incoming call. The secretary would then hopefully pass on the dic-tated complaint to the appropriate business agent. His intervention was usually more hurtful than helpful and was designed to undercut the au-thority of the steward.

If a steward did demonstrate an unusual degree of independence and discretion, he would be immediately "called on the carpet by the agent." According to a quarter-of-a-century union veteran, James Harris, the local "used to resolve everything through the BA [business agent]."[24] Harris, like other recently appointed 705 stewards, acknowledged how all-encompassing was the power of the agents under the previous regime. This centralization of power in the hands of agents meant they had total discretion on how to respond to complaints. Not surprisingly, it was common practice for the agents to visit the offending barns without ever speaking to either the steward or the grievant.

The very limited role of the steward is further revealed by the curious presence of the initials LFP, for local secretary-treasurer Louis F. Peick, scripted at the bottom of numerous grievance reports filed in the late 1970s. Despite the obvious demands that multiple offices placed on his time, Peick acted as a filter through which all grievances had to pass before they could be pursued. Preceding his monogram on the reports in question were the words "see" or "obtain ok from." The end result of denying the steward or the rank-and-filer any sovereignty in the process was to retard the ability of the membership to participate in their own governance. It was a minimalist version of participation, one that political philosopher Benjamin Barber has indignantly labeled "zoo-keeping."[25]

Since the trusteeship, stewards are now trained to do their jobs and are required to attend monthly steward meetings. Business agents, now referred to as "union representatives," have conducted some of the in-house trainings for stewards in their respective barns. As an added incentive for stewards to aspire to a higher ideal of membership representation, the executive board established the Walter Trakys Stewards Award. In announcing criteria for the annual honor, the board stressed the critical importance of taking action, by noting that it was Trakys's belief that "we all have a responsibility to lead by example."[26]

Educating union leaders and members also took place in a more mundane fashion. Departing from the days of membership ignorance and elite control, appointed officials began to visit their assigned barns and, more importantly, engage with the membership. An examination of 1998 Daily Activity Reports ($N = 158$) documents a daylight-shift representative's typical workday. He or she arrived at the work site between 5:30 and 6:15 A.M. The most common topics addressed with the membership were contract negotiations, grievances, benefit plans, rallies over full-time jobs, strike activity, and voting. Since every representative had more than three sites to visit ($X = 10.8$), these conversations were repeated, sometimes on a daily basis. In most cases, representatives are required to go on location at least twice a week. Unlike their pretrusteeship brethren, when they get there these days, they stick around. Conducting business with the members can take between 3.5 and 5 hours.

Steward Nick Slusher noted that "reps and stewards were now better in tune with one another" and that "the doors were [now] open." Access was a common resource. "Communication is now better and [stewards are] better informed," Robert Coleman explains. The result of a constant exchange between stewards, members, and agents was the development of work-site leaders capable of bringing rank-and-file concerns to the leadership. Rick Carlucci and Jim McKee pointed out that as stewards they also contributed to a host of other local policy areas. "Sitting on negotiation teams" was important to McKee, whereas Carlucci stressed the "health and welfare issues that they bring to the reps." Slusher took pride in noting that during craft meetings stewards were responsible for identifying "who was working scab [nonunion]" in their trade.[27]

In addition to the active participation in union policymaking and the interaction of stewards, which reinvigorated the union's presence in the workplace, the local took a radical step toward reform in March 2001: the membership approved a bylaw amendment to permit the rank-and-file election of stewards. Despite a long, difficult history of fighting for elected stewards, including a failed effort in 1997, local reformers managed to successfully campaign for the change.[28] Stewards were elected to represent members in more than four hundred collective bargaining agreements for three-year terms. The competition for slots was high: over 80 percent of the races were contested, and in most work sites multiple candidates competed for the posts. In a positive show of support for the reform movement, incumbents managed to beat back challengers in roughly 90 percent of the contests.[29] The first-time election of stewards meant not only that a record number of Local 705 members had actively pursued a political position but also that rank-and-filers had won a forceful means to leave their imprint upon the union.

The past inability to elect stewards did not reflect passiveness or submissiveness on the part of the rank and file. One good example of the internal debate generated by the ranks under the old appointment system involved the right to strike in a suit brought by UPS against the local. In response to the court's judgment, a proposal to strike UPS, "to stop [them] from stealing our work," was "submitted to the membership for discussion and vote" by a TDU member at the first fall 1998 meeting. In contrast to the way that the old regime responded to policy challenges, the reform leadership permitted a passionate, free-flowing, open discussion of the issue. Although the call for a strike was not formally voted upon, the democratic fashion in which opinions were received and strategy considered helped to set up the conditions for what would later transpire. On 9 December, just two months after the fall meeting, Local 705 conducted a one-day walkout against UPS.[30]

The enlarged contribution of the members and stewards to union action is possible only because they have been given opportunity and time to rationally think about what should be done. Perhaps the importance of such choosing is best appreciated by considering what it means to the union policymaking process. Allowing nonstaffers to elevate issues and perspectives from the ranks signifies that the truth about what is best for the local is not yet known. The best policy emerges from the deliberations of the many instead of the few. The outcome is a policy that has a better chance of serving the common interest of all union members.

Democracy Brings Results

Not every Local 705 member was actively involved in the union, but there were encouraging signs of participation. The expectation was that if more members were active in their union, then the organization would do a more effective job of representing workers. If democracy was to mean anything in the material lives of the membership, it would have to contribute to making Local 705 a stronger bargaining agent.

For union democracy to be worth the trouble, workers have to be materially better off because the means produce valuable ends. Union citizenship entails more than participation in a deliberative process; it also includes, in J. G. A. Pocock's terms, the "taking or maintaining of possessions."[1] Citizenship means the right and capacity to act on behalf of the things that one desires, wants, and needs, according to the classical Roman and modern Western concept. Citizenship is also what Michael Holland meant by a "kind of democracy that yields better trade unionism"; it is in that direction that this analysis now turns. The local's bargaining performance since the trusteeship demonstrates that acting democratically enabled the union to fight more effectively for the membership. Democracy made for a stronger union.

Democratic Bread and Butter

When the reform leaders took office, they found an institution bereft of formal polices for administering the local's business. Before the local could get down to critical representational issues, it had to take care of this more mundane issue. To address the accountability problems that were at the center of various IRB charges, the new executive board instituted a number of policies and record-keeping procedures. The first things it did were as substantive as they were symbolic.

Aware of the notorious Teamster practice of awarding multiple and extravagant salaries to union officials, the board ruled that full-time stewards' stipends would be reduced and set at $100 per quarter. More significantly, the board cut officer and agent salaries by a whopping $900,000 per year. In an unheard-of move, the board even reduced the secretary-treasurer's pay by a hefty 27 percent to $87,500. The reform board also addressed the past practice of indiscriminately awarding generous pay raises. The patronage-serving practice was replaced with a policy limiting staff salary increments to 2.6 percent, "based on a blended rate of increases under freight and UPS agreements." In a final administrative action, designed to bring the leadership back into contact with the members, the reformers approved a motion providing that no officer, representative, or employee would receive health or pension benefits from more than one union plan. In addition, benefits were not to exceed the top level received by "working members of 705."[2]

The board then addressed the former abuse of in-kind benefits by commissioning a "Local 705 Auto Expenses Analysis." Based on the findings contained in the four-page report, the board agreed to eliminate the purchase and use of union vehicles for officers and representatives. By shifting to a personal-car allowance, the local saved $75,000 a year. Sensitive to the old regime's preference for Lincolns and Cadillacs, it later added that staff should "make common sense decisions when purchasing their [personal] vehicles, keeping in mind the message we are sending to our members."[3]

In addition to the compensation of officers, the leadership took seriously the growing record-keeping needs of a modern office. Prior to the trusteeship, office clericals and staff worked with meager and antiquated information technology. The new leadership rectified this problem by installing facsimile and copying machines and by doubling the number of computers in the office. Upgrading the office technology not only made the filing and preparation of records more rational; it also enabled the leadership to keep track of how the members' dues money was spent. To ensure proper accounting of union expenses, the board mandated that all officers and staff maintain and submit time records to determine the "proper allocation of labor expenses between local and various pension, and health and welfare funds." For good measure, the elected leadership also reaffirmed that local union bylaws required "policies concerning vacation leave, sick leave, severance benefits . . . etc." This included salaries and bonuses, and the staff was further advised that "under no circumstances should personal expenses be charged to and/or run through the local union books."[4]

With regard to union dues, there was also a collection problem. For many years a significant number of local members had been paying less than the required monthly minimum in dues. Set at twice the rate of hourly earnings, the dues should have been adjusted each time a pay increase was negotiated. However, the dues "were not adjusted on a regular basis throughout the years," and consequently, Local 705 not only was in violation of the international constitution, but its treasury had been losing thousands of dollars for many years. The local's annual losses between 1986 and 1993 ranged from $300,000 to $1.4 million.[5] The board therefore undertook the unpopular step of adjusting dues payments upward.

Improving record-keeping and becoming more accountable was tedious work, but it was the kind of housecleaning that was necessary before the union could effectively represent the membership. With policies in place to restrain self-aggrandizing behavior, democratic accountability began to pay heavy dividends. In no area was that more apparent than in the local's record of grievance, arbitration, and NLRB awards. Before examining the union's posttrusteeship performance, it is worth noting one final act of considerable symbolism. The executive board added language to the oath of office that included, as one purpose of the union, "to eliminate corruption and to remember that it is the membership that is [to be] served."[6] The language was admittedly commonplace, but for the first time, Local 705 was formally acknowledging that acting democratically meant promoting the interests of the membership.

Representing Members through Grievances and Arbitrations

Rank-and-file members' identity with their unions is most often directly correlated with the way they experience the grievance system: the grievance system comes to represent the value of the union. Thus, a comparison of Local 705 grievance files from 1977 to 1992 and from 1995 to 1998 offers an authoritative account of democratic benefits. My analysis was drawn from the record of IBT 705–UPS joint-board hearings.[7] Joint boards have four or six members, evenly divided between union and company individuals. The panels are authorized to hear all shop-floor disputes that could not be settled at the first or second step in the grievance procedure. The local's relations with UPS were selected for study because from at least the late 1970s, UPS has been the union's largest employer.

In the Chicago area, there are eleven UPS facilities distributed north and south of the city, including the mammoth Chicago Area Consolidated Hub. Located near Chicago in the town of Hodgkins, CACH has nearly 2 million square feet of concrete and sixty-five miles of mechanical moving conveyor belts. The facility sits on 240 acres of land and is the world's busiest package distribution facility, sorting approximately "10 percent of the domestic ground packages in the UPS system every workday." On an average day, more than thirty-eight thousand trucks move in and out of the hub's 80 acres of paved roadway.[8] To the facility's roughly eight thousand in-house part-time workers, CACH is a noisy, fast-paced mechanical beast of medieval proportions. An aerial schematic of the hub resembles a giant spider with five long legs (docks) protruding from each side of its thick belly (warehouse facility). Although worker grievances occur throughout the UPS system, because of CACH's size, it accounts for a significant share of union-management problems.

On the basis of sheer volume of grievances taken to joint panels, the reform Local 705 has proven to be much more aggressive than its pretrusteeship model. From 1977 to 1992 the local averaged 85 cases ($N = 1,359$) per year. In comparison, since the election in 1995, annual board cases have more than doubled to 185 ($N = 924$). The difference in the yearly aggregate number of panel cases reflects the changing relationship among the rank and file, stewards, and staff. Prior to the trusteeship, agents possessed an unchecked power to settle all grievances. A case could not advance to a joint board unless an agent sent it there. Secretary-treasurer Louis Peick received numerous letters from frustrated members pleading for his intervention with an unhelpful agent. Typical were workers who wrote that an agent said "he'd check the records, but failed to do so," and they were now asking the union head "to help in this matter since no one else will."[9]

In one egregious case, thirty-nine workers explained that they had "turned in written grievances to [agent's name]" six months before contacting the union office, "and none of them [had] heard anything." Many workers penned multiple-page briefs to the local leadership, opening their appeals with the line "I'm writing to you as I can not get my business agent [person's name] to even return my phone calls." Some rank-and-filers pointed out, "As a paid member of Local 705 I am asking that [Peick] see to it that all agreements in our contract are totally enforced."[10]

Appealing to Peick was not very helpful, however. In addition to the plethora of internal appeals, individual workers often felt compelled to retain personal attorneys to attain a measure of representation. The case of denied medical payments for the daughter of a 705 member is a particularly poignant example of the deleterious effects of unaccountable business agents. "I am advised," wrote the worker's attorney to the union office "that [member's name] initiated a grievance [in regards to rejection of a medical claim] through your [agent] office." The attorney then notes that after the company dismissed the claim at a meeting at which the member was not present, "your office has undertaken no efforts to pursue further steps in the grievance process."[11]

Since the trusteeship, worker complaints about ignored grievances seemed to have dried up. A search of internal correspondence between 1995 and 1998 did not turn up a single appeal from a union member. This does not mean that every worker was satisfied with the outcomes of his or her representation. The record suggests, instead, that the triadic relationship among workers, stewards, and representatives is functioning to expand the defense of worker rights. Just how democracy is functioning to protect workers can be further revealed through a deconstruction of the grievance record.

A comparison of the types of grievances and the resolution of each charge indicates that posttrusteeship Local 705 has been enforcing workplace democracy with an unparalleled vigor. For instance, under the old leadership, 22.7 percent of all grievances ended up with the worker being discharged. In comparison, during the reform period, approximately half as many members have been dismissed (11.2%). In addition, before reform, 200 members (14.7%) "resigned" instead of going to the panels. Forfeiting the right to a hearing is no longer so popular. From 1995 to 1998 only 6 members (0.64%) have decided to accept the company's plea offers. During the same time period, the panels' rulings on company violations of the contract financially compensated 168 identified workers. In comparison, over the previous fifteen years, only 232 members were ever awarded financial payments by the joint boards.

Although each grievance resolution illustrates a general level of representation, the category called "back to work without pay" does so more effectively than others. According to figures from 1987 to 1992, the most favored panel response was an agreement to treat a dismissal as an after-the-fact suspension. A whopping 38 percent ($N = 516$) of all resolutions simply treated time off the job as an unpaid suspension. This compares unfavorably with the present regime's record of only 11.9 percent of workers ($N = 110$) forced to accept a suspension without pay. When we add to the above the 286 cases that have been "settled and withdrawn" to the union's "satisfaction" and an assortment of suspensions reduced to "written and verbal warnings" since 1995, we can reasonably classify an amazing 88 percent of panel verdicts as positive for the union.[12] Even including all the cases that were marked unidentifiable or part of a miscellaneous category, workers won only a meager 10 percent of all pretrusteeship UPS panel grievances. It is apparent that UPS now literally pays much more often for its infractions than it did years ago.

Perhaps the best indication of the union's ability to extract a financial penalty from the employer is its arbitration record. First let us consider that Local 705 has shown a robust willingness to "deadlock" joint-panel cases. When a majority decision cannot be crafted out of the panel's deliberations, the case is officially deadlocked. At this point the union has only two options: it can drop the case or take it to arbitration. Under the old regime, panel decisions were rarely split. Including the joint boards that heard grievances under the cartage and motor carrier agreements, from 1977 to 1992 there were only 62 deadlocked cases (4.1 per year). It would seem that at 0.6 arbitrations a year, the local's sizable legal bill ($400,000 annually) was a hefty price to pay for so little action. According to then in-house counsel Tom Carpenter, in 1993, the last year of Ligurotis's reign, "only three grievances were arbitrated."[13]

Democratic unionism has created a far greater propensity to act within the fullest extent of the contract. From 1996 to 1998, the union deadlocked 160 cases. During the same time period, the local filed for arbitration 45 times. At an annual rate of 15 cases, the reform leadership has dramatically increased the local's capacity to use contractual powers to act on behalf of members' rights. Most importantly, the local won a majority (56%) of the UPS cases in which arbitration rulings were handed down.[14]

The local's aggressive defense of member rights did not end with the exhaustion of internal dispute resolution mechanisms. The leadership also advanced its representational prerogatives through the National Labor Relations Board. Including all collective bargaining signatories, the local filed 103 NLRB charges between June 1995 and November 1998. By pressing contractual and legal violations, the local won approximately $2 million in arbitration and labor board awards. As the *705 Update* proudly proclaimed, "that's more than all other Teamster locals in the state combined have won in 10 years."[15]

Negotiating Better Contracts

In the workplace it is the collective bargaining agreement that best reflects the nature of union decisions. With the results of the 1995 officers' election verified, Local 705 took the first momentous step in transforming how it would bargain with employers. It is no surprise that the people involved in bargaining proved critically important to what got bargained. According to John McCormick, "before reform, contracts were bargained fast, with no rank-and-file input and far too often [they] came up short."[16]

A review of files covering 480 contracts, from 1976 to 1993, documents that the business agents and the Chicago law firm of Carmell, Charone, Widmer, and Mathews dominated the local's negotiations. Minutes for bargaining sessions rarely revealed the presence of any union representative other than an officer, an agent, or an attorney. Although there were occasions when a steward was present, there was no documented evidence of a rank-and-filer's participation. The involvement of the rank and file, furthermore, usually reflected the union's undemocratic nature. Typical were the workers at Transport Services Company who complained to the leadership about the "invisible [contract] talks with our Business Representative" or the thirteen members who signed a petition stating that "from the start of the negotiations [agent name] did not give our contract his best interest."[17]

The lack of membership input during the bargaining process was mirrored by the lack of input at the beginning. On only a small number of occasions did the leadership appear to solicit any ideas from the members as to what should constitute the union's bargaining agenda. It was customary for the leadership, before initiating bargaining, to request and dutifully receive from "the membership . . . approval to leave the negotiating in [our] hands." Although the reform leadership of Local 705 still assumes principal responsibility for conducting bargaining, the process of constructing a contract has been greatly opened up. According to Tom Nightwine, one of the local's three current contract administrators, the labor agreements are now "collaborative works."[18] Nightwine came to Chicago from an Ohio Teamster local after the 705 trusteeship was imposed and, along with his counterparts, assumed the major responsibility of leading the local's negotiating teams. His appearance meant the departure of attorney-driven bargaining and the introduction of rank-and-file participation.

Bargaining now takes a variety of forms. First, stewards solicit ideas from the members at meetings that are customarily held two to three months prior to negotiations for all barns. Members are encouraged to provide a written list of prioritized contract proposals. For example, UPS workers hold three separate proposal meetings, one each for feeder drivers, package-car drivers, and inside or part-time employees.[19] Before the 1997 talks, each of these meetings was attended by well over a hundred members. Ideas generated in this fashion are then shared with the union representatives and the contract administrator. Once proposals are crafted and selected, the stewards have the responsibility of educating the members in the barns on the local's position.

If steward and membership involvement had ceased at this point, the change would still have been dramatic. But it is within the actual process of negotiating the bargaining items that the union members must be represented. True to its reform, Local 705 provided seats at the table for its activist members. Although every bargaining committee has steward or rank-and-file representatives, or both, the bargaining committee for the 1997 UPS contract included 35 rank-and-file members, and a 5-person team at Airborne Freight involved 2 stewards and 2 members. In addition, the 1998 Trucking Management Incorporated negotiations included 3 stewards, 1 from each of the three major employer signatories to the contract. But presence is not participation. What role do the members play, once rough-and-tumble bargaining begins?

Nightwine admits that the Ping-Pong-like process of exchanging contract proposals requires that a designated individual conduct the bargaining at the table. He notes, though, that while "democracy should not be confused with anarchy," the members do play a significant part in separating fact from fiction. "Members are the first to ask for a caucus when the company says something they [members] know just isn't so," claims Nightwine. The contribution of nonstaff members to negotiations is perhaps best confirmed by examining their bargaining notebooks for the 1997 UPS agreement. What follows is a brief sampling of notes documenting how closely connected the nonstaffers were to the issues in play:

> UPS speaking on how they want weekend flexibility . . . we are asking for more full-time jobs . . . union has been cooperative over technology . . . pt [part-time] workers are not getting their slice of the pie . . . *Caucus—not true that UPS tells supervisors not to work* . . . UPS claims pt is where they have all the absenteeism . . . union is asking for a more specific "properly notified" . . . gave our new proposals on Articles 44, 45, 47 and UPS counters . . . company has not yet given us an economic proposal package . . . how many seniority lists are at CACH? . . . shouldn't have to prove innocence, company should have to prove guilt.[20]

After reaching either an impasse or a tentative agreement, the bargaining members are authorized to educate and take the pulse of the ranks on the contents of the last set of proposals. It is at this exit point that respect for democratic procedures is once again critical. When the committee decides that bargaining has ceased and a tentative deal has been reached, a rank-and-file vote on the contract will occur. Since 1994, postal as well as walk-in referendum voting has occurred within all bargaining divisions. By always bringing the tentative contract to the members, Local 705 has solidified what was at best a fluid, undependable past practice. For example, from 1971 to 1985, fifty-seven contracts were approved, apparently, without a membership vote. The contingent nature of contract ratifications occasionally generated a considerable display of membership anger. In one instance, a local trial committee hearing was held to consider internal charges filed by members against Louis Peick for "not informing [them] about the contract." In this case the charging parties further claimed that they "had to picket their own union" because they were denied entrance to a meeting called by Peick to discuss the contract.[21]

Union democracy continues to make a difference after the contract's approval. Ratified contracts are now provided, either in summary form or in full, to the people working in the barns. In the past, a member might not see any version of the contract throughout her or his entire career. When the trustee first arrived in Chicago, according to Gerald Zero, "he found stacks of contracts just sitting in the secretary-treasurer office."[22] Thus, one of the first orders of business for the trustee was to distribute the contracts among the ranks.

Local 705's inclusionary approach to labor negotiations undoubtedly raised the level of pluralism within the process of winning agreements. But did that matter to the quality of the contracts? It would appear that by every imaginable standard, contracts negotiated by the reform leadership were significantly superior to the ones they succeeded.[23] According to Nightwine, a review of some of the major improvements to pretrusteeship contractual benefits and language demonstrates that Local 705 is "successfully digging out of a deep hole" dug by their predecessors.

Before the trusteeship, in the cartage, freight, and package delivery units, there were at least seventeen permanent wage tiers paying $10 or less per hour. These tiers created separate levels of hourly pay for workers doing exactly the same things within and across firms. It is estimated that 170 multitier contracts existed. With the exception of a dozen posttrusteeship contracts, multiple-wage tiers have now been eliminated, and the minimum scale has been raised to $12. Before reform, the local's contracts were a patchwork of different company payments into the health and welfare and pension funds. Some companies were paying as little as $42 per week, while others were contributing more than twice as much. Contributions to the plans are now universally set by contractual terms.

In the days of unratified contracts, there were companies, such as TNT Transfer, that operated as union carriers without signed contracts for many years. Since the 1995 election, no 705 signatory company is functioning without having a signed agreement or being actively engaged in bargaining or sustaining a work stoppage. When attorneys and agents exclusively negotiated contracts, many employers repeatedly denied their workers raises. When those contracts were renegotiated after 1994, union members received their first wage improvements in more than five years. In other situations workers had received pay increases, but under old-regime contracts, such as MSAS Cargo's, they were denied health and welfare payments. Contracts now stipulate that benefit plan contributions are to be made for every 705 member.

There was also a time when part-time employees were not covered by any Local 705 agreements. Some old agreements further limited unit coverage by "red-circling" a flat number or percentage of employees. Any worker outside the red circle would be denied union coverage, regardless of the job he or she performed. In the posttrusteeship period, artificial restraints on union growth have been erased; it is now the task done, not how many hours the boss schedules you to work, that defines bargaining unit coverage.

The union's efforts to use the labor agreement can be best appreciated by a closer examination of one particularly outrageous old-regime-negotiated deal. As explained by union representative Richard DeVries, the local's pretrusteeship agreements covering the Movers' Association of Greater Chicago, which represented a group of moving-industry individual employers, was nothing more than a "great source of revenue" for the union's top brass.[24] Representative DeVries demonstrated how changes in contract language made between the 1987 and 1990 agreements significantly weakened the union in the moving industry.

For example, under the 1987 contract, union coverage extended to "all employees of the Employers," but in 1990 the bargaining unit was reduced to "all regular full time seniority employees." The previous contract also granted full benefit coverage to "Steady Employees," defined as anyone "continuously employed six months or longer." Not so under the renegotiated terms. "Non-regular" employees were now denied "any monetary fringe benefit" until they had worked "at least 120 hours on commercial activity in each of three consecutive months." As DeVries points out, however, the hours of work had to be accumulated under such onerous terms that it was practically impossible for any nonregular to qualify. As a result, from 1990 to 1995, only four nonregulars were added to the signatories' seniority list.[25]

In addition, the contract's definition of a covered employee was critical to a host of benefits. For instance, under the 1987 agreement, $50 per week was paid into the local's health and welfare fund "for each steady employee," but by 1990 such contributions were reserved for "regular full-time seniority employees who work *at least three days* [emphasis added] in the work week." Throughout the contract, the change from "steady employee" to "regular full-time" saved the employer money and, as DeVries pointed out, sharply reduced the number of unionized movers in the Chicago area. It also created an irresistible opportunity for union officials to personally profit. "How much would these changes be worth to an employer?" he asked rhetorically. The implied answer was "a great deal."

DeVries was not alone in his suspicion of these provisions. Approximately a year into the trusteeship, the local filed an unfair labor practice charge against five Chicago area movers. In a letter sent to the board's regional director, IBT attorney Peggy Hillman expressed the local's suspicions about "the movers contract." Hillman's correspondence was in support of the union's efforts to force the employers to drop their concept of "seniority employees" and to extend the collective bargaining agreement to all of the employees in the unit. The local's problem was further exacerbated because they could not discover "what if any collective bargaining negotiations went on before" the trustee was installed. Hillman continued by noting, "The complete history of Local 705's relationship to the moving industry is still unknown to us," and consequently, "we suspect that there are aspects which are improper and perhaps illegal."[26]

New and better contract language in the moving and other divisions has improved the capacity of the local to protect its members' rights, but Nightwine emphasizes that—as opposed to the thirty-odd years of union history preceding the trusteeship—"language now actually means something." His comment underscores the basic truth about collective bargaining agreements. The meaning of any regulatory document is determined by how it is acted upon. Thus, it is the union's enforcement record that breathes life into the contract. Union democracy demands that there must be limits on what the boss can do and that the boundaries of acceptable behavior must be fixed. Since 1995, Local 705 has thickened the borders between legitimate and illegitimate uses of management prerogatives.

705 Organizing for Social Justice

What a union does to draw others within the protective cover of a union contract is also relevant to its democratic character. Holding his index finger a millimeter away from his thumb, Local 705 organizer Paul DiGrazia mused that when he assumed his duties after the trusteeship, the "organizing file was this thin."[27] When the reform leadership was elected, they found that membership had badly fallen off from its peak period in the early 1970s. Throughout the 1980s the effects of national deregulation laws and the growth of "gypsy-drivers" had devastated the unionized trucking industry. Teamster drivers in Chicago felt their share of dislocation. In a proud, poignant essay written to the local in 1989, titled "Memories of a Trucker," an ex-driver sadly recalled that 349 "common carriers have either merged, sold-out or gone bankrupt" in the Chicago area.

Under extensive labor market transformation, organizing new members was a tall order. How the local responded provides an additional insight into the ways that an absence of democratic ideals handicapped the cause of industrial unionism. In the two decades or so prior to the trusteeship, it appears that the local conducted little external organizing. Membership and executive board meeting minutes in the late 1980s occasionally refer to a "new unit," but the last pretrusteeship report of any organizing activity occurred in 1989. According to one-time local organizer Gregory Foster, when the reform leadership examined the organizing files, they found that from 1989 to 1993 "there was only one three-man barn organizing campaign conducted." To rectify this deplorable condition, the local hired sixty-two-year-old rank-and-filer Frank Fosco to head its organizing efforts. Fosco was a thirty-plus-year veteran of the local before the trustee tapped him for the head organizer position. He was subsequently the first local organizer ever trained at the AFL-CIO's Organizing Institute.[28]

Shortly after creating the head recruiter post, the local elevated DiGrazia and Foster to full-time organizers. The appointments appeared to produce immediate dividends. One year after the local had emerged out of trusteeship, twenty-five hundred new members had been awarded a union card, and dues collections were up by $650,000. Organizing activity quickened in 1997 with campaigns for truck drivers at Jewel Foods and Consolidated Freightways. In early 1998 the local reported that it had won 13 out of 17 NLRB certification elections.[29]

Membership gains also resulted from extending union coverage to company employees who had been previously red-circled. For instance, when the reform slate took office, the moving company of Boyer-Rosene declared only 19 union workers on their roster. Three years later the union employee list included 93 dues-payers. During this same period, additions at six other moving firms raised the membership total by 33 percent. Gains were also achieved by the active enforcement of contractual language requiring that only union members perform bargaining unit work.[30]

The reasons for the modest yet discernible shift in local organizing activity can be mostly explained by the membership's support for the Volunteer Organizing Committee (VOC). The creation of VOC marked another radical break with a bad tradition. For the first time in the local's history, there were organizers who were not paid staff members. Led by trained volunteers, instead of pricey "ghost" staffers, Local 705 won campaigns in 1997 at Dobbs International and at Jet Star. "The VOC ran this campaign from start to finish," noted Zero about the model Jet Star drive.[31] With each success the use of volunteer organizers grew incrementally, and in some cases, such as the tank drivers, separate divisions have been formed and provided with intensive training.[32]

Membership does not come without conditions, though. There are behavioral rules and expectations for members. With regard to both benefits and obligations, the reform Local 705 appears to have embraced an expansive idea of industrial citizenship. Unlike their brethren of earlier years, they have moved to become more inclusive of the working community around them. Inclusiveness has, for instance, meant mobilizing the membership around political action. In 1998 the local made available to its members half a dozen different political fact sheets on the Illinois governor's and statewide races. Along with the previous congressional election, the 1998 campaign marked the first time in the local's history when candidates' records were put before the membership for consideration. The elections were also an agenda item at various steward and craft meetings. Stewards were assigned to precincts on Election Day, and local volunteers participated in get-out-the-vote phone banking.

Whereas in the past the local leadership made sizable contributions to local and state officials, the trusteeship 705 has since directly pumped $384,134.67 into political campaigns. The reform regime has successfully added a new important vehicle for rank-and-file involvement in politics. In 1997 the local signed up more than 3,500 members to the international union's political action committee. The additional contributors to the union's Democratic, Republican, Independent Voter Education (DRIVE) fund brought the local's number to nearly 5,000 and made 705 "the country's #1 [IBT] local in DRIVE contributions."[33]

The local has also established strong working ties with a variety of social groups dedicated to the cause of working people. Chicago area chapters of Jobs with Justice (JwJ), the Association of Community Organizations for Reform Now (ACORN), the Interfaith Committee for Worker Justice, and Operation Rainbow PUSH (People United to Save Humanity) have all partnered with Local 705 in pursuing a social justice agenda. Moreover, the union leadership has endorsed and facilitated the creation of a Hispanic workers' caucus among Teamsters who are not native English speakers. The outreach to minority members also includes the local's annual support for the Hispanic Law Students Association Fellowship Fund. In addition to providing financial assistance, the union has employed members of the association as 705 law clerks.[34]

Local 705 now actively supports the struggles of members of other unions. Solidarity, however, was not always an important union principal. Old guard Local 705 had for many years joined with the CFL and the building trades to thwart the desire of city public service workers to unionize. The Peick-led troop repeatedly clashed with the American Federation of State, County, and Municipal Employees' (AFSCME) efforts in the 1960s and 1970s to win representational rights from the Daley machine. But it was Local 705's resistance to a union drive of firefighters under the mayoral administration of Jane Byrne that best depicts the ideological differences between the prereform and reform leadership. In 1980 Chicago Firefighters Local 2 had staged a citywide walkout to pressure Byrne to fulfill a promise she had made while running for mayor the previous fall to recognize the union.[35] Local 2 had set up pickets at the city's premier convention venue, McCormick Place, during the Chicago Auto Show. Teamster drivers, many from Local 705, refused to make deliveries to the convention center as long as pickets patrolled the entrance ways.[36] In response, Peick, who was participating in negotiations with the mayor to generate a back-to-work movement and was a board director at McCormick Place, ordered two or three "car loads of thugs to confront the picketing firefighters with bats."[37] In what can only be described as a farcical scene of one-upmanship, the Teamster boss's hired hands were chased away from the center by axe-wielding firefighters. Despite Peick's best union avoidance efforts, Firefighters Local 2 successfully negotiated a labor agreement.

Contrary to the old regime's hostile attitude toward non-Teamster unions, the reform leadership has been represented at every statewide major workplace dispute. Letters of appreciation like the one from Chicago Brotherhood of Electrical Workers Local 134 officers, expressing their gratefulness that "no [705 members] union truck driver made a delivery or a pick up during the strike," adorn the union office's bulletin board. The local was also very supportive of the trilogy of striking unions engaged in bitter work stoppages during the 1990s in the Decatur, Illinois, "War Zone." And during the winter of 2000, Local 705 provided critical assistance to striking radio and television actors who had refused to do commercials without greater protections for their work. The Screen Actors Guild and the American Federation of Radio and Television Artists was so appreciative of the help they received from the local that when the dispute was settled, they sent a large cake, decorated as a truck trailer, to the local's office.[38]

Support for a broader working-class movement was further articulated by 705's appreciation of cultural symbols. The local's commitment to an inclusive labor community was publicly displayed with the commissioning and painting of a mural titled *Teamster Power*. The painting, spanning 127 by 28 feet on the wall of the 705 garage, depicts historic Chicago labor figures as well as an "old figure of the Industrial Workers of the World" and the "monsters of capitalism."[39]

After a prolonged spell of self-serving, inward-looking local control, the union has dared to once again offer itself as a productive mechanism for improving the livelihood of working-class nonmembers. Perhaps for Gregory Foster, Local 705 character is revealed in the words printed on a poster that once hung on his cubicle wall: "The ultimate measure of a man is not where he shall stand in moments of comfort and convenience, but also where he stands at times of challenge and controversy." At least for one Teamster organizer, the courageous words of Martin Luther King Jr. reflect the purpose that Local 705 communicates to nonunion workers.[40] In the light of democratic reform, it is hard to imagine a better message.

As the twenty-first century approached, Local 705 was a stronger and more honest and democratic union. The reform caucus led by Zero and McCormick had managed to sustain the direction of the changes implemented in 1993. They had overcome two electoral challenges, and as the union's transformation matured, the RPM team prepared for a third local officer election. The 2000 election would prove to be another important test of the democratic nature of Local 705.

▴ **PART TWO** ▴

Union Democracy, Elections, and the Politics of Local 705

The Reformers Split

On Valentine's Day in 1996, Local 705 held its monthly steward meeting. Before the session, United Party leader Dane Passo and eight other local members stood outside the union hall passing out pro-Hoffa campaign literature. As stewards entered through the glass doors and began to climb the first set of stairs up to the assembly floor, the Hoffa supporters moved inside the building and continued to distribute their flyers. Upon reaching the top of the staircase, Passo was met by union representative Donald Barnett. Barnett was one of a couple of union staffers who regularly served as guards at steward and membership meetings, ensuring that only union members or invited guests entered the twelve-hundred-seat Teamster Auditorium.

Recognized as one of the largest meeting facilities in the city, the auditorium has hosted political rallies, formal dinners, the University of Illinois at Chicago graduation ceremonies, and groups as diverse as the Chicago Federation of Labor and the Chicago Housing Authority. Van Barns, the local's one-time handyman who directed much of the building's $700,000 renovation work, took pleasure in also noting that "during the 1940s the auditorium was a premier place to hold dances for large groups."[1] It had also on many occasions been the site of fierce union struggles, and as Passo approached Barnett, the famed structure was about to become ground zero of a local political war with national implications.

Informed that he could not come into the meeting, Passo engaged Barnett in a heated argument over the right to politically canvass inside the hall. John McCormick and union representative Otis Cross then approached the Hoffa campaigners. As the debate grew louder and more profane, Gerald Zero made his way from the stage area of the hall to the back of the room. After an intense exchange of words with Passo, Zero ordered the uninvited campaigners to leave, and when no one moved, a fight broke out. As Passo later recounted for a trial judge in an assault and battery suit, the three-hundred-pound Zero "slammed" him "down to the ground." Passo further testified that after he rolled down the stairs, Zero grabbed him "by the hair, slammed him on the ground and threw him on the front sidewalk" in front of the hall entrance doors. Witnesses for Zero, however, directly refuted Passo's interpretation of events and instead portrayed the well-known Hoffa sympathizer as a provocateur.[2]

Nonetheless, at the conclusion of a tumultuous bench trial, Zero was found guilty of two misdemeanor counts of battery. Rejecting the secretary-treasurer's "affirmative defense" in the use of force to protect the property of Local 705, the court found that Zero was the "person that started all the physical fighting, the physical confrontation unnecessarily and without lawful justification," and sentenced him to one year of court supervision. Zero immediately appealed the verdict, but the appellate court upheld the conviction.[3]

Not only did Passo charge Zero with violating criminal laws, but he further accused him of violating the IBT Constitution, which "prohibits assaults on fellow union members or union officers." The Independent Review Board (IRB) subsequently recommended that Local 705's executive board charge Zero with "bringing reproach upon the IBT."[4] In response to the IRB's recommendation, Zero requested that the international office convene a trial hearing to consider the charge. The panel heard testimony on two separate dates in the fall of 1998 and determined that Zero was guilty. They then pronounced an unprecedented mild punishment of three months suspension from office. The short suspension was Zero's first bit of good judicial news, but his fortune was equally short-lived.

The IRB, as it is permitted to do under the 1989 federal consent decree, intervened and informed the international union that the "penalties imposed are not adequate." "Violence by anyone has no place in the conduct of the union affairs," the board noted, especially "regarding violence committed by a ranking officer of a local." The IRB did not stop with a sharp condemnation of Zero's actions. It also recognized that during the fight several participants threw punches and yet, despite court testimony that Passo and others suffered serious physical injury, no hospital admissions occurred. Nonetheless, during the court trial, evidence was presented that Passo and the "group that he was associated with, knew that they were not permitted to engage" in electioneering. Nor did Zero's unfortunate use of force interfere with the "internal political rights" of Passo, who ran unsuccessfully as a candidate for the local's secretary-treasurer position in 1997. The IRB also pointed out that the local succeeded in obtaining reinstatement of Passo after his employer terminated him. Passo was represented by none other than Otis Cross, a codefendant in the criminal action brought in Cook County Circuit Court. Finally, the board noted, "Passo and others engaged in the pattern of assaults dating back to the 1991 delegate nomination meeting," and in 1994 Passo had been suspended from membership for his disruptive behavior at union meetings.[5]

In light of the numerous mitigating factors, the IRB determined that Zero had been provoked by Passo and had never exhibited any premeditation to commit violence against any union member. They consequently recommended that Zero serve a "suspension of at least one year" from his union office and submit to "mandatory counseling."[6] It was a stiff sentence. Zero would be prohibited from conducting any official union business and would have to forfeit his $95,000 officer salary. Nonetheless, he felt fortunate; the final verdict could have been much worse. What Zero felt relieved about was that the board did not recommend the one penalty that would have ended his political career. They did not suspend his union membership.

If Zero's union card had been pulled in 1999, for any length of time, he would have been ineligible to run for local office in 2000.[7] While his imposed unpaid leave was a significant punishment, as long as Zero kept paying his union dues, he would be eligible to stand for union office when the suspension was lifted. Accepting the verdict of the international board, on 1 February 1999, Local 705 leader Gerald Zero stepped down from his position and turned the local over to the temporary control of president John McCormick.

Zero had no immediate plans for how to spend his involuntary vacation from the local, but he did mark the date of his return to Teamster City. Undoubtedly, so did McCormick, and he was committed to preventing it. Notwithstanding the success of a two-term democratic coalition, the two men had grown deeply uncomfortable with each other's union politics. It was a strange turn of events for two local dissidents who had once proudly been labeled fellow travelers on the road to union democracy.

The Mineworkers Dispute

On 14 January 2000, Local 705 executive board members met around a large oak table in a spacious and carpeted seventh-floor room overlooking the Eisenhower Expressway. In the comfortable surroundings of the union's offices, recording secretary and RPM leader Bennie Jackson made his intentions crystal clear. He would be bringing new union charges against Zero before the secretary-treasurer's scheduled return to office on 2 February. If the charges were upheld and the punishment was a loss of union membership, then this action would certainly disqualify Zero from running in the fall election. As devastating as that would be for Zero, Jackson was actually hunting for a more immediate political pelt; he wanted to "preclude Zero from reassuming his office pending the outcome" of those charges.[8] With Jackson's plans in the open, the rest of the executive board began the nearly surreal task of discussing how best to depose their one-time political partner and RPM leader.

Jackson's proposal to bring charges against Zero was supported by four other board members, including McCormick, and ex-RPM members Edward Benesch and Steve Pocztowski.[9] Disputes among union members and between officers and rank-and-filers are not uncommon, but this action was no mere internal squabble. A majority of the Local 705 board was, in effect, voting to throw out of office the union's highest-ranking elected officer. Zero knew something bad was brewing. The day after the executive board voted to file charges, the Chicago Workers School (CWS) sponsored a lecture. The CWS was a small, loose connection of city political progressives and labor and community activists that met periodically in a small space in Local 705's auditorium to hold lectures on various labor and political topics. On this occasion the CWS session attracted a good crowd, and extra chairs had to be found to accommodate the cramped attendees. The topic was democratic unionism, and the special guest was the soon-to-be-reinstated secretary-treasurer of Local 705.

Zero opened his talk by describing the early days of the local's trusteeship. He recounted the incredible fear and anxiety that existed within the local when the standing executive board was dismissed and the trustee was placed in charge. "I fully expected that someone would be killed," Zero admitted. "After all this [Local 705] was a real gem for the mob." Zero expressed pride in the numerous accomplishments achieved during the past two administrations but added that he had "heard charges might even be filed against me." Zero had already met once with his two-time running mate to discuss his return to office, and McCormick confided that perhaps it would be best if Zero "resign[ed] from office."[10] Zero dismissively rejected the advice. Ignoring the implications of Jackson's charges was another matter.

Michael Holland took Bennie Jackson's proposed charges very seriously. As counsel to the board and Local 705's principal legal officer, Holland had been responsible for matters of internal union governance since the 1993 trusteeship. Holland's role was to help construct a small-d democracy platform in order that the big-D democracy could flourish. A remarkable amount of positive change had occurred in seven years, but Holland now worried that what Jackson was planning would throw the local into turmoil and possibly undermine everything the reformers had accomplished.

Holland took the uncommon, unsolicited step of informing the board members that he "was profoundly distressed" by their plan to bring charges against Zero. "Charges brought against Gerry would almost certainly yield a round of replies and counter-charges," and if that were not bad enough, the counselor went on, it would create "dissension within the Executive Board and among the members." Holland closed his comments by announcing his intention to withdraw as counsel if the board persisted in their reckless endeavor. One week after the board voted to file charges, Holland mailed a resignation letter.[11]

Shortly after the January board meeting, IBT 1998 presidential candidate Tom Leedham offered to mediate the widening schism between Local 705's contending union democrats. Leedham spoke several times by phone to both men, and, sensing a rapidly approaching point of no return, he arranged a meeting of the three union leaders at a hotel near the O'Hare airport. As Leedham probed for the most serious points of contention, one issue appeared to operate as a channel for expressing all that divided the two men. McCormick and his board supporters had been adamantly opposed to the union's staff employees' organizing into a local of the United Mine Workers of America (UMWA). Zero and a large majority of the union representatives and clerical staff had expressed equally strong support for organizing.

For McCormick, there were a number of problems with directing a unionized staff.[12] His biggest beef was that Zero was building a kind of fifth column inside the local. As 1998 wound down, Zero privately resigned himself to an inevitable and substantial suspension from office. That meant the secretary-treasurer would be unable to govern the local and that Mc-Cormick would assume the principal governing authority. According to McCormick, Zero recognized his vulnerability and decided to construct a means for maintaining control over the local through his appointed unionized staff. The plan was to freeze in place an administrative team loyal to Zero, secure in their jobs and opposed to McCormick. Once unionized, the staff could function like a bureaucratic network undermining executive authority. They would also preserve what Zero most needed in order to win a third term of office: a full-time political cadre.

Zero understood the matter differently. He had proved that he was one of the Teamsters' most progressive leaders. During his tenure in office, Local 705 had earned a reputation for working with and supporting other Chicago area union members. Zero was also well known throughout the city as an active supporter of progressive political causes and candidates. Showing a willingness to work with a unionized staff was perfectly consistent with his deeply held union consciousness. In Zero's opinion, the question of whether the staff should organize was up to the staff. For what it was worth, however, he thought "unions were a good thing for everybody."[13]

Zero also was aware that with the Hoffa election the political landscape of the Teamsters was shifting once again. Zero was enough of a pragmatist to know that there was danger in this for a local that had derisively campaigned twice against "Junior Hoffa." As one notable labor attorney confided, "any labor lawyer worth his salt should be able to find a reason to put any local into trusteeship." The truth of this boast was not lost on the Local 705 staff. A number of them had come from other Teamster locals or unions where they had lost elections, been removed from appointed positions, or given new opportunities when political power shifted hands. Each Zero-recruited rep was very familiar with the Teamster rules of union governance; winners rule and losers leave town. McCormick knew this as well, of course.

Holland's view aside, the union staff feared that if Hoffa did take over the local, they would be dismissed. Staff members also recognized an increasing job vulnerability caused by the political competition within the local executive board. Katina Barnett, a fifteen-year local employee, explained that changes made in the union since the trusteeship had actually increased a person's job insecurity. During the pretrusteeship period, "no one ever worried about keeping their job," because among the staff there were no conflicting allegiances or contrasting political positions. Before 1995 "we never had any opposition up here [the office]," she continued. That changed during Zero's pending suspension, when it became very clear to staff members that the local leadership was not unified. "Where before you only had one leader at a time," Barnett went on to note, with Zero's suspension, the local now had warring chieftains.[14]

In order to inoculate them from the most severe scenario, staff members like Katina Barnett and her husband Donald contacted the UMW about representing the local's employees. Although some staff employees may have had their doubts about being members of the mineworkers' union, Don Barnett was an easy sell. Born in Powellton Holler, West Virginia, Barnett had deep roots in the mineworkers' union. His father was an executive assistant to the president of the UMW, and Ed Burke met the younger Barnett in 1991 while the Pittston Coal campaign wizard was teaching at West Virginia Tech. In coming to Local 705 as Ron Carey's appointed trustee, Burke needed help from someone whom he personally knew and deeply trusted. Chicago would be hostile territory for Burke, and in Barnett's terms, the trustee needed a "bullet catcher." Barnett was subsequently hired as an assistant to the trustee, and then before the trusteeship ended, he was appointed by Zero as a full-time representative.

In November of 1998, the NLRB held an election, and an overwhelming majority certified the UMW as the bargaining agent for Local 705 staff employees. Within less than a month, Zero and UMW regional director Jerry Cross had negotiated a tentative agreement. The contract would essentially preserve the employment status quo and add a grievance procedure. When Zero brought the deal back to the executive board, McCormick's majority rejected it and decried "all the coal miners shit around here."[15] The board also stripped Zero of his authority to negotiate any further deal and ceded the responsibility to McCormick and Jackson. When negotiations resumed, Zero's suspension had begun. John McCormick, a one-time agitator for union democracy and now a union-resisting union president, would represent local 705. And things were about to get more weird.

On 23 June McCormick sent a memo to the staff announcing that there would be a meeting "that you MUST attend." During the meeting contract administrator Tom Nightwine stood up and took exception to comments McCormick had made about the UMW negotiations. Nightwine accused the temporary union leader of creating divisions among the staff. A shouting match ensued, and McCormick adjourned the meeting. Six days later McCormick sent Nightwine the following letter:

> Dear Brother Nightwine:
>
> As you are aware, I am the principal officer of this Local Union and I have the authority to implement union policy. Your threatening outburst and temper tantrum on Friday, June 25, 1999 is adverse to our policy. I have decided to suspend you for the next three days.
>
> Fraternally,
> John B. McCormick, President

McCormick also informed the local accountant of Nightwine's suspension and directed him not to "provide wages for June 30, 1999, July 1, 1999 and July 2, 1999."[16]

Although the suspension did not threaten life or limb, Nightwine believed that it was a violation of labor law. His belief was confirmed when Region 13 of the NLRB issued a complaint against McCormick for disciplining an employee "engaged in protected concerted and/or union activities." The local was forced to post a notice declaring that the employer would not "interfere with, restrain or coerce our employees in the exercise of rights guaranteed them" by the National Labor Relations Act.[17] The posting of an NLRB notice on the bulletin board at Local 705, ordering it to cease and desist its union-busting behavior, was perhaps the most remarkable sign that the rule of law had crept within the once dictatorial walls of Teamster City.

The mineworkers' issue came to signify the fissures that had opened up within the RPM Party. It was evident to everyone working inside Teamster City that whether a union employee did or did not display "coal miners' shit everywhere," staff organizing operated as a kind of political allegiance barometer.[18] McCormick certainly thought so, and he accused Zero of raining terror down on staff members who were opposed to the miners. As evidence, he noted that Zero later fired the four staff employees who cast negative votes in the union election. One of the dismissed members, Sam Lodovico, filed a revealing set of union charges against his old boss that made it clear that the UMW vote was a proxy for an emergent political battle for control of Local 705.[19]

A three-person local trial panel appointed by McCormick adjudicated the Lodovico charges. Surprisingly, the panel found for Zero in a two-to-one opinion. In a rather uncommon maneuver, the executive board then proceeded to vote to disregard its own panel's decision and to rehire Lodovico and suspend Zero, not only from office, but also from his union membership for six months. Unlike Zero's yearlong suspension from office, this threatening penalty would pull his union card. The end result, of course, would be to make him ineligible to stand for reelection. Astonished by the boldness of the board's indifference to a finding not to its satisfaction, and aware of the "death penalty" sentence, Zero appealed the action to the international union.[20]

Despite their differences, both local leaders knew that reform had come to Local 705 from the adroitness of a political partnership. Compromise was still an option, and as strained as the Zero-McCormick relationship had become, Tom Leedham somehow found a way to knit together a cease-fire. Exactly one week before Zero was to take back the keys of his office, the "Leedham Accord" was signed. The RPM leaders agreed to abide by eleven conditions. Leading the list of conditions was that both men would jointly announce that the reform "slate will stay in tact" and that a meeting would be held "to begin to establish election plan[s]."[21] Responding to threats of a nasty round of internal union charges, both men also importantly agreed that "*all* potential charge activity will cease." This point appeared to remove the sword of Damocles that was hanging above Zero's head. In return, however, Zero agreed not to terminate any staff "as a result of" his reassuming office. With a distinct minority of the staff opposing the mineworkers and a number of stewards outwardly opposed to Zero, McCormick saw a prohibition on firings as a way to ensure some political opposition to the returning secretary-treasurer.

But three days after returning to office, Zero chopped for the second time, of all people, Sam Lodovico. In response, a now indignant and defiant executive board voted to file six charges against their secretary-treasurer.[22] McCormick defended the board's vote on the grounds that Zero was acting "like the guys [ex-705 board members] we threw out."[23] Zero had a more nefarious view of McCormick's action. It appeared to the secretary-treasurer that four board members had concocted unsubstantial and frivolous charges in order to disqualify him from the local election. The peace accord had lasted a paltry ten days.

Under the very best of conditions, an agreement between two politically competitive and viable union leaders would be difficult to sustain. These were two successful union leaders who had proven themselves capable of governing. They were part of a minority of rank-and-file committed union leaders in a Teamster world still characterized by elite, bureaucratic control. Both men had embraced democratic unionism while dodging flying metal chairs, hot coffee, and bare knuckles. Peace between them would have been preferred, but as Michael Holland reasoned, a three-part combination of "ideological conflict, differences on how to relate to the employer and simple personal animosity" turned past partners into present competitors.

Holland's Prophecy

Zero was now facing two sets of active union charges that could possibly strangle his reelection hopes. However disinclined the secretary-treasurer had been to govern on the basis of a bartered compromise, the board charges were too much to tolerate. Zero decided to do what his counsel recommend against doing and what counsel knew was inevitable when the board took its unwise and fateful step. Holland had warned the board that filing charges against Zero would trigger a round of reprisals, and if the local reformers were not careful, they would begin to devour each other. He was right.

On 20 April Local 705 members received a special letter from their secretary-treasurer. "Dear Sisters and Brothers," it began, "I am writing to inform you of emergency action I have taken on behalf of the membership of Local 705." The letter quickly got to the point: "On Monday, April 17th, I removed four Local Union officers from their positions as Union Representatives." In the letter, RPM leaders and Zero opponents John McCormick, Ed Benesch, Bennie Jackson, and Steve Pocztowski were accused of a number of deadly union sins. They "refused to fund the Local's successful organizing program," "worked to defeat proposals for a strong strike fund," arrived "unprepared at grievance hearings," and resisted extending "democratic rights and the full-time jobs owed" to UPS members. Zero

Teamsters Local 705 secretary-treasurer Louis Peick (left) and Mayor Richard J. Daley at the union hall in 1963 (on the right is Midwest IBT official Roy Schoessling). They were close political allies, and Daley appointed Peick to many city and county boards. *Courtesy Local 705.*

Teamsters general president James R. Hoffa speaking in 1958 at a Local 705 meeting. Local 705 remained independent after leaders refused to surrender their bargaining autonomy to the powerful union head. *Courtesy Local 705.*

Peick supporters within Local 705 preparing in 1983 to board a bus for a meeting of Teamsters for a Democratic Union (TDU) in Romulus, Michigan. The meeting broke up in a violent brawl after their arrival. *Courtesy Local 705.*

Local 705 activists and reform partners Gerald Zero (left) and John McCormick (right) with national Teamsters president Ron Carey at the Chicago Radisson Hotel in the spring of 1997. After placing Local 705 in trusteeship, Carey had persuaded Zero and McCormick to run as a team in the 1995 union elections. That arrangement later collapsed, leading to the divisive elections in 2000. *Photograph by Paul Waterhouse, courtesy of Local 705.*

Local 705 members picketing the Jefferson Street UPS facility in August 1997. Both Local 705 and the national Teamsters successfully struck UPS, gaining national attention and increasing the stakes in the struggle for control of 705. *Photograph by Paul Waterhouse, courtesy of Local 705.*

Rev. Jesse Jackson marching with Local 705 secretary-treasurer Gerald Zero outside the Jefferson Street UPS facility in Chicago during August 1997. After the victory of reformers in 1995, Local 705 established coalitions with Chicago community-based organizations, such as Jobs with Justice and Rainbow PUSH, to pursue a common social justice agenda. *Photograph by Paul Waterhouse, courtesy of Local 705.*

Local 705 representative Richard DeVries (in cap and glasses on left) in the fall of 1998 discussing a strike in the West Loop against moving company Knoffs-Atlas. DeVries was a veteran political activist and one of the local's most militant reformers. Like many other 705 union leaders appointed during or after the trusteeship, he was recruited from outside the Teamsters Union. *Photograph by Paul Waterhouse, courtesy of Local 705.*

International Teamsters Union special representative and former Local 705 member Dane Passo (hands in pocket) standing outside the 705 hall after the 2000 local officer nomination meeting. Passo was the most outspoken opponent of the Zero-McCormick reform drive. In the 1997 local officer election, Passo headed a unified opposition slate and was narrowly defeated for the union's top post.

Local 705 union representative Dan Campbell (center) talking with union members outside Teamster Hall after a local membership meeting in the spring of 2000. Campbell was on the national steering committee of Teamsters for a Democratic Union and played a key role in the local reformers' political success.

Local 705 union representative Bennie Jackson (center) outside the 705 hall in May 2000. A longtime 705 reform activist, Jackson had twice been a candidate for union office on the Reform Pride Movement slate. He later split with the RPM and sought to remove Zero from office, ensuring that the 2000 election would be particularly hard-fought.

Local 705 member and United 2000 Party candidate for secretary-treasurer Michael Deane (center, with right hand raised) at a 2000 campaign rally. Deane was a UPS driver who strongly opposed the local's trusteeship and believed that the Zero-led reformers had destroyed the union's famed bargaining independence.

went on to explain that the local's "positive progress was threatened" by McCormick's leadership of the union and that the four elected board members had adopted the "rhetoric of management" toward UPS. Readers were told that the indelicately labeled "Gang of Four" was removed from their positions because their actions were found to be "anti-member," and even worse, "pro-employer."[24]

Zero made one other point that later proved to be a contentious issue in legitimating his actions. He made clear to the membership that he "had to remove these four gentlemen from their positions as Union Representatives." Nonetheless, he reluctantly noted that the four "must remain elected officers throughout their term."[25] In other words, Zero was only discharging the four union employees from their nonelected positions. His letter implicitly recognized the local's officers as holding two distinct and separately compensated jobs. The distinction was of no minor concern. If McCormick, Benesch, Jackson, and Pocztowski were appointed union representatives as well as elected officers, then Zero had the authority under the IBT Constitution and Local 705 Bylaws to dump them from the payroll as appointed union representatives. If, however, the job of elected officer included the typical work of a union representative, then Zero had no authority to fire them from any position. In that case, he might not like what they had to say or the votes they cast on the executive board, but because members had elected them, they could be removed only by a vote of the members.

Armed with a definitive Supreme Court decision, *Finnegan v. Leu,* cited in nearly three hundred court cases, Zero fired the four union representatives with extreme confidence. In a unanimous opinion, written by Chief Justice Burger, the high court had ruled that the Labor-Management Reporting and Disclosure Act "does not restrict the freedom of an elected union leader to choose a staff whose views are compatible with his own." The court made the critical point that Congress sought only to protect "rank and file union members, not union officers or employees," from violations of the rights guaranteed under the act. The court found that the law only prohibits "retaliatory actions that affect a union member's rights or status *as a member* of the union." Burger added, however, that "discharge from union employment does not impinge upon the incidents of union membership."[26]

McCormick had correctly figured out that if action was not taken against Zero, he (McCormick) would have little opportunity to blunt the incumbent's quest for a third term. Since Zero had returned to office, the board majority had clashed with him over a number of union policies. It was clear that the local now had two primary parties and governing approaches. However, in order for the four fired agents to project themselves to the membership as a politically viable alternative to Zero, they had to maintain their union positions. With union staff jobs came the most important of political resources, access to union members. The fall election was still seven months away, but the immediate political goal was obvious:

McCormick and his UPS agents had to reverse Zero's firing. To do so they moved the conflict into the somber interior of a federal court.

McCormick and company immediately requested a preliminary injunction against their dismissal. In their court complaint, the four board members characterized Zero as a political tyrant engaged in a coercive scheme to silence political opponents. District Court judge Milton I. Shadur was asked to order Zero to restore the board members to their respective positions, resume paying their salaries, and provide them with all the benefits entitled to them as union officers. On May 18 the District Court judge complied, issuing a Temporary Restraining Order (TRO), and set June 14 as the date for a final status hearing.[27] After four days of midsummer hearings, Judge Shadur ruled that the TRO should be permanently enforced, effectively overturning Zero's actions.

Shadur gave considerable weight to the Supreme Court's *Sheet Metal Workers v. Lynn* ruling, which held that the removal of elected business agents in retaliation for exercising protected political activities was a violation of LMRDA. In *Lynn,* the court found that compared to the dismissal of an appointed business agent for political activity, discharging an elected employee in retaliation for his or her political activity had "a more pronounced chilling effect" on meeting the law's objective "to insure that unions are democratically governed, and responsive to the will of the union membership as expressed in open, periodic elections." In explaining his reliance on *Lynn,* Shadur noted that Zero's defense presented no documentary evidence that any of the four officers had ever been appointed to a separate business agent position. Shadur also noted that the four plaintiffs were only paid a single salary as full-time officers.[28] In the court's judgment, because the fired four were not appointed agents but were instead elected officers doing the work of a business agent, the principle set down in *Finnegan* was "wholly irrelevant."[29] Zero, Shadur forcibly insisted, had fired the four elected officers for criticizing the secretary-treasurer's policies and thus had violated the plaintiffs' free speech rights.

"I did fire them in part because of their political opposition," retorted Zero, but he insisted that "they were also let go because they refused to do their jobs" as appointed business agents. He pointed out that all four men were first hired as business agents during the trusteeship and only later were elected to executive board posts. In addition, he argued that the agent's work is far more substantial than any of the board offices. Except for the secretary-treasurer post, he said, "jobs of local officers by the IBT Constitution and local Bylaws are at best part-time work." To be sure, a formal job description almost never fully captures the actual work done by the person holding the position. Even the minimal duties of each officer require access to union records and members. "But how could you justify paying $86,000 to a local recording secretary or $76,000 to a trustee," Zero incredulously challenged, "Unless they were doing the real work of an agent?"[30]

Notwithstanding the compensation question, Shadur dismissed Zero's claim that he fired the four gentlemen because they were not doing their job. He based his evaluation of Zero's allegations solely on the union leader's sworn deposition. And to put it mildly, the deposition was a disaster. Zero was unprepared for the level of specificity that would be required to make a case of poor job performance against a particular employee. When asked to cite concrete examples of unsatisfactory work for each of the plaintiffs, the local's chief executive floundered for an answer. It may have been the secretary-treasurer's flippant answer to one particular question that sealed the case for the court, though. When asked how he came to know that on the day that he dismissed the plaintiffs, all four were performing inadequately, an obviously irritated Zero responded, "Just lucky, I guess."[31]

Zero's deposition performance was puzzling. Although he could not give a single concrete example of the fired four ever failing to represent the membership at UPS, his staff, led by representative Dan Campbell and contract administrator Tom Nightwine, had compiled a formidable record of misdeeds. More importantly, they had brought their discoveries to Zero's attention. What Zero knew at the time of his deposition was that approximately twelve hundred UPS grievances, extending back to 1996, had been badly botched by the four. To be sure, the finding was a real embarrassment to the union leader. The pre-1999 grievances that were mishandled had occurred under Zero's watch, and he could not now abdicate his responsibility for what had happened during his tenure in office. Armed now with a court ruling and a desultory record of performance, both McCormick and Zero looked to an upcoming membership meeting as an opportunity to win the hearts and minds of the voters.

Zero and McCormick Go to the Membership

Before an overflow and emotionally charged crowd gathered at the May 2000 membership meeting, presiding officer John McCormick condemned Zero's attempt to fire the four board members. McCormick could not have chosen a more inflammatory way to communicate his point. He paraphrased a quote from a fresh copy of Judge Shadur's temporary injunction. Standing alone behind the podium, McCormick shouted in triumphant tones that the judge had ruled that despite what Zero believed, "there should not be a czar in this local." As a small contingent of supporters howled their approval, the president went on to chronicle the undemocratic-like behavior of "Czar Zero."[32]

For a good ten minutes, McCormick brandished the court order like a hammer. He nailed and sank different points of the judge's decision into the meeting's rapidly heating atmosphere. When he was finished, the assembly was contorting like a giant snake by a mixture of cheering and jeering. Then Zero got up, hitched his pants, walked over, and grabbed the wooden podium as if it were a temperamental child. With his first four spoken words, the already excited house exploded into bedlam. "You heard that bullshit," Zero snarled, and the crowd leaped from their chairs wildly applauding their secretary-treasurer's blunt disregard of Mc-Cormick's comments. Barely audible over the repeated screams of "Gerry! Gerry! Gerry!" the Local 705 leader finished his sentence, "now hear the truth!" But the truth was not to be spoken; it was to be seen.

As supporters rhythmically shouted and stomped at their seats, Zero abruptly turned toward a back corner of the stage. He threw open a closet door and began to frantically remove boxes from the small storage space. Holding more than one box in his thick hands, he turned to face the membership and declared, "You people have been conned while I was gone." Zero then proceeded to angrily toss the multicolored paper contents of each box onto the stage. With each flying box, Zero explained to the now delirious crowd how badly McCormick and his fellow UPS board members had governed the local during his suspension. The boxes contained the twelve hundred grievances allegedly dropped by the four fired men. "Take a look, you've been lied to," he dared the members, adding, "If you don't come up here you don't have any balls!" Zero had literally thrown down a gauntlet. And every member with "balls" came up to take a look.

Zero's dramatic stunt had its desired effect. McCormick's favorable legal opinion was no match for apparent evidence of officer malfeasance. No matter that most of those dumped grievances dated back to before Zero was suspended and that most of them bore Bennie Jackson's signature. It was classic political theater designed to connect with a member's emotions in the same way that a civic voter is manipulated by giant, waving, red, white, and blue flags. McCormick understood the ploy to embarrass him. Zero had made a loud, dramatic statement that McCormick had been asleep at the wheel while UPS management was literally driving workers out of a job. The local president knew that he had to quickly respond with something that would expose the secretary-treasurer as a self-serving opportunist in democratic clothing. McCormick chose a trick that he had seen used against him for many years.

Shortly after the two local leaders had gone head-to-head, the meeting was opened up to members for comments and questions. Members who wished to speak were required to abide by some simple procedural rules. On this occasion one of the rules was that all questions about UPS matters would be held in abeyance for a separate meeting, which was to convene immediately after the regular session. All UPS members were invited and encouraged to attend. It was, according to local bylaws, the job of the president as presiding officer to manage the discussion, including enforcing the rules for debate.

As members gathered in a long queue to speak, the lineup began to look very suspicious to Zero. When the president then recognized a series of people critiquing the local's recent efforts at UPS, Zero became incensed. McCormick was resorting to the old Peick-Ligurotis maneuver of using the membership meeting as a device to discredit a dissenter. Zero heard workers criticize his role in a brokered UPS deal for creating full-time jobs at the local. Although he was never afraid to debate with the membership, Zero knew an ambush when he saw it. He yelled at McCormick to defer all UPS comments, but the president refused to use his gavel to redirect the discussion. "The members have a right to be heard," McCormick yelled back, and the next anti-Zero spoke person stepped up to the mike.

After once more demanding that McCormick rule out of order this character assassination, Zero also decided to take a page out of the old guard days. Frustrated by his political opponent's control over the microphone, he ordered that the hall's sound system be shut down. "Shut it off!" Zero raged as he stomped across the stage. It took a second for McCormick to realize that he could no longer be heard. When he became aware, his face contorted in pain and he began furiously pounding on the podium in an attempt to restore order and sound. But the show was over. Without sound McCormick could go no further. He screamed over the breaking pandemonium that he had "no mike" and consequently, that the meeting was adjourned.

The staged scenes were good campaign agitprop, but they also communicated something more than empty symbolism. They served to signal to the membership that the upcoming election would not be decided in a courtroom, but at the bar of rank-and-file representation. The membership meeting had been transformed into a soapbox debate with all the heated passion of an old-fashioned religious revival meeting. As witnessed by the membership, two believers in democratic unionism laid claims to governing what had been called the "crown jewel" of Teamsterland. Once what the men had in common had determined the local's fortunes. Now it was their differences that mattered most.

The Nomination of Political Parties

On 21 October 2000, the scene in the parking lot at Chicago's Teamster City was reminiscent of a political convention. Local 705's nomination meeting for local officers had brought out the solemn and the carnivalesque. Yellow T-shirts announcing the candidacy of Gerry Zero draped the tailgate of a pickup truck and the backs of many loyal partisans. Small groups of union members huddled in patches throughout the lot, with the stenciled blue and gold message "Local 705 Fighting for the Future" towering behind them from the side of Teamster Hall. Some people proudly wore black and white "Hoffa" shirts (referring to IBT president James P. Hoffa), while others flew the colors of the union's famed reform caucus, TDU.[1] It appeared that the democratic process, put in place by the one-time dissenters, had unleashed a union political free-for-all worthy of the "Second City's" street brawling reputation.

Contesting for Power: Parties and Candidates

On this Sunday morning, at least five proposed officer slates were represented in the hall, where nominations would be made for the ballot that would be mailed to all members on November 9. The unprecedented number of slates indicated to the assembled throng that the reformers had come unglued. Two-time RPM secretary-treasurer Gerry Zero, running on the Continued Reform Slate, and president John McCormick, heading up the True Reform ticket, were now competing for the right to lead the local. The executive board had ruptured, with McCormick and fellow RPM officers Ed Benesch, Bennie Jackson, and Steve Pocztowski uniting to oppose Zero.

The coalition that had brought reform to the local's leadership was a dead letter; now, oddly, enemies of the old regime faced each other in a contest for power. The split within the reformers' slate also provided opportunities for other established factions to make a run for the union's leadership. Recognizable candidates were proclaiming their fitness for leadership and arguing that the reform of Zero and McCormick had run amok. Opponents of the incumbents lumped Zero and McCormick together into one irresponsible leadership. The two may have been running separate campaigns, but in the minds of their protagonists they were inextricably and shamefully joined.

Although many in the audience were new to the electioneering business, most members were aware that the candidates, and the parties they were heading, were not born yesterday. The fall election was shaping up as a who's who of local notables. Since the local was put into trusteeship, no fewer than four full slates had competed in two local officer elections, and members had participated in two national union elections, along with two contests for international convention delegates. One obvious observation was that factions at Local 705 did indeed exist and that they seemed to have bred opposition movements. As the *705 Update* proudly and rightfully claimed, "Teamsters have had more experience with democracy in the last decade than any other union member, and probably any American in the country!"[2]

A large crowd of partisan and undecided voters poured into the 705 auditorium to hear election officer Bruce Boyens read the election rules and call for officer nominations. From the floor of the hall, most of the slate candidates were first introduced to the local membership. One slate, however, had been announced months earlier. It was managed not by an active union member, but by a well-known Local 705 retiree.

United Slate 2000

One-time Local 705 member Archie Cook had been asked to manage the United 2000 Slate, dedicated to healing a union that has "more factions among the members than ever before." Cook was a thirty-year veteran of Local 705 who had run unsuccessfully for local president in 1995 and for the local's recording secretary in 1997.[3] The elderly Cook had earned his living working as a UPS package-car and freight driver, but it was his side job that proved most lucrative to the local membership. In the 1980s he sued the local and consequently developed a reputation for being a "workplace lawyer," a reputation that paid off when the local was placed into trusteeship.

In 1992 he authored a $20 million class action lawsuit against the local's leadership and the trustees of the Health and Welfare Fund. Cook charged that the fund had been mismanaged and had subsequently bilked the membership of millions of dollars. The local executive board and the fund trustees could not have been more amazed that a truck driver had managed to gather sufficient evidence to warrant a civil action for damages. In truth, Cook was no simple cab jockey. The old leadership's arrogance must have dimmed their view, or it would have been clear to them that Cook had a head for numbers and was comfortable with legal proceedings.

Although he believed that he had a strong case of mismanagement against the fund's trustees, Cook found himself all alone while holding the tiger by its tail. "Nobody would join his lawsuit," stated attorney Robin Potter; "they all said they were scared."[4] Nor could Cook take his case to the union's standing counsel, Sherman Carmell. As the attorney paid to represent the Health and Welfare Fund and a long-standing Teamster legal fixture, Carmell was likely to be named one of the defendants in the lawsuit. Cook ultimately decided to engage Chicago lawyers Charles Pressman, Robin Potter, Joel Hellmann, and Stephen Seliger. As the Health and Welfare Fund case slowly unfolded, a second, related event turned Cook's initiative into something more than a truck driver's quixotic endeavor.

In February 1995, just two months before Local 705's first open election, the international union joined the Cook lawsuit and filed a separate action against the pension fund trustees. According to attorney Michael Holland, the international union's involvement was critical. The "case was languishing," and except for the work of experienced union attorneys possessing the "skill to figure out the fraud, the case would have at best been dragged out and at worst been dismissed." In the end, the combined effort of Cook's legal team and the IBT's attorneys eventually produced a $14 million settlement against the trustees.[5] On 13 March 1996 Ron Carey and Gerald Zero, who had become Local 705 secretary-treasurer, appeared triumphantly before the Chicago press to announce a settlement in both civil suits. It was a major score for the reform movement. Here in the heart of once-corrupt, mob-ridden Chicago Teamsterland, a blow for justice had been delivered. Still, something was missing from this celebration that suggested that democracy had to make room for old-fashioned party politics.

One of the reporters at the news conference was veteran *Chicago Tribune* reporter Steve Franklin. The *Tribune* writer noted in his published account of the settlement that "Archie Cook was out driving a truck." He also implied that the reason for Cook's absence might have been political. Not only had Cook run in 1995 for local president on the Leroy Ellis ticket against the Zero-led RPM slate, but he was now "on a slate of opposition delegates that will challenge Carey's leadership at the union's July convention." Cook claims that the first question Franklin asked at the press conference was "Where is Archie Cook?"[6]

Cook's legal finesse and retiree status aside, his involvement in the 2000 election was most notable for the curious mix of affiliations that colored his union career. Before running for an executive board office, he served the local for fifteen years as a union steward. In the late 1970s he joined TDU and served, for a short time, as its Chicago chapter cochair. He later became disillusioned with TDU and quit the organization. Despite supporting Ron Carey's international insurgency campaign in 1991, Cook was convinced that Carey and TDU had instituted a ruling "dictatorship." So in 1996 he ran successfully as a Local 705 Hoffa convention delegate.[7] Cook's association with the old guard leadership, the anti–old guard rank-and-file movement, and finally, the anti-Carey regime represented the fluidity of political thinking that would characterize some elements of this electoral competition.

Despite Cook's experience, as a retired member he could not stand for union office. He would instead apply his trade on behalf of the United

Party's candidate for the local's top post, who had also contested for office three years before. Michael Deane, a twenty-five-year member of the local and a UPS driver, collected thirty-four hundred votes and came very close to winning a 1997 trustee position. An expressive man with wide, sparkling eyes, Deane was the closest approximation in the race to a lifelong trucker. At the age of eight he was working on a milk truck for the Hamilton Milk Company, earning 25 cents an hour. By the age of twelve, he had graduated to an overnight shift, delivering milk at three in the morning.

Deane believed that under Ligurotis, UPS workers were not being represented. Yet, although he admitted that the local was not "on the path it should have been," he strongly opposed the trusteeship. Deane contended that instead of an imposed trusteeship, the members should have been given a chance to vote in a scheduled local election that was only six months away. Ligurotis may have been bad for the members, but Deane argued that "Teamsters should have decided what to do with him [Ligurotis]." In Deane's judgment, Carey took over Local 705 "to put his own people in" and not to advance democracy.[8]

By 1997 Deane had joined forces with Dane Passo, Arkansas Best Freight driver and Hoffa-friendly Local 705 member, in challenging a "TDU dictated" administration.[9] He decided at the time that the best way to return the union to local control was to campaign for James Hoffa in the 1996 national election. When Hoffa defeated Tom Leedham in the 1998 rerun election, Deane and other Hoffa supporters expected to benefit from the change of resident at the union's Marble Palace headquarters in Washington, D.C. But a series of events caused him to grow as unhappy with the Hoffa people as he was with the Zero-McCormick camp. As a result, his allegiances swung once more toward what he now defined as "local independence." "Since the trusteeship, who negotiates contracts for 705, professor?" he quizzed me. Deane quickly answered his own question by then noting the names of people who had been hired by Zero to conduct union business. Deane's contention about each of these staff members was that they had come from somewhere else. He was in this race, this time, to root out the "outsiders."[10]

Teamsters for Unity

Although the United Slate was the first group to organize publicly, it was not the last to promote unity. Much to the annoyance of the United camp, at the nomination meeting the Teamsters for Unity emerged. The United folks were not amused by the similarity of slate names and immediately filed an election protest, requesting that Unity be "enjoined from using this name or any other similarity [sic] name."[11] Undeterred, the Teamsters for Unity pushed forward; Eugene Phillips, a twenty-eight-year UPS driver, headed this second oppositional party.

Eugene Phillips worked out of the package delivery company's Northbrook facility. In the 1995 local election, he finished eleventh out of seventeen candidates running for one of three elected business agents. Unfazed by the poor showing, just one year later he collected 3,148 votes and was elected a Hoffa convention delegate. The international union's 1996 election proved to be important to the political path he was now undertaking. The Philadelphia convention was a raucous affair, with Carey and Hoffa supporters daily trading virulent hoots, jeers, and catcalls. Heckling actually broke out among the delegates on the floor of the Philadelphia Convention Center during the opening moment of silence. On another occasion, Hoffa supporters temporarily closed down the convention in protest over their belief that Carey was ruling contrary to the majority wishes of the delegates.

The behavior of delegates became so tumultuous that Pennsylvania senator Alan Specter was shouted away from the speaker's podium only to return and scold the assembly by declaring that "this demonstration does not bring credit to Teamsters." By the third day of the convention, the delegates had only advanced to page 3 of their 134-page book of amendments.[12] Carey's inability to manage the convention floor or move the union's agenda was a direct result of Hoffa's stunning success in winning the support of a wide majority of the delegates. Despite the power of the incumbent general president, delegates committed to Carey were in the minority. And no local was guiltier of weakening Carey's convention authority than Local 705. Local 705, the one and only Carey stronghold in the Central Region, had voted to send delegates to Philadelphia who were committed to the Hoffa team.

Phillips's willingness to run as a Hoffa supporter represented his first switch in political loyalty. In the 1995 local election, Phillips supported TDU member Leroy Ellis's run for secretary-treasurer. But by 1996 Phillips, a member of the Teamsters National Black Caucus (TNBC), had serious doubts about the reformers' agenda and rejected TDU for "standing for unproductive positions, that don't ever work."[13] Phillips's slate, if not his own candidacy, had been rumored for several months. There was a common belief amid the swirl of prenomination speculation that the local chapter of the TNBC was forming its first slate. The Chicago chapter was formed in 1999 and had approximately 170 members, the vast majority of them in Local 705. Surprisingly, however, the slate was not headed by, and did not even include, TNBC Chicago chapter chairman Ted Mullins. Running in 1997 for one of four elected business-agent positions, Mullins had actually collected more votes (3,414) than United Party candidate Michael Deane. More impressive was that Mullins's vote total in 1997 was two-thirds larger than what he tallied in 1995, while running for one of three trustee spots.

Despite Mullins's absence, two other caucus members joined Phillips on the Unity Slate. According to Phillips, however, he was not the black candidate. After two decades of union membership, he claimed to have acquired a reputation as the "union man." Although he never was appointed a union steward, he believed that "people felt more comfortable coming" to him than to the actual representative. He insisted that the strength of his candidacy was not based on the roughly one-quarter of union members who were black. Phillips declared that his legitimacy was a product of working at UPS because it had given him "a broad scope to see other problems."

The Membership Slate

Not to be left out of what was shaping up to be an intra-UPS electoral fight, the freight drivers had their own familiar political warhorse, Michael Husar, saddling up for the post. In 1995 the thirty-one-year "pick-up and delivery" driver ran fourth in a four-person field for secretary-treasurer. Husar had been a steward for eight years under Ligurotis and briefly served as an organizer prior to the trusteeship. Unlike many Ligurotis appointees, who were fired, Husar and close colleague Benny Leonardo were asked by Ed Burke to come on staff. Husar had a reputation for honesty and was familiar with the drivers in many of the freight barns. Because most of the union representatives dismissed during the trusteeship had come from freight barns, Husar and Leonardo gave the reformers a much-needed voice in a sector rocked by deregulation and links with a discredited past leadership.

The relationship between the Zero-and-McCormick-led reformers and Husar remained positive, right up to the prenomination stage of the 1995 election. Husar explained that his willingness to "work with the reform program" generated an offer from Zero to join his RPM slate. Zero needed some solid people in the freight division, and he believed that Husar "was a good guy." With the campaign offer hanging in the air and just two weeks remaining before the nomination meeting, Husar went to breakfast with Local 705 contract administrator Tom Nightwine. That breakfast turned into seven hours of coffee refills and intense talk about local union politics. Nightwine laid out the reasons for having Husar on the slate and, according to Husar, "went as far as to offer the president or vice president spot."[14] But Nightwine should have saved his tip money.

To Zero's surprise, the freight driver rejected the offer. Husar had sat in on a number of staff policy meetings and was frustrated by the constant "ripping of so-called old guard guys." It seemed to Husar that Zero and McCormick had a "divide and conquer" strategy for running the union, and he wanted no part of such an effort. What Zero did not know was that Husar had been quietly organizing his own slate. With the aid of individuals connected to the defunct IBT Central Conference, Husar led a Membership Slate of veteran cartage and freight drivers into the 1995 contest.[15]

During the local's freight-hauling glory years, drivers representing large national companies like Yellow, Roadway, Carolina, Preston, and USF Holland literally controlled the local's politics and culture. These men did not wear shorts and would not have been allowed to have nose rings. In the 1970s some UPS members and a minority of freight drivers were agitating for democratic reform, but Husar's constituency wore their Teamster membership as a badge of pride. Old-style Teamster leaders like Hoffa, Peick, and

Ligurotis may have had their faults, but they put the "fear of the Lord" into the companies they organized.[16] They were the "freight solicitors" of Local 705, resolutely standing against the "merchants of doom," and the membership was "in complete unison recogniz[ing] the efforts and results" of the leadership.[17]

For Husar the good old days did not include mobsters and union corruption. His remembered past featured a proud and powerful union that could deliver benefits to the members, intimidate U.S. presidents and corporate heads alike, and make the Teamster symbol of a gold and black horse team a statement of authority. In one distinct manner, Husar is a personal manifestation of the Teamster history that he yearned to see return. He is physically a giant of a man, six feet five inches tall and weighing more than 250 pounds. With weathered lines etching his face, brawny thick fingers, and even a slight limp caused by an old softball knee injury, he is a John Wayne–looking figure with a Teamster union card.

Husar's 2000 campaign was a long shot. Membership Slate candidates had fared poorly in the 1995 election, finishing near the bottom of each vote category. Putting together a viable campaign in 2000 was also handicapped by the inactivity of the slate since 1995. Husar had been fired by Zero shortly after the election and consequently lost a platform for campaigning among freight barns. When the second posttrusteeship election was held in 1997, in contrast to the one two years earlier, there was only one oppositional slate. And surprisingly, it did not include any Membership representatives.

In the aftermath of the 1995 contest, the oppositional leaders had cobbled together a group of members that embarrassed the pro-Carey forces by sweeping the local's 1996 delegate election. Nonetheless, it was at best an alliance of convenience, and according to Husar the delegate slate was formed out of three factions that "hated each other."[18] At a meeting in March of 1996, faction representatives discussed a plan to divvy up the local's allotted twenty-four delegate positions. Hoffa, who had declared himself a candidate for union president, made his recommendation for the composition of the delegate slate through local surrogate Dane Passo.

The proposed slate would include sixteen Real Teamsters and four each from the Membership and Leroy Ellis parties. Husar disagreed with the breakdown and suggested instead that a coalition be formed of three equal parts. His proposal was batted around for a while, and the meeting dragged on for nearly four hours; then Passo suddenly declared that the Hoffa plan had to be adopted. Knowing an ultimatum when he heard one, Husar immediately lifted his Bunyanesque body from the chair and "threatened to walk" if Hoffa got his way. The sight of this Teamster rising from his seat must have certainly punctuated the seriousness of such an undemocratic endeavor. In the end, Hoffa got more than his way and something he did not want. Although the Membership team got only two of the available delegate slots, old guard loyalists would now, perhaps for the first time in Chicago, have "nothing to do with a Hoffa."[19]

The meetings in preparation for the 1997 election proved equally futile. "Egos got in the way," and the discussions grew acrimonious. Husar decided that neither Passo nor Archie Cook "was the right guy to handle the job" of running the local. In the end a single "United" anti-RPM slate was formed without Membership participation. According to Husar, that was a fatal mistake for the slate. By the time the election was held, many veteran freight drivers, loyal to past Hoffa regimes, had developed a real dislike for the RPM oppositional camp leaders. Despite historically "always voting" in local elections, they decided to "trash their ballots."[20]

But Husar believed things would be different in the 2000 race. He saw this contest as an opportunity for a third-way option to grab the leadership reigns. Husar reasoned that the negative nature of the 1997 campaign, along with subsequent Teamster political events, had left many older and solid local freight members without a party or platform to rally around. Vehemently opposed to the Carey-Leedham-TDU forces and disdainful of the old guard elements that had failed to "keep their promises," these full-time freight drivers existed in a political purgatory. As explained by Husar, the strategy for the Membership Party would be to win the majority support of freight "fence sitters." Winning freight votes would mean promising to move the local forward by returning it to a proud past, when, in Husar's view, the "companies feared the union."[21]

Along with their antipathy for the reform incumbents, Husar, Cook, and Deane shared another common political characteristic. They were all former or would-be partners and eventually sworn enemies of Dane Passo, one of the more curious and notable players in 705's political fortunes.

The Passo Factor

Dane Passo was, without question, the most renowned enemy of the Local 705 reformers. When Carey imposed the trusteeship on the local, Passo was one of the first to be fired. But in 1998 his unyielding loyalty and hard work paid off in a big way when Hoffa was elected international president. Hoffa showed his gratitude to the one-time Christian Youth Organization golden-gloves boxer by appointing him as a special assistant to the general president. He was assigned to the Central Region; Chicago Local 705 was in his territory. The place where he was politically discredited on two occasions and twice involved in violent exchanges with Zero-backed allies would again be a site of struggle. With the fall 2000 election now approaching, whispers of Passo's shadow began to spread.

Passo believed that the fall election "was my best chance to win." The reformers had turned on each other, and there were a number of high-profile, anti-Zero members inspired by the election of Hoffa. Passo wanted to govern Local 705, and he claimed to have obtained Hoffa's blessing to make a third bid for the local's leadership. After a March 705 membership meeting, he arranged a summit at Hawkeye's Restaurant of key individuals, campaigners, and delegates from the 1996 convention. In attendance were fellow United Party stalwarts Mike Deane and Larry Hart. They had come to hear Passo lay out a strategy to finally wrestle political power from the outsiders. Instead, they heard Passo say the unthinkable. "I told them I wasn't running and that we needed to back Zero." At first the congregation was too stunned to respond. Then "they went ballistic."[22]

Passo claimed that his involvement in the local race would be uncontrollably divisive and thus bad for Hoffa. The newly sworn-in president badly needed a show of unity to win over those in and outside of the union who believed he would govern as a vindictive autocrat. To be sure, Zero had been an opponent, but if Hoffa inserted himself into the local's politics, it would be correctly read as a direct assault on union democracy in a nationally recognized, proreform Teamster local. Hoffa had campaigned on the issue of government interference into the union's affairs and had vowed to end the costly federal oversight. He wanted to create at least the appearance of an honest union no longer in need of "big brother."[23] Besides, in the context of political gamesmanship, he was holding a couple of aces.

When the executive board filed charges against Zero in February, the secretary-treasurer made a direct appeal to Hoffa to make a definitive ruling. By ruling against the embattled local leader, Hoffa could disqualify Zero from the fall election. But as the local campaign unfolded, Hoffa remained quiet. Local 705 would be left alone to settle their own internal differences—at least for now. Dan Campbell, a UPS union representative and Zero supporter, had his own less Machiavellian view of why Passo chose not to contest for power in Local 705. "He had everything he wanted." Campbell was referring to Passo's plum appointments as assistant to Hoffa and as trustee over a Las Vegas local. "Why come back here?" Campbell rhetorically asked. "Passo had arrived, it would never get any better than this."[24] In truth, even with his deft political skills, Passo would have a hard time beating Zero and a harder time governing, if he managed to win. Campbell's point seemed reasonable, and by the middle of the campaign season, every active slate supporter had an opinion of why Passo was staying on the sidelines.

After the tumultuous Hawkeye meeting, Passo flew back to Washington, leaving his partisans feeling deeply betrayed. They quickly spread the word of secret negotiations in which Passo had sold his soul to the devil. A meeting had in fact taken place in Washington between Zero, Passo, and Hoffa assistant Carl Scalf. The two 705 combatants concurred that they discussed the local's politics but that no deal was ever made to keep Passo out of the race. Zero fueled the gossip mill by attending a Chicago Anti-Defamation League dinner where James Hoffa was the featured speaker. When the local Teamster leader was asked by a newspaper reporter why he showed up at an affair where the spotlight was on Hoffa, Zero answered, "I haven't seen him do anything wrong."[25] Zero loyalists knew of the rapprochement with Hoffa and secretly hoped that Passo would sit this election out.

For his part, Zero said he never asked for assistance in the election and that Passo never offered to be helpful. But Passo admitted that he always intended to be more than a passive observer. As the campaign heated up in October, he acknowledged receiving daily phone calls from Local 705 members asking him for his advice on how to vote. "I told them to vote their conscience." But then, when directly queried about "whom I thought was the best choice, I told them what I thought." United chief Deane and Membership head Husar were certain that he answered, "Zero." Campbell was pleased that Hoffa had "called off the main dog" and would have been even happier if Passo "didn't bad mouth our guy."[26] He had little to worry about.

Despite Passo's violent previous encounters with Zero, he projected a pragmatic respect for the Local 705 leader. "I never disliked him personally, but he was a Carey guy and my fight was against Carey," Passo explained. He noted that Zero had good leadership skills and always "kept an open mind." Passo felt that Zero's appointing a number of "old RTS supporters" as union representatives was proof of the secretary-treasurer's willingness to consider different viewpoints.[27] He considered this good politics and also a sign that Zero wanted to unify the local. But while the combative 705 member found a cautious, moderating way to speak about Zero, he offered a much different tone for another election candidate: "McCormick was a slime!" Passo expressed a visceral disdain for the local president and, when speaking of him, ripped off a litany of derogatory comments; he was "sneaky, closed minded, lacked guts and couldn't deal with problems." But Passo's real hatred of McCormick was not fueled by any personal attributes.

Passo despised the local president because he was all "UPS, UPS, UPS and never cared a damn about freight." In Passo's heart, freight was still the soul of the Teamsters. He would not countenance any diminution of respect for the old-style Hoffa union he was still psychologically attached to. McCormick had also campaigned nationally as Tom Leedham's choice for international secretary-treasurer, and Leedham was endorsed by TDU. In the world of Teamster politics, there was nothing Passo had less tolerance for than "TDU Carey type piece of shits!" Now there was little substantive difference between Zero's and McCormick's commitment to TDU-style democratic reform.[28] But Passo believed that Zero had demonstrated the interpersonal skills and ability to work with those who disagreed with him. McCormick, he felt, "had his own platform."

Whatever Passo said to members who called him, he was once again an important player in Local 705's political affairs. Passo's way was never easy or mundane. For good or for bad, Passo could not be ignored. In the eyes of many local members, he was a Machiavellian figure with sinister intentions. To others he was a competent old-fashioned Teamster bureaucrat taking care of friends and punishing enemies. To others still, he was merely a bumbling, Hoffa sycophant without any regard for the membership. Whatever the truth was of this short, stocky, square-shouldered Teamster, Passo had already had an impact on the fortunes of the local and was believed to be playing a behind-the-scenes role in the upcoming election.

Continued Reform and True Reform

To opponents of the 705 administration, "Zero and McCormick" equalled one candidate. Any union member could have been forgiven for thinking that way. Both men had been 705 members for over two decades and had developed a working relationship that stretched back at least to the mid-1980s. "We became friendly on the floor of the hall," McCormick recounted.[29] His reference to location was essential to understanding what their relationship was built on. The hall in this case is more than a physical space; it is where, in the 1970s and 1980s, sides in ideological and hand-to-hand combat were drawn.

Inside 705's auditorium, members like McCormick and Zero courageously spoke out against corrupt leaders. Sometimes for their trouble the dissidents got beaten up, or their cars were vandalized, or worse yet, their families were threatened. If workers stood against the reign of Peick and Ligurotis, they were brandished as labor traitors. Workers who stood for union democracy were part of a crazy insurgent group, meeting in private homes to plan a revolution with only the camaraderie of others to sustain their effort. From such struggles partnerships can be formed, and within such struggles the flaws of partnerships are hidden.

For two terms Zero and McCormick played a winning cooperative hand. "We discussed everything at first," McCormick noted, and "we never argued." Zero acknowledged that he worked harmoniously with his president and always "included him in every meeting and decision." For both men the goals were the same; rid the local of corrupt people and push the reform agenda established by Carey. "Power," according to McCormick "was never an issue." And "to the outside world," Zero admitted, "it looked as if there were two people running Local 705." The temper of union governing from 1994 until the commencement of Zero's suspension in 1999 was businesslike and productive, because in McCormick's terms, "we were fighting for our lives."[30]

The local had also weathered more than five years of restructuring since the trusteeship, and a successor election had been run without major incident. By 1999 the local had established a six-year record of support for democratic unionism. Zero and McCormick had beaten back antireform opponents in 1997, and one year later, Tom Leedham's meagerly financed Local 705 Rank and File Team had decisively stomped the well-heeled Hoffa machine. Leedham's source of support among midwestern drivers and UPS employees was centered within Local 705. Leedham had raised money at numerous 705 events; the local was also prominently represented on the slate with John McCormick running for the secretary-treasurer's office. Although most experts considered Hoffa's candidacy to be an unstoppable juggernaut, if the Leedham candidacy was to stand any chance of upsetting the much better known and financed favorite, it was absolutely essential to keep a strong proreform force alive in Chicago. Reformers also believed that maintaining a very large outpost of anti-Hoffa Teamsters in Chicago was necessary to preserve a democratic movement within the union.

When the rerun election results were finally certified, Hoffa had won a clear victory around the country, and, except for Local 705, a sweep of locals in Chicago. Zero and McCormick had not only brought the local in for Leedham, but the anti-Hoffa vote had actually increased since the initial corrupted election. The cumulative effect of proreform votes at Local 705 provided sufficient evidence to believe that the old guard forces had lost their political legitimacy and that democracy had become the status quo. It appeared now that the union's only significant enemies were sitting in corporate boardrooms. By Local 705 standards, a modicum of calm had befallen the Teamsters.

But then Zero was suspended, and reform itself was divided between "Continued" and "True" advocates. Zero and McCormick would now try to do what neither man had done before: win political office without the other. More importantly, they would risk the unity of the democratic movement, painstakingly developed for over twenty years, by running as competing reformers. Each man knew that in the past, divisions within the dissident ranks had handicapped Teamster reformers' attempts to win local office. Both leaders were betting that roughly seven years of rank-and-file unionism had changed the political culture at Local 705. Not everyone was fully committed to reform, but Zero and McCormick believed that everybody was chasing democratic votes.

The fracture in the reformers' ranks was an ugly separation, but it was not an antidemocratic turn of political fortunes. Prior to the Zero-McCormick split, there was only one concept of democratic unionism. For two terms Zero and McCormick had stressed procedural changes and providing better union service to the members. Now the meaning of democratic unionism included a debate over the degree of rank-and-file involvement and levels of labor militancy. The test for anyone wanting to lead this Chicago Teamster union was to transform the idea of democratic unionism into a coherent political agenda and a governing philosophy. The campaign had been joined.

CHAPTER SEVEN

The Campaign Begins

The Zero and McCormick leadership had held constant through officer elections in 1995 and 1997 with only small changes in the ticket. Each of the board officers was a veteran member of Local 705, well known to the union rank and file, and a proven vote-getter. Over the past five years, they had proved to be a formidable party with a majority bloc of supporters. But that was then.

A majority of the board was now at political war with Zero, the local's highest-ranking officer. More importantly, the ability of the majority faction to wage a separate campaign was substantial. As Local 705 UPS Division chief, McCormick collected more than six thousand votes in the central region in 1998 as an international candidate for secretary-treasurer on the Leedham slate.[1] Although McCormick obviously represented a well-established and solid base of political support within the local's UPS members, Bennie Jackson had perhaps the deepest political experience of anyone in the group. In 1975 he was a candidate for office and three years later ran for president on a Rank and File Slate. Taken together, the new faction had heady political credentials. The combined vote of the four executive board members and a supportive business agent in the 1997 elections was equal to the vote of Zero and the trustees and agents who remained Continued Reform Party members.[2]

As the campaign season was about to begin, it appeared that Local 705's factions were more than mere vehicles for ambitious individuals; they were instruments for expressing contrasting forms of union leadership and union ideology.

Zero versus McCormick

Although there were five candidates contending for the local's position of chief operating officer, members were initially faced with the odd task of separating Zero-McCormick into Zero and McCormick. The two men had twice successfully campaigned and governed as one; now they were asking members to associate them with distinct political records. To the average rank-and-filer, the differences may not have seemed obvious. In 1997 Zero and McCormick ran for reelection as a unified leadership team touting their accomplishments. Both men were portrayed as "Life Long Teamsters, Honest Hard-Working Leaders." Campaign literature stressed how "They've Delivered Top Notch Representation, Good Contracts, Better Pensions and Clean-Effective-Honest Leadership." To further ingrain the idea that both men had equivalent reform credentials, campaign material regularly featured a picture of Zero and McCormick embraced by a smiling Ron Carey.[3]

The call to reelect the "Zero-McCormick Reform Team" was loud and unequivocal. Together McCormick and Zero had led the reform effort, and over and over again Local 705 rank-and-filers were reminded that both men were real working Teamsters who deserved continued membership support. Now three years later, union members were asked to deconstruct the past in order to find a more democratic future. As difficult as it was to unravel the reformers' record, after putting aside the obviously hyperbolic campaign appeals, there were important differences between the two. What ultimately shattered Zero and McCormick's working relationship was that they began to reflect opposing ideological definitions of competency.

McCormick and Zero had developed different philosophical approaches to union governance and trade unionism. The local president was inherently more cautious in his manner and actions. He was a solid administrator who treated his job as local president and UPS coordinator with seriousness and honesty. McCormick was by all standards a very serviceable and valuable democratic union officer. But he was also less willing to draw a clear line between the company and the union on bargaining demands. Instead of a combative stance, McCormick preferred a common-interest "fair accommodation" approach to the employer.

The former UPS driver was also resolutely focused on what was happening at UPS. The regular column he penned for the local newsletter underscored his attention to the package company. McCormick's "UPShot" appeared in every edition of the *705 Update* and addressed issues relevant to UPS members. As the chief union officer responsible for managing affairs at "Brown," he believed in a kind of union leadership domino theory: as labor relations with UPS went, so would the fortunes of Local 705 go. McCormick was a soldier in the war between labor and capital. It's just that his tour of duty would be served as a member of a single Teamster unit, largely disconnected from the larger goals of the labor movement.

Although McCormick was committed to reform and was a fierce partisan against the "old school" Teamsters, he was a small-*d* union democrat. He had fought against corruption and for procedural justice in the union, but he was never comfortable engaging with the rank and file. He showed impatience with their questions and demands. Reform had unleashed the members' long-simmering frustrations, and as the new leadership made progress, expectations rose enormously. The union now had a more confident membership, and with that confidence came a willingness to challenge authority. Although McCormick respected the idea of the rank and file, he was afraid to give the real thing free rein to influence the direction of the local. He stressed order and paternal control as the way to achieve enlightened leadership and productive policy. Membership debates over union policy should be tolerated, but leadership decisions should never be subjected to a plebeian defense. In other words, rumbling with the membership was a formula for chaos, not democracy.

Zero, in contrast, liked to rumble. He understood and agreed with the power that the IBT constitution had given him as local secretary-treasurer, but he believed in using that authority to empower rank-and-file members. That meant creating the structures that gave members a voice in their union. Sometimes the sounds from the ranks were hostile, but Zero never flinched from a membership debate over his actions or decisions. His was a more grassroots approach to leadership and trade unionism. To Zero, a good labor union leader promoted worker solidarity across internal divisions, industries, and unions. Although his critics on the campaign trail saw him as a divisive force, the secretary-treasurer actually had a good relationship with every constituent group in the local. He was a freight guy with a broad, class-conscious understanding of labor-management relations, which made it possible to relate to workers of all stripes.

Personality was also important, and here differences were understood, rightly or wrongly, to reflect how much respect the official had for the membership. McCormick was rather stiff with the members and never seemed comfortable with spontaneity. He was easily irritated and earned a reputation for being self-serving and rather snobby. Some members went so far as to call him nasty and surly. Zero, however, enjoyed an off-the-cuff conversation. He readily embraced the opportunity to debate with members and was as much at ease walking through a garage shaking members' hands as he was sitting behind an office desk. A sign of just how their differing personalities shaped the way that they were thought of can be found in the way many members referred to them in conversations with the author. More often than not, members would speak of the secretary-treasurer as "Gerry," whereas the more formal "McCormick" typically identified the local president.

Zero and McCormick had been a productive leadership team in a time of extreme internal turmoil and worker distrust. Their split was nothing for the Teamster democratic reform movement to applaud, but history had been kind to the local. Having advanced from the oppressive days of bureaucratic and corrupt feudal union lords to two successive free and open elections, the local was now the setting for a five-way political struggle featuring two dedicated reformers. In a fashion rarely seen in Chicago and Teamster politics, multiple contrasting philosophies of trade unionism and leadership styles would compete for membership support. Issues would sometimes get lost in campaign hyperbole, but the impressions left on members during the previous seven years of dramatic change were unmistakable. The RPM division had let loose different and oppositional political forces. Democracy had become less neat and orderly, but it was still a vibrant way of conducting union business. Workers would once again vote for their brand of workplace empowerment and for a way to struggle with their employer.

Campaign Strategies

Dan Campbell had a reputation to uphold. At the IBT's 1991 Orlando convention, he was aspiring presidential candidate Ron Carey's delegate floor captain. He was also the first delegate at that convention to suggest the idea of voting to increase the weekly strike support pay to an unheard-of $200. The idea easily passed as a resolution. In 1991 Campbell was also a member of a Michigan IBT local and a TDU activist. By the time of his arrival at Local 705, he had become widely known as a national cochair of TDU's steering committee. He had aggressively campaigned locally for Carey and Leedham in the disputed 1996 national elections and was now ready to do political battle for Gerry Zero.

Campbell was one of two dozen members of the "Breakfast Club" that met once a month at six thirty in the morning, beginning in March, to plan an electoral strategy for the November vote. Although club members were often bleary-eyed when they met, they were unflinchingly serious and engaged with the task of beating McCormick. The other slates would get some support, campaign director and Airborne Express representative Mark Postilion believed, but it was McCormick's challenge that had to be repelled. Between bites of the Racine Café's best scrambled eggs and French toast, the club constructed a campaign strategy that was designed to both destroy McCormick's credibility and highlight Zero's accomplishments. No one working on the campaign would do it better than Campbell.

To look at him was to know that this guy was playing to win. Replete with "Zero Continued Reform" shirt and ball cap, and with cell phone, pager, and dangling key chain adorning various parts of his clothing, Campbell was a one-man tactical campaign zealot. His political work on behalf of union reform was part of a larger personal theology, which prioritized a lifelong commitment to social justice. Campbell was a long-standing member of the "Re-Organization" branch of the Mormon Church, and in his own words his faith was "the only way to understand why I do what I do." Faith to Campbell was predicated on a personal "calling" to build a better society consistent with the biblical teachings of the Book of James. As a matter of faith Campbell took seriously James's notable admonition to "Be ye doers of the word and not hearers only."[4] Campbell was compelled to act in the world, and everything he did inside the labor movement was underscored by his belief that "a person is justified by what he does and not by faith alone."[5]

From March until November Campbell was never without a briefcase or box of campaign literature. His white Chrysler van was converted into a rolling command center that went everywhere a Local 705 member vote was to be found. He got excited about union elections, and, fortified by his Mormon faith, Campbell believed that he had always fought on the right side for the right guys. Principles aside, Campbell was also driven by the realization that, unlike the runner-ups in civic elections, union election losers "go back to being some bosses' employee." He was convinced that Zero's team would have to outwork their opponents "by any means possible"; but he quickly added, "as long as it's legal and moral."[6] "Relentless campaigning," he called it: his own unique style of salvation.

The first thing that had to be done was to raise money. Postilion estimated that the campaign would have to come up with about $50,000 to get its message out to the members. Money would be needed principally to produce campaign flyers and assorted political paraphernalia, as well as to operate a phone banking system and to conduct two large mass mailings. Postilion informed Breakfast Club members that they could solicit money from anyone except employers. He also reminded them of their own financial obligations. Club members included all of the appointed and elected representatives who had remained loyal to Zero. According to Postilion, that was at least three-quarters of the staff; much would be asked of their loyalties, including a monthly contribution of $50. Out-of-pocket contributions by campaign supporters and candidates were common in union elections. These were not well-heeled individuals with large campaign donors and no PACs to grovel before. The candidates led by McCormick (True Reform), Deane (United), Husar (Membership) and Phillips (Teamsters for Unity) also each paid their own union version of a poll tax for the privilege of running for office.[7]

In addition to personal donations, money would be raised through fundraisers. The Membership Party, for example, planned to hold four rallies and a number of "meet the candidate" events. At these events visitors were tempted with a collection of campaign material to purchase. Hats, buttons, and bumper stickers were common. Selling $10 T-shirts proved to be a big hit. But it had to be done carefully. Union elections must abide by rules governing when, where, and how candidates can solicit for money. Postilion encouraged his group to "sell [their] shirts on the street and off the clock [not while working for the union]." He also warned them that they could not "go into a barn [workplace] and sell," although they could "wear the shirt inside" —unless of course, they "were meeting with an employer"; then they could either "throw something over it or turn the shirts inside out." The staff had apparently heard the message, because by the May membership meeting, more than twelve hundred bright yellow Zero shirts were in circulation. Two months later, Zero supporter Mike Colgan had somehow figured out that the number of shirts sold was proportional to the percentage of members represented by divisions. The campaign staff agreed that this was a good sign. The party flag was now planted throughout the union territory.

The United Slate had its own $10 lettered shirts out on the streets, but its solicitation efforts had, unexpectedly, left the slate with a nasty bruise. Apparently, it had escaped the attention of someone in the campaign that the first batch of printed shirts was not made in the United States. The campaign had embarrassingly had their name stenciled onto a piece of fabric that was made in a foreign sweatshop. At least that's how contributors to Teamster Web chat site Teamster.net saw it. The Web site was a favorite place for debating the local's election. Although many of the postings were blunt, crude, and inflammatory, they roughly approximated the nature of the electoral debate that occurred in conventional handbill and face-to-face forms. Most of the comments appeared to be generated by Zero, McCormick, and Deane partisans. Each had his favorite electronic author serving the party as either a hatchet man or a white knight. There was the Deane "Concerned Member," the McCormick "705 Man," and Zero's "Molly Maguire." Not everything these spokespeople had to say could be considered an intelligent exchange of views, but they were pioneers in utilizing a new communication method for campaigning. Now that the electronic door was opened, free and unfettered political speech came rushing in.

Postings about the scandalous shirts flew back and forth. The best example of the heat that United campaign coordinator Archie Cook and the slate took is the following piece, reprinted exactly as it appeared: "Lets tell the truth Archie, you ordered the shirts and never gave it one thought about where they came from. You told your non-union printer to get the least expensive shirt you could by. You gave no thought to the fact that fruit-of-the-loom assembled products in El-Salvadore, the country with a reputation of having the highest density of sweat-shops in the world."[8] Cook dismissed the gaff and claimed that the printer had misled the campaign about the shirts' country of origin. Anyway, Cook proudly noted that new shirts with "Made in America" labels were now selling faster than he could order them, and that nearly "2,000 of the originals had already been bought."[9] United 2000 needed every nickel of all that shirt money if it was going to reach its fund-raising goal of $30,000.

Along with the hawking of shirts and hats, the campaigns held social events to attract attention to their candidates and to poach for dollars. On a political calendar posted on the jerryzeroslate.org Web site, campaign socials were scheduled from April to September. And the first major fundraiser stirred up a bit of discontent. The club had agreed to hold a golf outing on one of the most unlikely days to draw a crowd, July 4. Campaign staff groused about the difficulty of getting a foursome together on a holiday at $100 a person for a day of golf and hotdogs. "People had families" was the most common complaint. Postilion was unmoved. He and Airborne colleague Mike Colgan insisted that this was the only day available and that the event had the potential for raising $8,000. Unfortunately, it fell short of expectations. Despite a nice day for golf and a cache of attractive door prizes, the event made only $2,500, and Postilion admitted that it was "a little disappointing."[10]

He also made it crystal clear at the July campaign meeting that the staff would have to do much better at the next two major fund-raisers if it expected to have the money to campaign through the fall. The campaign's last event was a "Cosmic Bowl" scheduled at the end of the month at Centennial Lane in Tinley Park. Participants would be treated to dinner and all-night bowling for $40 per couple. Although the late-night food and strobe light pin-bashing was selling well, everyone on the staff looked to the final fund-raiser as the potentially big moneymaker. The approach this time would be a September 10 picnic at one of Chicago's south side forest preserves. In scheduling the social gathering, Postilion was counting on a time-tested fact. If there was one thing certain about union elections, it was that free food and drink brought out the voters.

The United Slate, however, beat its opposition to the punch by scheduling an early campaign kick-off pig roast in late July. The affair was held at a slate member's home and featured an "aloha" theme. Everyone was dressed in the soon-to-be-infamous T-shirts with colorful Hawaiian leis draped around their necks. Cook saw this affair as an opportunity to introduce people to the slate members. Unlike the other four slates, United 2000 decided to publicly identify its candidates well before the nomination meeting in October. Believing that it needed to start earlier than the two well-known incumbent parties, United 2000 organized the party in order to create excitement about the slate before competitive campaigning began. Even though the day was gray and there was intermittent rainfall, a disc jockey kept the music coming for dancing children in straw skirts, and a Teamster, known only as Babalou, served as master of ceremonies, announcing to the attendees that "United Slate 2000 was in the house!" As Mike Deane and the rest of his slate took their bows from a small back porch, Cook wore a happy face. And why not? The pigs were succulent, the mood was festive, and seven hundred aloha tickets at $5.00 a head had been sold.

The Zero bash, coming nearly one and half months after the United fund-raiser, also attracted a very large crowd of union members and their families. The day started off cold and wet, but by midafternoon the weather had turned hot and humid. Kids jumped up and down inside an inflated carnival playground and ran around swinging at a piñata, while adults sat on lawn chairs and leisurely strolled the ample park grounds. Different races were well represented in the group of members from each of the local's bargaining units. UPS part-time workers were particularly conspicuous in their attendance. Everyone knew that part-time workers made up the largest pool of potential voters, and their attendance today was considered a positive sign by the campaign staff. By the late afternoon, yellow Zero T-shirts were evident everywhere. It was retail politics in the finest American tradition. Share a hotdog, talk a little work, and ask for a vote.

The United Slate held a second shindig two weeks later. Deane's picnic also drew an impressive turnout on a much less inviting day. A cold morning rain gave way to dark skies and falling temperatures throughout the afternoon. By early evening people were huddled together wearing United Slate 2000 sweatshirts and drinking hot cocoa. But the lack of heat did not cool anyone's spirits or resolve. Enthusiastic supporters stepped over muddy patches and queued up for food. Everyone brought a dish to share and a story of why they "wanted Zero and McCormick out." Eventually each slate member and many individual supporters spoke out on behalf of their cause. Although the day grew colder and colder, no one seemed in a hurry to go anywhere. As darkness eventually enveloped the pavilion, the cheers of hardworking union members continued to punctuate the chilly night air. It appeared that these people were in the campaign until the end.

There were drastic differences in the weather conditions that they faced, but the Zero and Deane campaign events shared some similarities: they offered enormous amounts of good barbecued beef and chicken and an assortment of baked beans, chips, tacos, and soda. Music was a big part of each event. Zero's group mixed contemporary rock artists like Stevie Ray Vaughn and Bruce Springsteen with a little of Frank Sinatra's big band ballads. Deane's patrons preferred a 1970s retro sound and an unmistakable repeat playing of "Eye of the Tiger," from the third *Rocky* movie. In an obvious nod to popular taste, both camps played a few cuts from one of the year's biggest recordings, Santana's *Supernatural*. It was the only recording that the two camps had in common. Whether the festive mood was set by Texas blues-rock, Latin soul, or a rousing sing-a-long version of *YMCA* by children at the United party, participants at both campaigns' events danced, sang, played softball, and professed the righteousness of their slate.

They also raised money. Both slates sold T-shirts and held a number of fifty-fifty and door prize raffles. One of Zero's prizes was particularly impressive and unexpectedly controversial. Two fortunate ticket holders would win a twenty-six-inch color television set. Nice prize for a $1.00 donation. Too bad it came with a red flag attached. As everyone in the country, and certainly in Local 705, knew, there is no American-made television. That means the prize was vulnerable to the "nonunion" foreign-made label. And no doubt remembering the flack raised over the United Slate's sweatshop T-shirts, people involved in the electronic campaign launched a series of attacks on the Zero camp. One posting, likely contributed by a delighted United partisan, asked the Zero team, "Why do you refuse to tell everybody where those scab televisions were manufactured?"[11] Postilion had no idea where the sets were built and explained that they were purchased through an AFL-CIO Web site called workingfamilies.com. He was unapologetic for the prize and thought that the United folks were ridiculous for criticizing a union-approved buying service. But in the world of union elections, Postilion knew that every slight appearance of insufficient commitment to true unionism was a potential insult to the rank-and-file voter. Although he shrugged off the "scab" television comments, he never rhetorically let go of the T-shirts made in El Salvador.

The television flap aside, the Zero picnic was a big success. Postilion walked home that day with a pouch strapped around his waist containing $15,000. Contributions nearly doubled the campaign's treasury and ensured that campaign publicist and *705 Update* editor Paul Waterhouse would have the means to put out two mailers right before the ballots were mailed to members' homes. Each of the mailings would stress the slate's union credentials and past accomplishments. They would cost about $10,000 each, and given the good working relationship the campaign had with the printer, Waterhouse did not want to put the order in unless he had "the money up front."[12]

The other slates were facing similar money needs for similar reasons. Along with numerous flyers and campaign items, the McCormick True Reform Slate and the United Slate produced at least one mass mailing each. Husar's Membership Party never raised enough funds to mail a campaign brochure. Nor did Phillips's campaign, but, like the Zero camp, the Phillips candidates did construct a Web site to promote their candidacy. The site featured pictures, biographies, and personal statements of each slate member, as well as the "Unity Pledge" that served as an issue platform.[13] Although Phillips's crew was the least well funded, it did have the distinction of holding the campaign's only live Internet interactive forum.

Zero's slate never held an on-line rally; nonetheless, its use of electronic campaigning was unprecedented in the history of Local 705 politics. Designed and maintained by Kankakee representative Jeff Dexter, the jerryzeroslate.org site featured six options including an E-mail address to contact the candidate. As of September 10, the site's 1,341 visitors had clicked onto pages informing them of the slate's platform, upcoming campaign events, and facts about the Zero record. Interested union voters could also download a series of leaflets pounding the opposition candidates on their respective records. At least a dozen of those negative leaflets targeted the McCormick slate, none more so than the infamous *Wanted Poster*. This piece displayed a picture of McCormick, Jackson, and Benesch and provided various examples of "trading members rights for personal gain." A wood shaved border, designed to look like an old western outlaw poster, framed the photos and narrative.

Not only did these negative leaflets harshly criticize the opposition, but the Zero camp also got enormous mileage from them. Visitors were invited to print out each political advertisement and reproduce it at their work sites. Considering that the campaign staff was blanketing work sites with the same information that was found on the Web site, it amounted to a blizzard of voter contacts. The site also featured a clever function that reminded the viewer of the campaign's reform qualities. When a person entered the site's home page, titled *Ground Zero*, the entire screen shook for a few seconds, and the words "Gerry Zero—Shaking Up the Labor Movement" appeared. If people were suitably impressed or at least entertained by what they read, they could then download a form enabling them to volunteer either time or money to support the Zero campaign. There is no proof of how any of the various Web sites influenced the election, but the information electronically communicated served notice that this election was the first to tap into the democratic potential of electronic campaigning.

Old-Fashioned Campaigning at the Barns

If the Web sites suggested a new format for reaching the voters, they did not signal a repudiation of the old face-to-face paper exchange. To a great extent, the entire campaign can be read through a successive distribution of written literature. Local union contests are in many ways throwbacks to the eighteenth-century American political tradition of street parades and outrageous pamphleteering. Anyone with access to a printer or a copier could speak repeatedly to each member of the union. Candidates could introduce themselves without being censored, and issues could be addressed as thoroughly as was desired. And with each new day, an announcement hot off the press would reinvigorate the campaign and remind voters that an election was about to happen. At Local 705 political speech not only came in different languages; it also came in various colors, sizes, and parchment types. In reality the campaign flyer was a powerful democratizing agent; it actually made being a candidate for union office possible.

Once again Archie Cook struck first. At the heavily attended May membership meeting, the United Slate handed out a double-sided flyer mocking the lack of "responsible leadership" at Local 705. In what would become the slate's primary message, the flyer pointed out that Zero and McCormick had jointly mismanaged the local and that neither officer was mature enough to claim responsibility for the union's past performance. The effect of seven years of irresponsible leadership was a divided union with "more factions among the members than ever before." After premiering on the sidewalk outside of Teamster Hall, the flyer quickly spread through roughly half of the UPS facilities. It was followed by a one-sided sheet that alerted the reader to "some of the things we [United 2000] stand for." This modest, nondescript white piece of paper had the distinction of being the first issue platform published in the campaign.

Additional flyers issued by the United Slate made it clear that its strategy was to tie Zero and McCormick together. With both officers throwing accusations at each other, the United camp believed that the two groups would be mortally wounded. But just in case the ex-RPM disputants failed to strike each other a fatal blow, United issued two additional negative flyers. Both also bundled Zero-McCormick into one unfit officer and reflected on important campaign themes. "This Union Belongs to You!" shouted one announcement. The other was no less alarmist in stating, "Your Union Representative Is Your Business." Both broadsides sent the message that Zero and McCormick had willfully ripped the union away from the membership.

United candidate Michael Deane would return over and over again to this idea that the local had lost its autonomy. Deane alleged that TDU extremists and Carey supporters had swallowed up Local 705. One inflammatory handbill charged that "When Zero & McCormick Took Over . . . They Turned Local 705 into a Dumping Ground for Friends" of ex-IBT president Ron Carey. Deane's brief was that, beginning with the trusteeship, Zero had hired "outsiders" to run the local. In fact, Zero had brought on board a cadre of talented, experienced, hardworking, and dedicated unionists. They also happened to be either TDU members or Carey supporters. But these union employees were not Local 705 members. To Deane, these intruders were unwelcome because they had been hand-picked from other Teamster locals around the country. Worse yet, some of the hires had never even been in the Brotherhood.

In addition to electronic and paper handbilling, the campaigns directed their people to hit the streets and talk up their candidates. Candidates, too, had to be seen, and they needed to be where the workers were. In the case of freight drivers, that usually meant rolling out of bed at 3:30 in the morning to get to an initial work site by 4:30. Campaigning would then continue until the overnight shift climbed into their cabs. By the end of the day, candidates and their supporters would have "hit" three or four freight barns and, in the case of the Membership Slate, passed out more than five thousand pieces of literature. For Membership chief Mike Husar, this was no walk in the park. A battered knee caused by a three-night-a-week softball schedule had made moving around difficult. Bad knee or not, the freight vote, according to Husar, was the key to winning the election. "In 1997 freight drivers stayed home, because they hated Zero and Passo."[14] Husar believed that with Zero and McCormick now fighting each other, the non-freight vote would be divided. Freight, however, would vote as a bloc. Husar aimed to win that bloc, and he knew that vote-getting in the trucking business meant politicking in the dark.

Zero and Deane were there also. Campbell went to CACH. He and other Zero supporters had a standing Tuesday and Thursday early-morning and late-night date with the eight thousand union members who were herded in and out of the megacomplex. During campaign sessions at the Racine Café, Campbell had worked out an elaborate military–like strategy for capturing the local's largest vote pool. He sketched out a daily plan of campaign visits on two large easel-size sheets of paper, taped together to hold all of the information. Campbell's targeting of CACH was predicated on his belief that the 1997 election was nearly lost because Zero had underestimated the voting potential of the facility's part-time members. CACH, not freight, according to Campbell, held the key to victory.

From the middle of May until two weeks after the ballots were mailed out on November 9, the five campaigns kept pounding the pavement. Just as Zero and McCormick had continued to wage an offensive against each other, they both managed to mail colorful multiple-page glossy brochures to the membership. McCormick's message, emblazoned in green and gold, reminded members that his was the True Reform Slate. Zero answered with an eight-panel, red and gold mailing hailing his "Continued Reform Team." United put together its own red and white glossy, eight-by-eleven-inch mailing. In bold red lettering it emphasized a list of campaign promises under the heading "WE BELIEVE . . ." Although Husar never conducted a mass mailing, he did have an ample supply of flyers, as well as a solid contingent of forty campaigners working around the clock for his election.

The campaign would at times bring out the best and the worst of union members. With equal parts creative, fundamental, electronic, face-to-face, informative, hard-hitting, negative, and positive, the campaigning was done in full-throttle Chicago style. It was also familiar to any union member anywhere in the country who had ever been politicked by civic candidates, with one important difference from a large municipal, state, or national election: Local 705's candidates or their closest surrogates would personally communicate with every likely voter. This was genuine retail politics, a politics not controlled by big dollars or catchy sound bites or neat public-relations packaging. A union voter could actually get close to the candidates bidding for his or her allegiance. Nothing so radical, so democratic could ever have been imagined for the working citizens of Local 705.

Candidates and voters alike had good reason to expect that the 2000 local officers' race would be another big step for democratic unionism. Since the 1991 international referendum vote, the share of Local 705 ballots for reform candidates had steadily increased. In 1991 only 31 percent of Local 705 members cast a vote for upstart Ron Carey, but in the disputed 1996 race, reform ballots dramatically increased to a majority 53.6 percent. Perhaps the most critical sign of how the tenor of political debate had been invigorated was the local's turnout in the 1996 and 1998 national Teamster elections.

Carey's narrow and overturned 1996 win was bolstered by majority support from more than seven thousand voting Local 705 members. The turnout at 705 was the largest of any single unit. But with Carey's disbarment from the subsequent rerunning of the election, local reformers were asked to now put their democratic faith in the dedicated but decidedly unknown Tom Leedham. Local reformers had rallied considerable energy around Ron Carey, and for many rank-and-filers a cult of personality had developed around his exploits. Now merely five short years after the 1991 vote, Chicago Teamsters were being asked to forget Carey and throw their trust toward a nearly phantomlike figure. Local 705 reformers faced a daunting task.

Despite Carey's popular image with local activists, an internal union poll revealed that over half of the membership could not even name the international president.[15] No poll was taken on Hoffa's name recognition, but there was little doubt that union members would more easily identify him than the Western Region vice president Tom Leedham. How would reformers quickly raise Leedham's profile in old guard Chicago when, after five years of governance, a majority of union members did not even know the name of their international leader? With Carey forced to the political sidelines, mobilizing votes against the high-profile Hoffa shortly after the heroic champion of Teamster reform had fallen from grace would require considerable grassroots organizing and a strong commitment from members to the cause of democratic unionism. As it turns out, both requirements were met.

In the 1998 Teamster presidential rerun, challenger Tom Leedham's source of support among midwestern drivers and UPS employees was centered within Local 705. Leedham had raised money at numerous 705 events and had slept on the couch of the local's "Rank & File" campaign director, Richard DeVries. The local was also prominently represented on the slate, with John McCormick running for the office of secretary-treasurer. Since Carey's 1991 victory, Local 705 had always had a local representative serving as a Central Region vice president on the international executive board, but if elected, McCormick would hold the prestigious number-two post in the union.

Although most experts considered Hoffa's candidacy to be an unstoppable juggernaut, keeping a strong proreform force alive in Chicago was absolutely critical if the Leedham candidacy were to stand any chance of upsetting the much better known and financed favorite. Reformers also believed that maintaining a very large outpost of anti-Hoffa Teamsters in Chicago was essential to preserving a democratic movement within the union. When the rerun election results were finally certified, Hoffa had won a clear victory around the country, and except for Local 705, where a majority of votes went for the underdog reformer, a sweep of locals in Chicago. More impressively, an examination of vote totals revealed that despite the crisis caused by the Carey electoral scandal, for the second consecutive national election, Local 705 cast more ballots ($N = 6,897$) than any other local.[16]

Now, two years after the 1998 international rerun election, the rank and file were again embroiled, for the third time, in a local political campaign. In choosing a slate of officers, the membership would have to reconsider the torments of the past before determining which slate had the legitimate claim on a democratic future.

CHAPTER EIGHT

Campaign Platforms and Rank-and-File Votes

Local 705 elections had never been the subject of any conscious planning. Before the trusteeship the local barons simply handpicked a successor. There was never a need to develop a political strategy, because intimidation of the rank and file worked perfectly well. Campaigning under Peick and Ligurotis was mostly a test of brawn and fealty to favored benefactors. Democracy changed all that. Of course, there remained a fair amount of huckstering and mudslinging, but these were no longer sufficient to win elections.

Since 1995 competing slates of officers had organized campaign staffs, raised money, and, most importantly, plotted how to win. It was an indirect benefit of democratic reform that political parties formed at Local 705 and learned how to aggregate voter interests, shape a political message, and construct political coalitions. In the 2000 campaign, each slate embodied a platform of ideas about how to protect the union's future and constructed divergent strategies for winning rank-and-file votes. For Zero and McCormick, getting to the future would mean struggling over and appropriating the past.

The Pledge

Eugene Phillips was the lowest of underdogs in the fall race. But one of the things his Teamsters for Unity did was to put up a Web site where voters could download the "Unity Pledge." The Pledge consisted of nine items. A brief statement explaining the party's position followed each item. Under "Strong Leadership" was a pledge to do what no other slate had promised: "We will do site visits with more than a BA. Our entire executive board will visit your work site."[1] Every party referred to the issue of leadership, but none had offered to take executive-board field trips. It was, however, a sign of what the parties believed mattered most to voters. Campaigning became a bidding war for stronger and stronger acts of leadership.

McCormick accentuated his leadership skills by stressing, "Within the next 3 years every major union contract, including UPS is set to expire." The union president pointed out that the local was "facing a critical time in history" and that he was the one best situated to "fight for new contracts that protect the benefits and the dignity of our members."[2] Husar had his own leadership appeal. The Membership Party accused Zero and Mc-Cormick of never accepting responsibility for any of their actions. "They blame anyone but themselves" and foment "divisions amongst us." The critical question every member had to ask was "Can we live with three more years of inept leadership from Zero and McCormick?" If the answer was no, then it was time "for positive change."[3]

The Zero Breakfast Club agreed that leadership was important and provided a constant drumbeat of messages touting their guy's credentials. The Continued Reformers had more than promises to offer: they had a record. They pointed out, in numerous pieces of literature, that strong union leaders like Zero "rolled up" their "sleeves and fix[ed] the mess." Most importantly, "Zero's actions brought results." Reflecting the campaign's focus on McCormick, they never failed to note that "McCormick talks a good game, but his actions tell the *real* story." In a flyer featuring a graphic of a fist with thumb turned downward, the Zero camp simply posed the question "John McCormick's Leadership?"[4]

Mike Deane also embraced the mantle of leadership. Members were told that a "strong union leadership represents all the members." Unlike what Zero and McCormick had exhibited, the United 2000 Slate would "stand for" and bring "responsible leadership" to the local. Deane and company went on to urge the members "to decide who will lead [them] into the first decade of the 21st Century." A group of Local 705 members from the UPS Jefferson Street facility offered some assistance to voters struggling to answer that question. They distributed a flyer that included, along with a picture of the United leaders, the title "Deane: Portrait of a Company Man." The implication was that a good union member would never be well served by following someone who was "UPS approved."[5] In the posttrusteeship world of Teamster politics, bidding for leadership was now possible. That was the good news. The bad news was that it was no less a contact sport than before. For every claim there was a counterclaim. It was up to the members to sort it out.

Beyond the leadership qualities of the candidates, there was also the volatile issue of determining who was a legitimate Local 705 member. Since the trusteeship the union had made many personnel changes, and a number of high-profile people had been hired into the local. This issue was not about the union's bread-and-butter performance. This was about protecting borders, promoting your own, and being part of the clan.

The United Slate addressed this issue directly by distributing a flyer with the heading *This Union Belongs to You!* It made two provocative if unproven claims: first, that the local had once negotiated "its own contracts for its own members" but that now, under Zero and McCormick, it had given up that right; and second, that Local 705 had been turned "into a dumping ground for friends of the general president [i.e., Ron Carey] who lost elections in their own locals." Deane, the United candidate, charged that this blatant assault on the local's famed autonomy could never have happened before the trusteeship. "Louis Peick would have told them [i.e., the international union] to take a hike."[6] Thus, instead of preserving the local's character and identity, Zero was bartering it away at the behest of external powers. According to Deane, the real "company man" was Zero.

"Nobody Dies and Forget Your Kids"

Postilion seemed edgier than normal. During most of the Breakfast Club meetings, he spoke in tense, demanding tones. He confided that he never wanted the staff to believe that they had enough votes. "I start from the point that we need another 200 votes to win." With a week to go before ballots were mailed out, he delivered his final trenchant marching orders. "Nobody dies and forget your kids, your wife, your dog and going to sleep." Staff members were expected to use up all their vacation time to squeeze out every available vote. "Look folks," he intoned, "if we lose there will be plenty of time to sleep and lay around the house." This election was "a game of small numbers," and Postilion warned that there were votes still to be earned.[7]

Campbell helped him get an idea of where those votes were by estimating the likely turnout and pro-Zero vote for every barn in the UPS system. The local's newspaper editor, Paul Waterhouse, appreciated the projection but thought it inadequate. As a veteran of Chicago city politics, he knew the value of personal commitments. Waterhouse insisted that each staff member identify which members were solid for Zero. He was often frustrated by the ambiguous responses he heard. With each unsatisfying answer to his plea "Anyone got a hard count?" his question grew distinctly more vulgar, "Anyone got a fucking hard count?" Waterhouse wanted to know who, in less-than-pure Chicago fashion, would definitely "vote for us, unless they were dead."[8] Throughout the campaign, Breakfast Club foot soldiers assured the *705 Update* editor that they had the hard count. But Waterhouse never saw a list.

A decision was made early in the spring to build a campaign around two dominant messages. First, Zero's team would emphasize Zero's record of accomplishments. Particular attention would be given to pension gains, health and welfare improvements, contract advancements, and successful organizing drives. Stressing good deeds alone, though, would not win the numbers game. A low road would also be devised and implemented with unrelenting precision. Although the campaign viewed McCormick as their most serious threat and, consequently, heavily targeted his candidacy, none of the opposition escaped a trip behind the political woodshed.

Zero's people pounded the McCormick, Deane, and Husar camps for their lack of skills, leadership credentials, and trustworthiness and for their recent conversion to democratic unionism. The idea, according to Campbell, would be "to drive their vote down." The plan was to mobilize Zero's "hard count" and to deter the undecided from even voting. Breakfast Club discussions bristled with talk of "core groups," "our people," "McCormick's faithful," "drivers for Deane," "tight group of freight for Husar," and "our enemies." Loyalists and antagonists were further identified by location, division, and job status. Postilion never failed to remind people of the need to combine different groups of likely pro-Zero supporters. This was sophisticated coalition politics, and the rule was simple: if you can't get a vote, then keep it away from your opponent.

Oddly, part of that electoral strategy included how the campaign would handle the issues surrounding a second local election that would occur after the officer contest. In the summer of 2001, every Teamster local would send elected delegates to the international union's convention. The IBT convention was held every five years, and one of the most important responsibilities of a convention delegate was to cast a vote for a candidate, nominated to run later in the fall for the union's general presidency. The 2001 race was expected to rematch incumbent James P. Hoffa with 1998 challenger and TDU favorite Tom Leedham. To qualify for the ballot, a nominated candidate had to receive at least 5 percent of the votes cast by the convention delegates. In addition, before a presidential candidate could be nominated, the candidate had to obtain the signatures of at least 5 percent of the membership.[9] In the period before the local officer election, getting signatures at Local 705 would prove to be a delicate matter.

Like so much else that the fractious Local 705 executive board touched, the timing of the delegate election became a hotly contested item. Zero had proposed that the two elections occur simultaneously, thereby saving the local about $70,000 in administrative cost. For reasons never fully explained, McCormick's executive board overruled the secretary-treasurer and voted to separate the elections. At a combined cost of $158,460, the officer election would occur in the fall and the delegate race in March of 2001.[10] In this case the McCormick-led board opposition may have been a fortuitous break for Zero.

Zero was well aware that Hoffa had supporters within the membership and the staff. He also knew that some of his most capable employees and campaigners were fiercely opposed to Hoffa and unconditionally committed to Leedham. What both groups had in common was that they represented potential Local 705 officer votes for the Continued Reform Slate. This political mixture made it clear to Zero that he had to walk a fine line: he must avoid alienating rank-and-file supporters of either presidential candidate, while at the same time appearing not to be endorsing or rejecting anyone. The issue of the general election and collecting signatures for Hoffa and Leedham took center stage in the following exchange between Breakfast Club members:

Mark Postilion: We're in our election. If the only support we got were from Leedham backers we'd lose the election. Look at Freight—a lot of solid Hoffa people. We really ought to focus on our election.

Joe Allen: Reform and Hoffa slates are fractured. But hard line Hoffa people believe their time has come.

Paul Waterhouse: It's a matter of common sense. Be careful not to turn this election into UPS against freight. It must be between Zero and McCormick. Don't be so obvious with Leedham or Hoffa petitions.

Rick Rohe: It's a little confusing for the average guy. I mean McCormick and Leedham are linked. So what happens if we endorse Leedham?

Otis Cross: I don't understand mixing the elections. The members are voting for reform in this local. Period.

Tom Nightwine: We need to keep reform going, however, we can't do it from the outside. I would rather not hear "Hoffa-Leedham" until after our election.[11]

Zero's task became much easier when McCormick split the elections. If the elections had been held simultaneously, as Zero wanted, his campaign's ability to steer between the rocky shores of both presidential candidates would have been compromised. Zero, of course, was also still under the threat of a union suspension, and Hoffa had yet to issue a verdict. In private, most campaign workers thought that Zero would have endorsed Leedham if not for the fear that it would have generated a punitive Hoffa ruling on the McCormick-filed charges. For his part, Zero expressed some reservations about Leedham's candidacy and noted that he was "no Ron Carey."[12]

In any event, the McCormick board rendered the touchy item moot. Now the local officer's election would be only about local leadership and not whether a member was a Hoffa or a Leedham supporter. When asked why he proposed something that would have likely made his candidacy more difficult, Zero stated, "To be honest I didn't think I was smart enough to know what would be best for us. I just knew we would win and I wanted the elections combined simply to save the money."[13]

Fighting the Last Fight

Andrew Speck understood Zero's "good cop–bad cop" approach to winning votes but thought it was a loser. Speck, a University of Chicago graduate, had worked for the prestigious Chicago-based Democratic Party consulting firm Strategy Group and was now a consultant with Advocacy Media. Since 1991 he had provided political assistance on numerous Illinois state campaign races, as well as in Chicago ward contests. In the spring of 1999, McCormick hired Speck to direct his party's public relations. It was Speck's first foray into union politics, and he was not only genuinely impressed with his candidate's political skills but also struck by the sharp contrast between McCormick's and Zero's campaign approaches.

Speck saw Zero's negative campaigning as old-school, top-down Teamster electioneering. Bashing McCormick was "just a lot of white noise." More importantly, he predicted that, given "all the negative history these guys [the membership] have had with their union under Ligurotis," the Zero strategy would backfire and turn voters away from him. Speck also reflected on the campaign's positive message. "Zero's material," he noted, "screams 'I'm the boss.'" The campaign literature "was all about him [Zero]," and this one-dimensional framing of the local's success was a throwback to the days when business agents anointed the union's chief operating officer and "manhandled the voters."[14]

Speck also claimed that Zero's campaign strategy was "dishonest" because of the way it defined the candidate as a union leader. Although there was much to brag about in the area of labor relations, the secretary-treasurer had another proud record that he was curiously ignoring in his appeals to rank-and-filers. Zero was well known to progressive forces around the city. Along with a small number of other local union leaders, Zero articulated a social democratic vision of unionism and politics. For instance, he endorsed third-party politics and served as the president of the Chicago-Metro Chapter of the Labor Party. Speck's contention that Zero's unionism was tied to his political philosophy was supported by the Teamster chief's use of his 705 newsletter column to promote the Labor Party. In one issue, the *Update* informed members that the "the legislative Update page will highlight some of the political changes the Labor Party will be fighting for in the coming months."[15] The paper went so far as to include a membership form that Local 705 people could clip out and send in to join the party. Zero's support for working-class politics was even noted by the *Wall Street Journal,* which wrote that he was the kind of union leader who was likely to forge "alliances with left-leaning religious and social groups."[16]

The local was also well known for providing aid and support to community groups, religious organizations, and local politicians addressing poverty, housing, and economic justice. The organizations the local has actively supported since the 1995 election include, among others, the ecumenical union-based Chicago Jobs with Justice, of which Zero was one of three founding members, the housing and poverty organization ACORN, the Jobs for a Living Wage Campaign, Operation Rainbow PUSH, Comite Latino, the Peotone Airport Alliance, and the Interfaith Committee for Worker Justice.[17] At the forefront of all these and many other efforts was Zero, a labor leader who intended to have a larger citywide political impact.

Why, then, Speck mused, did Zero not tout his political and social activism? Instead of pointing out the leader's commitment to social justice and economic equality, his campaign material was all union "bread and butter," with not even a hint of social activism. Speck was not critical of Zero's political work, but he did feel that the secretary-treasurer's record was deceptive. McCormick, not Zero, according to Speck, was the union's day-to-day administrator. Zero was just the public face of a once-corrupt, now-democratic union. They were a great team, a kind of inside and outside dynamic duo. Speck believed that everyone knew that McCormick was the guy who was responsible for the local's bargaining accomplishments. Yet there was Zero, in all his literature, projecting himself as a leader that delivered the goods.

Speck argued that Zero's repackaging of his identity would not work, because local union elections were, in the last resort, built on personal relationships. Money would not substitute for handshaking at plant gates and trips to the local bar. Speck noted that Local 705 members were exceptionally well informed about the issues and the candidates. Instead of Zero's divide-and-conquer approach, McCormick would run a positive "just the facts" campaign. He would stress the future while Zero reminded everyone of the past. McCormick would ask voters to consider which man was best able to lead the local while Zero was busy "surrounding himself with people who could him keep in power." In the end, Zero was campaigning like the Teamster demigods of old, and in that sense he was "fighting the last fight."[18]

Ironically, that did not keep the True Reformers from trying to appropriate the past for their own benefit. It was McCormick, not Zero, who filed internal charges and lawsuits to void the electoral process. Attempting to remove Zero from the race before a single vote had been declared was hardly a case of positive campaigning. The McCormick-inspired intrigue was undoubtedly designed to remind voters of the strong-arm, unlawful practices of past administrations. McCormick publicly stated that he took action against Zero because the union chief was acting like one of the bad boys they had once fought together to depose. It was McCormick's allies who at a spring stewards' meeting passed out copious copies of a flyer titled *Just the Facts,* summarizing Judge Shadur's findings. Printed in bold black letters against a Teamster gold background was Shadur's claim that "Reformers such as Zero give the label reform a bad name." The True Reformers appeared to have veered off the high road, and their driving was about to become dangerously reckless.

Early-morning listeners to Chicago radio station WBBM-AM were aroused from their slumber on 16 October by the following bombshell: "Zero embezzled $150,000 from the members." The voice crackling through the fall morning air belonged to none other than John McCormick. He alleged that Zero had misused more than $500,000 in union dues by borrowing against a line of credit without the executive board's approval. By noon of that day, about a dozen loyal McCormick supporters had organized in front of the union's auditorium. They carried pickets that urged "Zero!! Put The Cash Back" and charged, "Zero leaves 705 empty." One of Chicago's daily papers, the *Sun-Times,* was alerted to the demonstration and the next day ran a story under the headline "Union Members Claim Official Misused Dues."[19] It was news coverage fit for a stereotypical thuggish union. And it came directly from Speck's desk.

One reason the scandalous scoop occurred may be because McCormick appeared to have a political identity problem. He had been linked with Zero for nearly seven years, and in the eyes of many members, the two were jointly running the local. After the two-term partnership, Zero had taken on the difficult tasks of peeling off his sidekick and claiming ownership of the local's good deeds. McCormick also wanted credit for the union's recent history, but as the local's second in command, he had to find a way to legitimately claim it. What McCormick needed was a way to create the appearance of a fair, legitimate comparison with Zero. The loan scandal was the True Reformers' chance to simultaneously club their opponent and promote their candidate.

McCormick pointed out that before Zero's return the local had accumulated a $200,000 surplus but that now the local was "more than $300,000 in debt." The True Reformers were playing rather loose with the facts. The local was in debt, but there was nothing inappropriate about Zero's accessing the line of credit; the state of the local's finances was badly mischaracterized by the local president. First consider the issue of the loan. Amalgamated Bank of Chicago had first granted the line to the local in 1997 after the dramatic summer strike against UPS.[20] By contractual agreement the company had the obligation to deduct union dues directly from each worker's paycheck and then promptly, by the end of each month, transfer the funds to the union treasury. But since the strike concluded, UPS had often failed to transmit the funds on time, generating a temporary deficit on the local's monthly balance statement. As the local's largest employer, UPS's monthly withholding of the money drained the union's treasury of nearly $400,000. The loan was first taken out and later renewed in the summer of 2000 with executive board approval to provide a temporary means of meeting payroll.

The *Sun-Times* story also quoted McCormick claiming that Zero "took $500,000 in dues money and threw it down the drain with fat salaries for his friends and political allies." The charge made the secretary-treasurer appear to have converted a healthy surplus into a burdensome deficit for crass political ends. To be sure, the local president had left the union with a cash surplus when he stepped down from his one-year assumption of power. The surplus, however, was less than half of what McCormick claimed and about one-third as large as he found it when he stepped in for Zero.[21] A closer examination of the local's 1999 and 2000 trustee reports also reveals that the union's monthly cash balances moved up and down in strikingly similar fashion. In addition, just sixty days prior to the time McCormick loyalists picketed outside the union auditorium, the local had a positive cash balance of nearly $300,000.

Nevertheless, the local was spending money faster than it was collecting dues. In only two of the nine months since Zero's return did the local not experience a decrease in its cash balance. Zero defended his more aggressive use of dues money by accusing his board opponents of wanting "to run this union like a corporation for the good of the stockholders."[22] In contrast, Zero appealed to the membership to support an increased investment in such things as organizing and education. Although the local's spending in these areas was up, the increase explained only a small portion of the spending differential. The biggest item in the local's shopping cart was salaries. McCormick was correct that Zero had increased the local's workforce. But then, so had Judge Shadur.

When Zero resumed the leadership of the local in February 2000, he moved to widen the union's presence at UPS's CACH facility. Dan Campbell took the lead in restructuring the way the local would represent its members at the facility and recommended that the union create a part-time business agent post. After completing a four-hour work shift, a part-time worker would then go to work for the local, representing members for another four hours. The local would pay roughly $20,000 in annual salary for each part-time agent. All health and welfare benefits would continue to be paid out of the joint union-employer fund. Zero liked the idea of a low-cost way to increase the union's presence among part-time workers and agreed to hire ten people. Salaries, consequently, did go up by $200,000.

Now recall that Judge Shadur had ordered the four fired agents reinstated to their positions with full restitution of pay and benefits. While waiting for Shadur's court judgment, Zero had hired people to fill the four vacancies and refused now to cut them loose. When the local fully complied with the order, the monthly payroll shot up 65 percent. The four rehired agents would cost the local nearly $500,000 in additional annual compensation costs. Zero was now forced to carry four staff members that the local had not budgeted for, and worse yet, according to the union head, "they weren't working."[23]

Along with the part-time agents, Zero also began to appoint new full-time and part-time "alternate" stewards at UPS. The idea at UPS, according to Campbell, was to match each part-time supervisor with a Teamster alternate steward, as part of a Members Power Program. The program also divided the UPS system into three distinct branches based on the operations performed. The biggest operation was the "hub" system at the giant CACH facility. With thousands of part-timers working at a feverish pitch, CACH was not only the heart of UPS's national delivery business; it was also the belly of the beast. Worker complaints came as fast and furious as the packages. The work site desperately cried out for an expansion of union representation and was tailor-made for a specialized, concentrated approach to handling workers' problems.

Members Power proved to be a controversial issue that further split the executive board. In reorganizing how the local provided services within the UPS system, Zero had effectively stripped the four UPS agents of their jurisdiction. With the creation of separate hub, feeder-car, and package-car divisions and the assigning to each their own union representative, the four fired agents lost their territory. Under the old system, the union's representatives operated from a narrower assigned area of coverage. Power was spatially determined, and representatives functioned with a good deal of autonomy. Each representative also had his or her party machine of loyal lieutenants (i.e., stewards) to manage the affairs of the institution. Each representative handled one or more entire facility, and all of the stewards within those designated areas reported to the union staffer.

The new structure brought work of similar character under one umbrella organization. Now hub, feeder, and parcel delivery operations would be managed as separate centers with their own extended hierarchical structure of stewards and representatives reporting to a principal officer. In addition, each division would establish a stewards' council to coordinate policies and practices. By reorganizing the UPS system in this manner, the union intended to respond to members according to their job classifications. It would also attack a thornier problem that the delivery firm had fostered. UPS had mastered the art of whipsawing the local from one facility to the next, creating an often-unintelligible corporate labor relation standard. It had consequently become increasingly difficult for the local to keep its "eyes on the ball," given the autonomous site-based approach to labor relations. To address the problem of identifying systemwide problems, the union decided to focus its representational function around the actual work performed. Member response to the reorganization was better than expected. Within two weeks of initiating the program at CACH, more than one hundred members volunteered to be "Hub Stewards."[24] On the surface it looked like a winning move, although not everyone felt like a winner.

No union official lost more in the restructuring than McCormick. For seven years he had been director of the mammoth UPS division. With the fortunes of eleven thousand members dependent on his leadership, the one-time feeder driver directed the local's largest constituency. It was an enormous responsibility that also offered an equally large political opportunity. McCormick selected stewards and representatives throughout the UPS system. Each one of those people would be expected to solicit votes, come election time. But with the reorganization, there was no longer a UPS division.

Zero's firings and new appointments generated a bevy of critical comments in the union's discussion forum, teamster.net, expressing the suspicion that the local leader was "desperately trying anything to keep his cushy job."[25] The issue was polarizing, and with five slates contesting for political power, there were multiple vantage points for exploiting the turnover that had occurred within the local's staff and system of stewards.

Although the record of steward appointments at UPS revealed that Zero had kept his pen warm, the net nominal impact on the union's representational function was hardly extravagant.[26] From early April until late August, he issued appointment letters to 131 new UPS stewards and removed or replaced 67 stewards, thereby increasing the number by 64. In half a year, then, he added approximately 10.6 stewards per month to help service a part-time workforce that had grown from 6,000 to 8,000 union members. In addition, out of the 131 hires, 73 percent ($N = 95$) were alternates assigned to assist part-timers. Zero's use of his executive powers to widen the local's reach with part-time workers was ambitious but not unreasonable for a union looking for ways to strengthen its hand against an employer incrementally increasing its employment of part-time labor. Furthermore, increasing the steward base was not limited to UPS. Zero incrementally added representation in other crafts wherever it appeared to be needed. Considering the secretary-treasurer's authority and need to construct a "first line of defense against employer misdeeds," the appointments and removals at UPS and other crafts did not seem to be without merit.[27]

Nor did they appear, as McCormick charged, obviously political. Of the 67 replaced stewards, the secretary-treasurer had forcibly removed only 16. Most had resigned for personal reasons, retired, changed employers, suffered an injury, or taken a supervisory position with the company. Nonetheless, there were suspicious removals. The case of John Boettinger looked like a political lynching. A mild-mannered, intellectual guy, Boettinger was an atypical part-time worker. He held a college degree and worked as a chemist during the day before reporting for his evening shift at CACH. Boettinger had worked as a local steward since 1997. His work was good enough to bring him to the attention of Campbell, who tried unsuccessfully to recruit him for one of the part-time union representative slots. Boettinger refused, telling Campbell that he thought that the Members Program was a "political patronage network."[28]

Boettinger had once been a Zero supporter and had even campaigned for him in past elections. This time around the Teamster chemist decided to endorse the Membership Slate. He began to wear a Membership button and to show up at the CACH facility to hand out leaflets. On a number of occasions, he verbally jousted with Zero campaigners before crowds of workers rustling outside the CACH Number 2 entrance gate. Membership chief Mike Husar was sufficiently impressed with Boettinger's skills that he asked him to be the party's candidate for recording secretary. Boettinger agreed, then immediately got a bad feeling about his decision.

On 25 September, nearly one month after he was announced as a Membership slate candidate, Boettinger got an oddly worded letter from Zero. It read in part, "I understand you no longer support our Member Power program at UPS. Imagine my surprise that you would take such a position. I assume that you are resigning your position." Zero accepted Boettinger's "resignation" and reminded him that he was of course free to "oppose this or any other program."[29] Boettinger scoffed at the idea that his criticism of the UPS restructuring was tantamount to a resignation. He admitted to opposing the plan but challenged Zero to find any evidence that he had not been a conscientious and dedicated steward.[30] To his mind he was the same steward that had once been solicited for a promotion. All that had changed was that he was now opposing the reelection of Gerry Zero.

The firing of stewards like Boettinger suggests a mixed motive for Zero's actions. On one hand, stewards who oppose the administration have a platform to spread an anti-Zero gospel and to campaign for precious votes. On the other hand, a steward who voices resistance to the secretary-treasurer's policy and also campaigns to remove him from office is a poor ambassador for the local's work. Certainly McCormick remembered the hard-fought early days of the trusteeship when Ligurotis bodies were figuratively being tossed to the pavement. Nothing Zero was now doing approached that level of housecleaning, and it was undeniable that additional representation among part-time workers at UPS was a priority for the local. Zero was, by all accounts, acting consistently with his union and political values. To preserve those values, it would sometimes be necessary to fire staff. No one died, lost paid employment, or was physically threatened or hit by a chair; no one had his or her vote rejected or was silenced at a union meeting. If this was a purge, surely it was one of the mildest in the embattled history of the Teamsters Union.

Campaign Issues

Contesting political voices echoed wherever Local 705 members congregated. Candidates and their campaign staff passed out flyers and preached the good word about their commitment to the rank and file. Sometimes plant gate campaigning turned into soapbox debating with two or more representatives of different parties jawing ferociously at each other. Most often it was an outstretched arm offering a piece of political literature and a request to "vote Gerry," "vote Deane," or "vote McCormick for the future." To the rank-and-file member, the constant political barking may have, at times, looked and sounded like a carnival. But behind this carnival atmosphere, there were three substantive and symbolic issues that served to group members around particular slates, old grievances, and new leadership approaches.

From Carolina to Arkansas

In any union political campaign, the issues that get addressed come from divergent sources. Not surprisingly, the nonincumbents draw attention to events, practices, policies, and outcomes that they believe best demonstrate the need for political change. Typically it is the challengers who push first and hardest to frame the issue debate. The issue agenda is also influenced by the coalitions that are formed to develop each party. Party advocates may agree on opposing other party candidates, but they do so for different reasons. United 2000 is a good example of this phenomenon working itself out in the Local 705 election. A close examination of two issues and two constituency groups will demonstrate how union parties can grow out of plural interests and how diverse voting blocs can be formed around single issues.

In 1995 Arkansas Best Corporation (ABC) entered into an agreement to merge its subsidiary, Arkansas Best Freight (ABF) with the freight delivery company WorldWay Corporation (formerly known and referred to here as Carolina Freight). ABF would acquire WorldWay through a cash purchase of all outstanding shares of Carolina stock; WorldWay informed the union that "without the WorldWay acquisition . . . Carolina Freight would not survive, and by purchasing the company, [WorldWay] would allow for more jobs to be saved than if they had gone out of business." In announcing the deal, Robert A. Young III, chief executive officer of ABF and chairman of the trucking association that negotiated the 1994 labor pact, stated that the acquisition would give his company "one of the premier LTL [less-than-truckload] motor carriers in the United States."[1] The motor carriers were also signatories to the union's 1994 National Master Freight Agreement (NMFA), and Local 705 had a "white paper" (i.e., independent of NMFA but inclusive of it) contract with ABF and Carolina, representing 96 and 81 workers, respectively.

As required by the NMFA, in any change of ownership or operations, the method for bringing two or more workforces together must be consistent with jointly negotiated procedures. The union's principal concern with mergers, acquisitions, and buyouts in the transportation industry was the application of job seniority. To cope with the problem, the 1994 NMFA gave rank-and-file members in each area the right to vote on Area Supplemental Agreements. This power of ratification was "intended to give members greater autonomy over working conditions in their own area."[2] But implementing the area supplements proved to be a logistic and legal nightmare for the international union. Things were not any easier in Chicago.

Drivers and dockhands at the older Carolina held considerably more seniority than their union peers employed by the rapidly expanding ABF, and they were very concerned about how the local was planning to protect their seniority rights.[3] Some Carolina drivers were well aware that in IBT locals around the country, disputes had arisen over whether the workforces of the two companies would be "dovetailed" or "endtailed." Dovetailing involved a merging of seniority lists, which would have strictly honored years of service. In other words, the more senior worker would be placed higher on the seniority list regardless of which company she or he had previously worked for. Endtailing would mean that all of the workers from Carolina would be placed at the bottom of ABF's seniority list, regardless of their years of service. The latter option was a bad choice for older Carolina drivers, because if the reconstituted company had to lay off workers, the first to go would be from Carolina.

Dealing with mergers is always a maddening process for unions. In most cases some jobs are lost, and no matter how the union manages the affair, it will be accused by some members of selling somebody out. Ron Carey, the Teamster president during the merger, adopted the position that seniority lists should be dovetailed, even where area supplements called for endtailing, because otherwise they "don't meet the needs of members." His respect for the time-honored union principal got him involved in at least five lawsuits from members who believed that ratified area supplements calling for endtailing trumped ideals. Local 705 Carolina drivers, however, expected that because a "Carey guy" (i.e., Zero) governed the local union, they would end up with a dovetailing agreement.[4] They were wrong.

The disposition of the companies' combination and seniority application was determined at a Chicago area change-of-operations meeting. At that meeting, Local 705 contract administrator Tom Nightwine and a company representative had the following exchange:

> Mr. Nightwine: For the record, we need a couple of clarifications. It may be semantics but it's important because of our language at 705. First of all, are we correct in assuming that ABF's acquisition of Red Arrow [purchased along with Carolina] is considered a buyout?
> Mr. Little: Yes, sir.[5]

In the more than three hundred pages of meeting transcripts, no lines had a greater impact on the lives of Carolina drivers. As Nightwine further explained, Local 705 was not a signatory to the NMFA and therefore had no area supplement. Although the local had negotiated a standard trucking agreement, it did not include any change-of-operations language. "In fact," Nightwine noted, "the company was not obligated to follow any process, other than what was in our [Local 705] contract."[6] The absence of such language at Local 705 highlights the importance of Nightwine's brief exchange with Mr. Little.

But before Nightwine asked his question, he telegraphed its implications with the following statement: "We would request that no issues of implemented changes or conditions, including the seniority application—we have a unique endtailing application in Chicago—we'd ask that none of these circumvent or be in contradiction to Local 705's TMI [Trucking Management Incorporated] negotiated agreement."[7] A "unique endtailing application" was bad news for Carolina drivers. "It wasn't fair [to Carolina drivers]," Nightwine acknowledged, "but the contract was clear."

Despite Nightwine's understanding, Carolina drivers were confused. To add to their agitation, they learned that the change-of-operations committee had ordered dovetailing in 167 of 170 union locals. Local 705 was one of only three exceptions. Shortly after the change-of-operations decision, Carolina drivers Mike Sweeney and Jim Askin sent letters to the executive board signed by twenty-five Carolina employees, requesting that their "years of service be considered when assembling a seniority list which is used to determine work assignments."[8] The matter remained largely unresolved until December 1997, when a federal court in Maryland ruled that ABC's purchase and subsequent consolidation of Carolina into ABF Freight Systems was a merger, not a buyout. Armed with the court interpretation, Sweeney and Askin led a renewed charge of Carolina employees back to Zero's office, but they left disappointed.

Sweeney and Askin then tried to sue the local. They presented more than twelve hundred pages of documents to their attorneys and raised more than $50,000 "to pursue our claim through litigation in Federal Court." But after a prolonged period of inactivity, the two drivers received a letter from their legal counsel recommending "that you not proceed in this matter." Along with the disappointing letter, the legal team returned to Sweeney and Askin the funds that they and their brother drivers had raised. More than half of the 81 drivers who could contribute made at least one $300 payment. Sweeney and Askin had written checks for $1,500.[9] In the end they could be proud of their doggedness, but the threat of job loss still hung over the Carolina drivers.

In response to their failed legal efforts, Sweeney and Askin became "political" and joined the United Party. Sweeney was running as an elected business agent and found a political motive for the local's decisions not to dovetail. "I believe Zero took the action that he did because Passo had been a Carolina driver." Again Passo was interjected into the local's political machinations. But if Zero was not worth supporting because he had acted out of a desire to hurt Passo, the Hoffa aide's actions were even more intolerable. Sweeney and Askin angrily recalled that in the spring of 1996, Passo had made a promise to the Carolina drivers that "When Jimmy [Hoffa] gets in we will help you." Jimmy got in, but all Carolina drivers got "was fucked."[10] This incident was but one of a number of events that undergirded the United Slate's formation and its members' belief in a conspiratorial Zero-Passo pact. Another matter would deal with a loss of pay and brought a smaller, but more vocal, anti-Zero group into the party's corner.

The Shot System

For nine years Midwest Terminal had productively provided services to the Burlington Northern–Santa Fe railroad. Midwest was hired by the rail freight company to load and unload tractor-trailers from its flatbeds coming in and out of Chicago's rail yards. Most of the work involved shifts of thirty crane operators moving the giant containers from the train beds to storage space in the rail yards. Midwest had always been a good union vendor and had developed a reputation for paying its roughly two hundred Local 705 members very well. During the busiest transportation periods, Midwest offered a special incentive to workers to speed up their production. Known as the "shot system," to describe how quickly operators would move about the yards, Midwest would pay workers a premium rate during regularly scheduled hours. It was a Cadillac piece-rate system, and from 1997 to 1999 it was not unusual for a worker to earn $100,000 annually.

But as Glenn Pomonis emphasized, the money was hard-earned. "Guys would zip up and down the yards, working their asses off."[11] Pomonis had been a steward for Local 705 since 1997 and had worked in the yards for eight years. He was proud of the human effort that went into moving containers around the rail property. Operators would run cranes nearly three stories high along a mile of railroad track. One particular yard had acquired near-legendary status. The Corwith Yard, at 43rd and Kenzie Avenue, was the star among the railroad's four facilities. During the 1990s it had an unheard-of 98 percent on-time job completion record. Times were prosperous under Midwest, and the local's rail members benefited. But the good times took a turn for the worse when the Midwest-Corwith contract expired in the spring of 2000. The railroad decided not to renew its vending agreement with the company and instead granted the work to a new company, Rail Terminal Services (RTS). Unlike one other bidding company, RTS was willing to recognize the union. They insisted, however, on one change.

RTS agreed to everything that was written in the previous Midwest labor pact, but it refused to honor the shot system. The local now had a touchy problem. If it opposed the RTS offer, the railroad would sign an agreement with the nonunion contractor, thereby putting 215 workers' jobs at risk. But entering into a successor agreement with RTS that did not include the generous incentive arrangement could cost individual workers as much as $25,000 a year in lost income. It was a big concession, and when union rail yard negotiator Otis Cross discussed it with the Corwith members, they became very hostile. Cross's position was made more untenable by the fact that the shot system was an informally honored side agreement. "The deal was solely between Midwest and the members," Cross stated.[12] Because it was an "in-house" agreement, the local was in no position to insist that a new employer honor the practice. Cross did attempt to negotiate a substitute codified incentive plan with RTS, but the Corwith operators voted down three proposals in forty-five days.

In the end the local ratified an agreement calling for a prosperous $2.00-an-hour increase in pay. The agreement also set up a mechanism for developing a productivity incentive plan for individual yards.[13] Cross believed that with the hourly increase in pay and the expected incentive deal, yard workers would maintain most of the income they had grown accustomed to. But a vocal group of Corwith members, occasionally sporting United T-shirts, felt differently. It seemed to them that Cross had given away an enormous benefit without even a struggle. Despite his insistence that "nothing in fact was taken away or lost," some rail yard workers believed Cross had sold them out.[14] Their suspicion of Cross was also aggravated by the nasty feelings that some of the Carolina drivers expressed about him. He had been part of the discussions with the drivers over the change of operations and was therefore guilty by association. Cross had been a rail yard representative for only five years, but in that time he had managed to become, for United members, a symbol of treachery.

Before Zero appointed him to the staff, the Chicago-born Cross had been a Local 705 member and a freight driver for twenty-two years. He was also a third-generation Teamster who had undergone a political conversion. Ligurotis had made him a steward in 1993, and when the first posttrusteeship election was held, Cross supported the Husar-led Membership Slate. Despite his opposition to the RPM Party, Zero appointed him as a representative for the rail units, and he was now a candidate for president on the Continued Reform ticket. For the length of the campaign, Cross would be a favorite target for the United Party's most colorful criticisms. At the summer United luau, visitors were served generous portions from two succulent, open-pit-roasted pigs. One pig was named "Dane" and the other "Otis." Cross was a decorated Vietnam veteran who had learned to overcome adversity, but the personal attacks caught him a little off guard. In a quiet moment just days before the ballots were mailed, Cross confided, "I never imagined myself in this position." He then added, "God had been good to me, but still this was mean."[15]

UPS, UPS, UPS

Along with the particular grievances that brought groups of workers together under political banners, there was one issue that all of the slates debated. Much of the campaign discussion centered on the local's relationship with UPS, specifically on how it treated the company's sizable bloc of part-time workers. The core of the debate grew out of the local's and the international IBT's historic 1997 strike against the delivery firm. After a one-week shutdown of all package delivery business, the company agreed to a national settlement that most industrial relations experts interpreted as a big union victory.[16] As good as the national contract was, Local 705 held out one additional week before signing a deal. In the context of the 2000 election, the most popular, important, and contentious part of the local's contract was the requirement that UPS create six hundred full-time jobs in Chicago: popular because the union built its public relations campaign around the issue, important because the company was rapidly shifting its work away from full-time workers, and contentious because how the agreement was interpreted could shift many votes from one slate's column into another's.

In July 2000 the local sent a one-page leaflet to every member proudly proclaiming, "The amount of full time jobs won by Local 705 far exceeds the amount achieved by any other Teamster Local union." It also included a celebratory Zero pointing out that his administration "kept its promise to UPS Teamsters who are Part timers. . . . We got our hard working members the justice they deserved—with no compromises and no watered down settlement." These jobs had not been easy to come by. It took a fifty-four-page arbitrator's ruling that one local staff member described as "thick enough to stun an ox" to force the company to make good on its agreement.[17] The ruling adopted an implementation schedule that identified the part-time jobs that would be "combo-ed" to create a number of full-time jobs within a five-year time period. It also led to an agreement between the company and Local 705 that set forth in exacting detail how these full-time jobs would be created. On the surface the contract, arbitrator's ruling, and subsequent implementation plan looked like an unconditional win for local UPS members. However, for a bargaining relationship that on balance was already far better for UPS union members since the trusteeship, the local's behavior toward the delivery company was the subject of a remarkable amount of trash talking.

Membership stalwart Mike Husar, for example, blasted the incumbent leadership for not raising the part-timers starting pay. The starting scale was $8.00 in 1982 and "over the last 18 years has only increased 50 cents." "The truth," he claimed, was that "McCormick and Zero made a lot of things worse for 705 members at UPS."[18] He also demonstrated his awareness of the importance of the UPS vote by placing three part-timers on the slate and offering the Membership's ticket's second spot to Dan Shaughnessy. Shaughnessy was a bright, intense, and very popular UPS member. Husar described him as an "in-your-face kind of guy," and the Zero camp considered him to be the slate's strongest candidate.[19] Shaughnessy had once worked on the local's staff and had served on the 1997 local UPS negotiating committee. He now used his experience and popularity to hammer the Zero administration for "turning their backs on the part-time workers," and he derided the incumbent leadership for practicing "Teamster light!" If Shaughnessy had his way, he would have UPS members mad as hell and looking to "kick their asses [i.e., Zero's and McCormick's] to the curb."[20]

Teamsters for Unity's Eugene Phillips also felt strongly enough about the local's relationship with the company that he placed six UPS employees on his eleven-person slate. His biggest complaint about the recent agreement was that it "was not farsighted enough" and "left too many things wrong." In Phillips's analysis, Zero and McCormick had "rushed the contract language" and, though the new jobs were good, "important matters got dropped."[21] Criticisms from both the Membership and the Teamster for Unity parties were constant, but no party candidate was more damning of the union's relationship with the package delivery firm than United's Mike Deane.

Deane's list of grievances began early. "In 1993 the local negotiated away a twenty-cents-an-hour progression pay for part-timers." He then went on to explain how Local 705 trustee Ed Burke had put out a memo after the 1993 contract was already signed that permitted UPS to use "part-time employees to perform shifting work [i.e., move trailers around the yard] at CACH."[22] This agreement, Deane alleged, opened the door to the company's use of part-time workers. But Deane's biggest argument with the leadership was over a single detail in the full-time-job settlement.

Package-car drivers were excluded from bidding on any of the new combo jobs, and Deane bitterly complained that by "cutting them off from the opportunity," the local had sacrificed the drivers' seniority rights. He passionately explained that the package-car job was "brutal, unbearable and members with more seniority should have the chance to move into a less stressful job." He was not opposed to part-timers being placed into full-time spots, but he was adamant that it should not come at the expense of a "person's years of experience." He suggested, instead, that part-timers should be given full-time work on the docks loading and unloading trailers. This would promote an internal job progression from dockworker to package-car driver to a near-retirement post as a feeder driver. Dean's harsh feelings about the UPS deal also led him to add five other company employees to his slate. In the end, it seemed that his campaign was more than a pragmatic struggle for union leadership; it was a mission to preserve the status of UPS drivers.

McCormick may not have been on a mission, but he built his entire campaign around his ties with UPS members. To begin with, he constructed a slate of candidates that consisted of seven members with a combined total of more than 150 years of experience working at UPS. In the True Reform's two major mass mailings, accomplishments at UPS consumed more than half of the printed pages. But McCormick's message was not all positive; he found space to accuse Zero of various shenanigans harmful to UPS workers.[23] Conversely, the Breakfast Club repeatedly trumpeted every Zero UPS accomplishment and highlighted each UPS failure as a shameful blotch on McCormick's record. The Breakfast Club took particular pleasure in pointing out that despite McCormick's stated concern for part-timers, somehow when forming his slate, he "forgot to put a part time UPS'er on as an executive board candidate."[24] Zero's slate had two UPS part-timers running for executive board positions.

In "going negative," both Zero and McCormick dabbled in distortion. One good example of this was the Zero camp's charge that while McCormick was the local's acting principal officer, he "gave up the right to strike UPS over supervisors" doing the work contractually reserved for union members. It was referring to a court-brokered arrangement, which settled a dispute over a one-day strike against UPS in 1998. The local called the brief work stoppage after the company refused to uphold its "pledge of compliance" to stop supervisors from performing bargaining unit work. Complaints about the company's actions went back to before 1995, and even though the union won a favorable court ruling, supervisors continued to perform bargaining work.[25]

The problem of continuing "Article 3, Section 7" contract violations was aggravated by the 1997 agreement to create new full-time Teamster jobs. Pressure from the union ranks to act defiantly against UPS's apparent disregard for the earlier and recent job-compliance language quickly mounted. With the embers of the previous summer's strike still smoldering and the busy 1998 Christmas season approaching, the local determined that it was a good time to pull the picket signs out of storage. Shortly after midnight on 10 December Local 705 called for a seven-hour walkout. Zero explained that the local took the action in order to "fire a shot across the bow of the UPS ship and let them know we want to talk seriously about getting some more jobs."[26] As a result of the costly interruption of business, the company dragged the local back into court.

By the time the legal proceedings unfolded, McCormick had assumed the local's leadership post, and he did surrender, for the life of the present contract, the right to "engage in any strike or work stoppage over the issue of supervisors performing bargaining unit work."[27] But the secretary-treasurer was wrong to call it McCormick's blunder. "Zero overstates his case," Michael Holland admitted. Holland was present during some of the settlement talks and recalls that the lawsuit was a "significant threat" to the local's financial health. It was typical for large, economically powerful companies like UPS to use court challenges to "put restraints on union job actions." The company alleged that the 1998 holiday strike caused sizable monetary damages, and the judge appeared anxious to bring in a verdict. According to Holland, the judge "was doing a significant amount of jawboning to get this thing settled." It was clear to everyone present that the court was willing to force a settlement; the court warned both parties that it would be "in your best interest to settle." Although Holland concluded that McCormick had "done a poor job negotiating," he admitted that the settlement was inevitable.[28] Maybe so, but with a smoldering political campaign throwing off sparks in every direction, such fine distinctions were rarely made or understood.

White Sheets, Racism, and Politics

UPS was a dominant issue, but all of the parties addressed their own laundry list of items. The United campaign excoriated Zero and McCormick for making the local the target of a number of lawsuits. Deane and Cooke argued that these legal actions siphoned scarce resources from the union that could have been better spent on representing the interests of members. Undeterred by the issue of lawsuits, Zero openly emphasized his record of financial management. McCormick and Deane preached the need for a viable strike capacity, while Zero pointed out that neither man endorsed his proposal to create a permanent strike fund.[29] Phillips campaigned on improving communications with the membership, but it was Zero who pointed out how membership rights had dramatically expanded since the trusteeship. Deane stressed the need for "elected stewards," and Husar spoke out against Zero and McCormick's "unfulfilled promise of elected stewards." But Zero answered by calling attention to his proposed 2000 bylaw amendment to construct a "self governing Stewards Council."[30]

Most encounters between candidates and with rank-and-file members were quiet, mundane affairs. But not all campaigning went so uneventfully. On an unseasonably warm night in late September, workers moving through Entrance 2 at the UPS CACH facility were buzzing about the most controversial political exchange of the campaign. They had recently been informed of a phone message delivered by a Membership candidate to Tony Gatson, an African American running on the Continued Reform Slate. Gatson was one of the slate's part-time UPS workers, and he was also appointed as a union representative. While attending to his staff office duties, Gatson decided to listen to the phone messages that had accumulated from the previous day. What he heard left him wondering, "if this what you have to go through . . . then I'm not sure it's worth it."[31]

The message began with an obvious reference to Gatson's staff position being racially motivated. "Hey you *token* business agent that doesn't know shit." It then went on to issue a frightening warning; "Next time you open your mouth about me and next time I see you I'm going to *BBQ your fucking ass.*" As if the initial language and threats were not enough to conjure up a disturbed imagery of racial terrorism, the message was repeated. "OK *token boy,* that's it . . . the *pig* is on the *rotisserie* and you are the oinker."[32] Although Gatson was stunned by the threats and confused as to why he should be the target of such anger, he was not uncertain as to who had left the message.

Gatson was sure that the voice on his answering machine belonged to Dan Cassidy, assistant union representative and Membership Slate candidate. Among his supporters, Cassidy had a reputation for being a fearless, uncompromising defender of worker rights, but to his distracters he was "just plain nuts." Sometimes his manic-like approach had its benefits for the union leadership. "They would send me to the biggest shit-holes and let me straighten it out," Cassidy boasted. Straightening things out usually meant taking a "worker was always right stance" and doing a lot of yelling at the boss.[33] His record of successful grievances gave him some reason to feel confident, but his uncompromising attitude often created as many problems as it resolved. Cassidy had a history of combative relations with both Zero and McCormick, and until two weeks before the fateful phone call to Gatson, he was serving his second term of duty as a union representative.

On 8 September Cassidy had received a letter from the secretary-treasurer removing him from his responsibilities, in part for his inability to "channel [his] frustration into being more effective against company transgressions rather than blaming [his] colleagues or finding fault in the method or style of others."[34] The letter infuriated Cassidy. He believed that Zero had acted out of political malice because of his involvement with the Membership Party. It is possible that Cassidy's removal and his belief that he had been the victim of a political show trial triggered his racially charged comments. The political effects of the disturbing message on the Membership Slate were immediately felt.

The Breakfast Club had initially disregarded Husar's candidacy. But as campaigning unfolded, the Membership Slate proved a more formidable adversary. As expected, Shaughnessy was having some success in UPS barns, and the Continued Reformers determined that the Membership Slate's ability to attract votes was escalating. It was possible now that Husar could siphon off enough votes from Zero that McCormick could win the election. The Continued Reformers responded with a flyer characterizing Husar as a political spoiler. It screamed, "Husar . . . You're Handing This Election Over to McCormick." Zero's message was meant to send cold shivers down the spines of freight members. In *A Special Message to 705 Freight Teamsters,* the Zero camp claimed that the unintended consequences of voting for Husar would be to produce the worst possible scenario: electing the antifreight

UPSer McCormick.[35] Zero's campaign strategy was based on having to fight McCormick for votes; now he had the unexpected problem of competing against Husar. But then Cassidy's message changed all that.

Dan Campbell quickly saw possibilities. With tape in hand, the Continued Reformers would not only be able to bludgeon a Membership candidate with his own words, but they could do it with his actual voice. One day after Gatson shared the message with his party colleagues, Campbell took the incriminating tape to the streets. The mostly young and black CACH employees were treated to a personal twenty-four-hour broadcast of Cassidy's diatribe on a pocket-size tape player. It sounded as bad in the UPS employee parking lot as it did in the union hall. Workers were stunned by the vile tone of Cassidy's voice. Sensing that Husar was badly damaged by his fellow slate member's words, Postilion and Campbell decided to broaden the audience and ratchet up the racial barometer. They released into UPS circulation a yellow flyer with Cassidy's exact message reprinted within a speaker's balloon, as if the character depicted was speaking the words. The speaker was obviously meant to be Cassidy, but the Zero camp took some dangerous liberties with their characterization. Cassidy's words appeared to be spoken by a white-sheeted Ku Klux Klan member. On the Klansman's sheet was a black Membership button with these words printed: "Anti Membership Klan Slate, Vote for Us, Positive Racism."[36]

If Postilion and Campbell were hoping to make people really angry, they succeeded. But some of that anger blew back at Zero. Both white and black workers leaving the CACH facility condemned the use of KKK imagery. While Cassidy's reference to Gatson as a "token boy" was viewed as patently racist, many black workers were also alarmed that any party would dangerously exploit someone's insensitivity for political ends. "The KKK shit spread among a largely teenage shift of black workers could have a caused a riot," one very agitated member commented. Election officer Bruce Boyens agreed and ordered the Zero camp to cease distribution of the inflammatory flyer. The words were already out, however, and Campbell called the attack against the Membership Party a "direct hit."[37]

Husar, however, never flinched in his support for Cassidy. In response to calls that he dump Cassidy from the Membership ticket, Husar explained that "it was just a guy making a mistake in the heat of battle, that's all." He further noted that Cassidy had been successful in representing a large number of white and black UPS workers. Husar stood valiantly beside his political partner, but he may have paid a high price for his loyalty. Angered by Cassidy's remarks, Shaughnessy demanded that Husar get rid of the former union representative. Husar refused. Shaughnessy was also upset to learn that, if elected, Husar did not intend to turn the UPS division over to him.[38] Shaughnessy had coveted the UPS prize, and with just days to go before the October nomination meeting, thirty-eight of the Membership Party's top campaign workers held a tumultuous gathering to discuss the issue. Shaughnessy again demanded that Cassidy step down and repeated his desire to be the party's choice for UPS chief. But Husar rejected this "personal demand for power and authority" and watched as his party's number-two man "walked out of the meeting," taking "a couple of guys with him."[39]

Husar admitted to feeling "personally hurt" by Shaughnessy's decision, but he remained very confident about the people who remained with his candidacy. Nonetheless, he had a real problem. As the electoral season was about to head into the crucial postnomination phase, the Membership Party had lost a high-profile candidate and its strongest UPS campaigner. To keep the party's chances viable, Husar needed to find a new presidential running mate. He found a little-known UPS package-car driver out of the Westmont barn by the name of Judy Fanning.

Fanning's ability to attract votes to the ticket was uncertain at best, but her selection was precedent-setting. For the first time in Local 705's history, a woman would be running for the union's second-highest office. Oddly, a racial incident had served to break down an important electoral door to local female union members in an international union that had refused to drop "Brotherhood" from its name. Fanning and Lauren Hill, the Teamster for Unity recording-secretary candidate, were the only women campaigning for board seats, but they would be joined by five other union sisters running as trustees or elected union representatives. A dozen African American and five Latino male candidates accompanied these women on party slates. Local 705 elections had never looked so well balanced in terms of race and gender. Full citizenship was coming to the union, it seemed, whether it was ready or not. Now if only rank-and-file citizens would vote.

CHAPTER TEN

The 705 Vote

By early November of 2000, the electoral season at Local 705 was already eight months old. Parties like the Continued Reform and United 2000 had been campaigning since early winter, and the others shifted into active campaigning with the October slate nominations. From early morning to late-night workplace visits, candidates and issues were scattered like falling leaves throughout the union's jurisdiction. Party loyalists publicly predicted victory for their side and discounted the credibility of other candidates. But privately no one was so certain. This election was expected to be close, and turnout among party supporters would determine the outcome. Although no party activist knew for sure how many members would cast a ballot, they acted as if every Teamster in good standing just might. But member sovereignty was still a new phenomenon at Local 705, and with so many candidates, issues, flyers, phone calls, arguments, and counterarguments to consider, a rank-and-filer could become overwhelmed and fail to vote. Democracy in principle was a good thing, but a returned ballot was even better.

Votes Not Cast

Richard DeVries was not about to mince words. With one week to go before the ballots were mailed out to members, he wanted his Breakfast Club brethren to imagine the postelection headlines reading something like this: "The winner is the I'm for you Gerry, but my fucking ballot is sitting on top of the refrigerator."[1] Despite the party's campaign efforts to build support for the Continued Reform Party, DeVries thought it more than possible that members would simply forget to vote. At the last strategic party session before the votes were cast, DeVries was animated and very vocal. But he was not giving the party faithful a pep talk. He was there to staff a phone banking operation.

DeVries had established a phone center nearby at the United Electrical Workers hall on South Ashland. A room on the first floor had been rented and equipped with fifteen phone jacks. DeVries intended to staff the phones twelve hours a day for the first week after the ballots were mailed to members. He estimated that sixty people would be needed to make phone calls to members' homes, from nine in the morning until nine at night. Crews of fifteen would work three-hour shifts and then be replaced by another set of party volunteers. If it was done correctly, each phone operator could make a dozen calls during his or her shift.

Operators were also responsible for keeping a running tally of responses on a large chalkboard. Plus signs would designate pro-Zero calls, minuses would indicate anti-Zeros, and circles would mark the undecided. DeVries made it clear that a diversity of callers was necessary. "We need women to call women, Spanish speaking to call Spanish speaking." Callers would also reach out to workers in their barns and divisions. A special effort would be made to make twenty-five hundred contacts with mostly female CACH employees. "I prefer that we have women calling these women at home." De-Vries also expected each slate member, including Zero, to spend some time on the phones. Admittedly, dialing phone numbers "was not glitzy stuff," but according to DeVries, it was "real important to combat any apathy."[2]

While the other parties worried as much as DeVries did about voter turnout, only the Continued Reformers decided to do mass phone banking. McCormick's campaign director, Andrew Speck, believed that phone banking in a local union election was an unproductive search for last-minute votes. Likely voting members already knew the candidates very well and had probably made up their minds early in the campaign. Thus, McCormick's membership contacts during the waning days of the campaign, according to Speck, were not about "winning votes," but instead about getting the slate's committed voters to mail back their ballots. Membership patrons agreed and took relentlessly to the streets. They stayed there from two in the morning until nine in the evening. Campaigners organized into three different crews to handle the multiple shifts worked at UPS and into two teams to cover the city freight barns. Party activists worked from a three-day advance schedule developed by Membership Slate members Joe Bates and Nick Ponivich. For all the slates, winning or confirming votes now was like hand-to-hand combat, and in battle casualties sometimes occurred.

After an early October morning round of campaigning, Husar and other campaigners stopped for breakfast. Before ordering his food, Husar became light-headed and passed out. He slumped down in his seat, and "the guys dragged me out of the booth," immediately drawing the alarmed attention of the restaurant staff. A waitress ran over and, after listening to Husar's heart, began to administer CPR. An emergency medical team then quickly arrived and transported Husar to Christ Hospital in Oaklawn. Doctors diagnosed him as having very low blood pressure and ordered him to remain in the hospital for two days and to avoid campaigning for at least two weeks. Husar wanted to be Local 705 secretary-treasurer and figured this was his last and best chance to win. He was ready to "campaign, campaign, campaign," but for the next few weeks, he agreed that perhaps it would be smart to "just cool my heels."[3]

Deane also kept up a busy schedule of campaign stops and believed that he had seen signs of an impending victorious United coalition. His winning scenario came in three parts. First, "Zero dies after CACH," and second, "McCormick dies out at freight." Deane would then pick up little bits of vote support from everywhere. The game plan was "to shake the trees in all portions of the union." He expected that UPS members would determine the election. It depended on how they felt. "If UPS wants a change, I'll win, but if not, McCormick wins." Deane never considered that either Husar or Phillips's Teamsters for Unity were likely to attract many votes. Surprisingly, he had completely written off Zero's chances.[4] McCormick, however, had not. Zero was the "other" candidate to beat, and to do so McCormick would have to build support from not only UPS, but also freight. To that end, on the second day after ballots were mailed, the campaign distributed a special brochure targeted to freight drivers focusing on health and welfare and pension improvements.

The Zero team expected campaigning to be heaviest from November 1 to 17. A final search for Zero votes had been developed around the concept of "craft campaigning." Equipped with a pager and a cell phone, the Zero loyalists moved in small blocs among the local's various crafts. Each craft team had developed a schedule of barn visits, and campaign chief Postilion coordinated the blocs' movements. Postilion insisted on knowing where everyone was in the final days, because he wanted to "parachute Jerry in" if it was necessary to win a member's support. In order for Zero to win, Postilion believed that votes had to come from every craft, and that meant Zero had to be "where he needed to be."[5]

The Continued Reform Party's vote projections were predicated on building a broad-based electoral coalition. Postilion was looking for large blocs of UPS, freight, and city cartage votes, along with significant support in most of the other crafts. The strategy was coalitional because Postilion was not confident that Zero would carry a majority of either UPS or freight workers. The campaign chief had done the math, and though Zero was not likely to finish first in any one of the UPS, freight, or cartage divisions, he stood an excellent chance of finishing a strong second in all of them. Adding his runner-up large divisional votes to his expected dominance among the smaller units of tanker, mover, city cartage, liquor houses, municipal, air freight, and Kankakee-area workers would result in a winning coalition.

Even after the ballots were mailed, Postilion believed there was a window of opportunity where the election could be won or lost. Ballots would be mailed out on November 9, and all returns would be counted on December 2. But because the Friday after the mailing was a holiday, ballots would not start to arrive until Saturday. Most of the membership had a light work schedule on Saturday. Thus, the first big opportunity to remind members to return their ballots would be Monday, November 13. On this day thousands of workers would have "their ballots in hand." Postilion advised the staff to "work out from the core" and visit "your strongest barns first."

Since 1993 Teamster Local 705 had come a long way. From a deeply contested trusteeship through two combative elections, the local body politic absorbed the structural and social shocks of democratization. Rapid change had first been imposed from above, then twice afterward had been endorsed from below. Elections in 1995 and 1997 transformed the local from a dictatorship to a burgeoning democracy. In both cases voting had contributed to union citizenship by incrementally undoing the constraints of the pretrusteeship years. Rank-and-file members were moving away from being subjects of the union, but they were not yet full members of the local. In this sense the 1995 and 1997 officer elections had looked to the past for motivation. They were realigning elections that condemned the past and called out for something different.

The 2000 contest was fundamentally different. It was the first free election that challenged rank-and-file voters to draw inspiration from the future. After seven years of reform, union members could now genuinely speculate on how to broaden their membership instead of simply thinking of ways to undue their oppression. Casting a ballot in 2000 was not a choice between democratic values and self-interest. It was a choice between various alternative versions of how best to defend and further democratic trade unionism. The first two posttrusteeship elections had been nail-biters, but they were transparent. Reform squared off against the status quo. In 2000 every party called for steward elections, better contracts, expanded membership rights, unity among the ranks, more militant opposition to the employer, greater organizing efforts, and honest, independent, responsive leadership. It was a brave new world, and 2 December had finally arrived. The voters had chosen, and all that was left to do was to count the ballots.

Local 705 Elects Reform Again

It was an exceptional day. The temperature hovered a little above freezing, and the ground was free of snow. Owing to the good weather, Local 705 election officer Bruce Boyens's midmorning ride from his office to the Chicago Main Post Office on Harrison and Canal Streets was uneventful. Once Boyens arrived at the central facility, postal employees immediately proceeded to drag large mailbags of returned union ballots out from a secured area. Observed by three carloads of invited slate representatives, Boyens loaded up his truck and within five minutes pulled into the parking lot of the Teamster City Auditorium, where ballots would be counted.[6]

Carrying the oversized mailbags, Boyens and his appointed staff entered the auditorium first, followed by one member from each of the five slates. Upon climbing the two sets of winding stairs that lead to the main floor, the election team and observers found a collection of twenty tables arranged in a square. At each of the tables were six chairs. One chair, pushed up to the edge of the table, would be occupied by a neutral "vote teller" hired by Boyens. The other five chairs sat a foot or two behind the teller's chair; they were for a single representative, or "observer," from each slate. When the balloting actually began, there would be one hundred party activists bird-dogging every movement and every utterance. Boyens brought the mailbags to the center of the squared-off area and unceremoniously dumped the contents on the floor. What piled up on the hall tiles, like logs on a bonfire, were postage-paid envelopes, each carrying a union member's ballot sealed in a special secure envelope. Party observers were ordered not to enter the square or even to touch the tables.

One person from each slate could "walk thorough" the hall, though. The walk-through was an opportunity for party officials to check the hall for any security problems. United hopeful Mike Deane raised some issues, and Postilion took offense at most of them. The two began to argue, and Postilion accused Deane of being "ridiculous." Their exchanges became so disturbing that Boyens threatened to remove them from the hall if they did not stop bickering. Both men relented, and the walk-through was completed. Boyens and his staff proceeded to cross-check the digital code numbers printed on the outside of the envelopes against a four-inch-thick roster of union members' names. The envelopes were then sorted by the first initial of the last name and distributed to tables designated by a placard bearing a letter or a range of letters of the alphabet. With stacks of envelopes in front of them, tellers performed their first critical function, determining the eligibility of the voter.

By cross-referencing the code number with the previously submitted and approved membership roster, tellers were able to determine whether a member was in good standing. Here is also where the slate observers got their first opportunity to influence the count. Any one of them could challenge the eligibility of a voter. Envelopes that were challenged were set aside, and the election officer then ruled on their status. Boyens ended up throwing out approximately 800 ballots, many more than the average of 500 in the two previous contests. The tellers began sorting and checking eligibility at 10:00 A.M., and they finished a few minutes before noon. After breaking for lunch, they returned to the hall and took their assigned seats, each one followed close behind by five very self-interested party activists.

With everyone's eligibility settled, the tellers were directed to tear open their packages and remove the sealed ballots. Freed from their secure pouches, Local 705 ballots were now ready to be examined. At 1:00 P.M. Boyens ordered the count to begin. As the tellers commenced the laborious task of eyeballing the ballots and recording the votes, the contesting slate observers were also busy keeping their own scorecards. Union members had five slates of candidates and three voting options to choose from. Option one allowed a voter to cast a vote for every member of a single slate by marking a single box (slate voting).[7] Option two permitted the voter to place a mark next to the name of every candidate on a single slate (candidate voting). The third option was to pick and choose among slate candidates and offices (bullet or split-ticket voting). As tellers examined the ballots, they would identify the vote by calling out the option chosen. For example, if a member chose to vote a straight slate for Zero, the teller would say, "Continued Reform Slate" and then put the ballot on a Continued Reform Slate pile. In the course of the count, an observer could get a pretty fair idea of who was winning by noting the relative size of the slate and candidate piles.

Continued Reform representatives had organized a simple way for getting regular updates on how their candidate was doing. Each observer went into the hall with a pencil and twenty pieces of three-by-three-inch yellow paper stapled together. On each slip, written in pencil, were the initials of the last names of each secretary-treasurer candidate. The initials were written in the same order as the names appeared on the ballot.[8] Observers were directed to listen to the teller's call and to record a vertical line for the declared candidate. In accordance with the election rules, each party could designate one person as a "floating observer." Postilion floated for the Zero slate. He had planned to go to each table every fifteen minutes and tear off the observer's top tally sheet. Postilion kept to his schedule, but after floating the first time he knew the rest of his rounds were purely for show.

"I knew after fifteen minutes that we had won." Postilion's collection revealed that after 1,000 ballots were counted, Zero was up by more than 100 votes. "If you're ahead by 100 after 1,000 votes, you're going to be ahead by 1,000 after 8,000 votes," the campaign chief revealed. The official count went on until roughly 5:00 P.M., when Boyens unofficially declared the Continued Reform Party the winner of Local 705's officer election. Before Boyens certified the election results, he had to dispense with nearly one hundred election protests. The most significant one and the most bizarre was a protest submitted by candidates from both the United and True Reform slates pointing out that a number of the carrying envelopes were received without "proper postmarks." Despite the hyperbole surrounding the controversy, Boyens rejected the protest and subsequently certified the results.[9] The final tally revealed a surprisingly big win for Zero and his entire slate. Table 1 shows the vote for secretary-treasurer.

An Analysis of the 705 Vote

Before the vote, a few of the Breakfast Club members took up a betting pool to predict the actual vote count and the order in which the slates would finish. Postilion won. He had guessed that Zero would receive 2,700 votes but had never expected the incumbent to win by such a wide margin. No one else in the Breakfast Club had either. So what produced this impressive victory? Since there are no "exit polls" taken in union elections, a vote analysis must rely on a few facts and a lot of firsthand impressions.

TABLE I—**The Final Tally**

Candidate	Vote	Percent	Slate
Gerald Zero	2,719	38.9	Continued Reform
John B. McCormick	1,798	25.7	True Reform
Michael Deane	1,065	15.2	United 2000
Michael Husar	1,063	15.1	Membership
Eugene Phillips	358	5.1	Teamster for Unity

Postilion believed that he had a good idea of how the campaign had performed and where Zero's votes had come from. "A couple hundred of votes came out of the Kmart people in the Kankakee area." The Kmart Corporation warehouse members had been a "secret weapon" for Zero ever since an Illinois Circuit Court judge had ruled that the retailer had spied on the workers during a six-month organizing drive. After a close pro-union vote in the summer of 1993, the local solidified its standing with the Manteno-based employees by winning a $50,000 settlement from the company, for hiring Confidential Investigative Consultants "to pose as workers and spy on the activities of union members at the center."[10] Jeff Dexter, a Kankakee representative, had been reporting solid support for Zero throughout the campaign.

Based on a very detailed estimate of likely UPS voting, the slate also believed it had a shot at capturing approximately 800 part-time votes out of the CACH facility. Campbell had figured that only about 60 percent of the site's 8,000 part-time members would be eligible to vote. But even in the best scenario, Postilion believed that McCormick could walk away with nearly 2,000 UPS feeder- and package-car-driver votes. In the end, Postilion estimated that neither Zero nor McCormick did as well as expected at UPS. "We did about 700 votes, and McCormick took around 1,600." Although Zero's total missed the target, McCormick's shortfall was more damaging. Based on observations made by Continued Reform Party representatives during the vote count, roughly 3,100 votes came out of UPS.[11] Even if this figure is just a good estimate, it seems likely that despite McCormick's appeal to full-time drivers, he only won a bare majority of support from within UPS. And few if any of his UPS votes were from part-timers. On the contrary, the majority of Zero's UPS votes were certainly from part-time workers. Given the 921 votes separating Zero from McCormick, it seems the lesson Passo taught in the 1997 election had been well learned.

The UPS strategy worked reasonably well, but Postilion underestimated how successful Husar would be in the freight division. It is likely that the vast bulk of Husar's 1,063 votes came from drivers at large carriers like Roadway, Yellow, and Holland freight. Including some support at ABF-Carolina, Deane also drew roughly 800 votes out of freight barns. The result, according to Postilion, was to suppress Zero's non-UPS support by at least 400 votes. However, without a unifying candidate for freight drivers to rally around, their vote appeared to be carved up into three factions.

Like any civic election, Local 705's officer race served up a number of "what ifs" that make entertaining fodder for political junkies. For instance, what would have happened if Ron Carey had not been barred from the international rerun election and had won reelection? To begin with, Dane Passo would never have been appointed a special assistant to the general president. Would he then have run in Local 705's officer election? Or perhaps if Carey had stayed in office, the reformers would have remained united, and no serious political challenge would have emerged.[12] But there is one undeniably impressive fact about Zero's win that links his political leadership with democratic reform. His electoral coalition truly represented the divisions among the membership. Zero drew support from every craft in the local. The Continued Reform slate took first prize because it took a pluralistic approach to winning votes. Zero was not beholden to any special interest. His party members and supporters represented the depth and breadth of the union membership. It was a distinction that elected union officers of any stripe should be eager to emulate.

The Strength of the Reform Movement

For the third time in seven years, Local 705 members had participated in an open and honest election. An election seriously affecting the lives of more than 18,000 people had been successfully carried out with many of the same types of regulatory oversight that are necessary to protect the legitimacy of the civic voting process. Electoral politics had dominated the local for nearly a year, and at the end of the process 7,003 union members used the power of the vote. That total was only slightly up (4%) from the local's first brush with open elections in 1995, but it did represent 47 percent of the eligible body politic. A good chunk of the membership had cast a ballot, and an overwhelming 65 percent of them had voted for the reform candidates. Zero and McCormick may have held down different lines on the ballot, but they were clearly identified with the local's democratic transformation. Democratic unionism had not only been endorsed again, but this time it had taken up two places on the ballot and had provided the framework for the entire campaign. Since the trusteeship, 20,753 votes had been cast in Local 705 officer elections. Approximately 52 percent of those votes went to either Zero or McCormick. The margin was narrow, but reform was winning.

Despite what Michael Holland called attempts to "govern the union by litigation," to run an "election by protest," and to make "policy by charge and counter charge," at the end of seven years reform had proved to be a good vehicle for "asserting worker rights in respect to the employer."[13] Democracy was productive, empowering, and desired by the membership. Union members were now directly participating in, or at least were better aware of, the governance affairs of their local. By democratizing, the local redefined its purpose from self-perpetuation and elite self-interest to doing what is necessary for improving the working lives of its members. In other words, Local 705 was now a liberating tool of the membership rather than a mechanism for fulfilling the alien interests of nonworkers.

Internal democracy also increased the number of people who were willing and able to stand up to the employer and demand justice. As a result of reform, Local 705 was fighting the employer with rank-and-file organizing and negotiating committees, and there were hundreds of educated stewards protecting the rights of workers. Stewards filed grievances, representatives argued cases at panel hearings, union lawyers arbitrated contract violations, and the local struck, held rallies, and engaged in an assortment of corporate campaigns. Democracy has freed the membership and encouraged the leadership to regularly confront the power of the employer. Compared to the pretrusteeship period with its authoritarian control, democracy at Local 705 has increased the local's level of efficiency.

Union Reform: A Local Comparative

In the internal democratization of Local 705, we can identify some of the common elements involved in the historical and contemporary transformation of local unions. It is worth noting again, however, that although "cleaning house" is essential to good union governance, democratizing unions is not principally about ridding them of criminally implicated individuals. Instead, the larger democracy project within the labor movement is dedicated to redefining local and international unions into rank-and-file-driven movements for workplace and social justice. The focus is not on extralegal union behavior as much as on irrelevant or meaningless union behavior. In many cases union reform efforts have been sparked not by outright violations of the law, but instead by policymaking that has left members with less power in the workplace. Union members have then turned toward greater political involvement within their organizations as a response to ineffectual leadership.

In the case of Local 705, democratizing meant taking punitive administrative and legal action against officials, as well as creating mechanisms for union members to contribute to the organization's fortunes. An examination of a few other national and local reform movements reveals, to one degree or another, the presence of one or more of the following eight common elements:

1. Government intervention or the threat thereof occurs.

2. There are criminal indictments or convictions of incumbent union officials.

3. A trusteeship is imposed on the local by the international union.

4. A perceived undemocratic act by the incumbent leadership triggers the formation of a reform caucus outraged by the loss of democratic rights.

5. Initial reform procedures alter the relationship between the leadership and the membership.

6. Meaningful behavioral change follows the organization and mobilization of a grassroots dissident group.

7. Reformers first focus on representational and bargaining issues before competing for political power.

8. Local democrats ultimately build the capacity to win elections.

An example of how government-protected reform at the international level can trigger dramatic change throughout the union structure is the case of the United Mine Workers. In 1972 a dissident worker group called Miners for Democracy rallied behind the martyrdom of slain reform candidate Jock Yablonski and, with the help of federal intervention, defeated an incumbent president who was convicted of hiring two men who shot Yablonski. As with national Teamster reform, the adoption of democratic procedures in the miners' union was the end product of a rank-and-file movement—in this instance, one that emerged in the coalfields of West Virginia, Ohio, and Pennsylvania.[14]

In the UMW case, however, dynamic currents of cultural and political change also conspired against the autocrats. In the early 1970s, a large number of Vietnam veterans and civil rights battle-tested African Americans entered a rapidly expanding coal industry. Once there, these groups expressed little patience with "bossism" of any kind and added significant fuel to a democratic fire already kindled by a murderous act. Influenced by the civil rights and Black Power movements, and by radical elements opposing the country's involvement in Southeast Asia, young workers entered industrial workplaces determined to challenge the lack of democracy wherever they found it. Although there were no dramatic international leadership changes in functioning unions like the United Autoworkers and the United Steelworkers of America, dissent caucuses did emerge across the labor spectrum with the help of similarly focused civic groups.[15]

The Teamsters Local 560 represents a critically different reform case. Brutally controlled by mobsters connected to the Genovese crime family, New Jersey Local 560 was the target of the first union-related RICO suit. In 1982 the Justice Department filed charges against the local leadership for extortion, bribery, and the murder of political opponents. But the eventual elimination of mob influences did not depend on rank-and-file opposition. Despite a trusteeship, which removed corrupt officials, subsequent open elections simply put in power individuals closely aligned with the discredited leadership. In this case, the old guard union leadership was so savage in its assault on worker rights that the cleanup resulted principally from the work of a troika of third-party individuals, wielding substantial legal authority over the local's affairs. It was the efforts of court-appointed officers, independent of the union establishment, that finally brought change to the local—and the process took nearly thirteen years.[16]

In the 1995 federal monitoring agreement of the Chicago Hotel Employees and Restaurant Employees Union (HERE) Local 1, an outside election officer was appointed to supervise all local elections and establish rules for political campaigning. The local was also forced to remove its incumbent chief operating officer for illegal actions and behaviors that violated union members' rights. Holding a free and open election, as in both Local 705 and the miners' union, was a seminal event in legitimating a reform agenda. Under independent monitoring, an insurgent HERE Local 1 caucus won 40 percent of the vote in officer elections and began to propose bylaw amendments to increase the level of rank-and-file involvement.[17]

Through a unique 1995 agreement with the U.S. Department of Justice, mob-related activities within Chicago-based locals of the Laborers' International Union of North America have been weeded out. Over the past few years, a number of local union officials and the entire Chicago-area district council were removed, and new, supervised elections were held.[18] The story of local transformation was similar at the Service Employees International Union (SEIU) Chicago Local 25, New York Local 32B–32J and Local 144, and Boston Local 254. But in the SEIU cases, a federal order was not necessary to push the international union to act against renegade locals.

Corrupt influences, including misappropriation of funds and intimidation of union dissidents, forced the international union to remove the local presidents and to completely reorganize the local unions' structures. Each situation, however, did include a group of dissidents who had publicly agitated for expanding the rights of union members. Local 254, for example, had a twenty-year history of grassroots opposition. Groups like Service Employees for a Democratic Union and Put Workers First had been active around contract issues and membership rights. At the 32B–32J Local, fifty thousand members strong, an eighteen-month trusteeship was followed by a contested officer election featuring three slates.[19]

In 1999 the American Federation of State, County, and Municipal Employees Union, New York City District Council 37, was placed under trusteeship for a series of incidents of financial misconduct and election impropriety. The effort of the international union against its largest district body was prompted, in part, by the dogged efforts of the reform-minded Coalition for Real Change in DC 37. Made up of members from each of DC 37's fifty-five represented locals, this group held public meetings calling for all elections and contract referendums to be conducted by outside agencies, and for the direct election of district council officers. The public nature of the district's scandals led the international union to remove the incumbent executive director and to appoint an administrator of the council. With the support of the Coalition, the new administrator has encouraged rank-and-file rallies around contract talks, brought lawsuits against the city's use of welfare recipients to replace civil service employees, held steward trainings, conducted audits, and adopted a code of ethical conduct.[20]

A contemporary example of how a reform movement can be sparked by controversial internal union decision making is the case of the New England Regional Council of the United Brotherhood of Carpenters. Angered by an international edict dramatically reducing the sovereign power of local union members, reformers organized the Carpenters for a Democratic Union (CDU). CDU quickly petitioned members throughout the six New England states, demonstrated at labor council meetings, and, most importantly, elected prodemocracy delegates to the regional council. The reformers' mobilizing paid off when a Boston union official associated with the rank-and-file caucus was elected to the region's highest executive office.[21]

Local activist organizations can also succeed without international involvement. Union members in the country's largest transit local built a bottoms-up movement that eventually led to a dramatic change in leadership without outside help or inspiration. Frustrated by the lack of respect for membership opinions and burdened by ten years of degrading labor agreements, in 2001 New York City transit workers at Transport Workers Local 100 elected the oppositional New Directions Party to 37 of 46 executive board seats.[22] New Directions had been around since 1984, agitating for contract issues and defending rank-and-file workers against severe employer abuses. Along the way, with the help of a favorable court ruling and Department of Labor intervention, it slowly developed the means to win elections.

Finally, reform efforts can operate at the subelection level. Organized in 1989 to oppose the United Food and Commercial Workers' concessionary bargaining in the meatpacking industry, Research-Education-Advocacy-People, or REAP, was formed. A nonprofit organization of union members, REAP has principally fashioned itself as an informational tool for local activists. It has published numerous briefing papers on matters relevant to the industries in which UFCW members work and to the internal governance of the union. Forming an oppositional electoral "party" is not at the moment the organization's principal goal. REAP is attempting to prod democracy forward through membership education and advocacy—not unlike the reform trajectory within the Teamsters.[23]

Although there are different elements involved in each of these reform cases, each union's strategic direction is dependent on the quality and quantity of democratic participation. The ability of unions to advance both their moral and their instrumental objectives is linked to their responsiveness to membership aspirations. Identifying and pursuing those needs requires that members assert effective control over their union's behavior. Thus, Local 705's success in improving the working lives of its members points to a critical motivation for embracing union democracy. For democracy to matter to union members, it must produce a more just workplace and contribute to a more egalitarian society. Bill Fletcher, one-time director of the AFL-CIO's Education Department, states the issue this way: "Union democracy is a dead letter if the members believe that the union is irrelevant to their principal concerns."[24] Simply put, union members become involved when they believe that it matters, and at Local 705, union involvement is now relevant to the rank and file.

A Perspective on Local 705 Democracy

Local 705's impressive reform record is built upon a number of conventional measures, yet there are a few likely reasons why democracy has developed in this Teamster local and not in others. First, the tectonic shift in membership away from heavy freight workers to package delivery workers, set into motion by unrelated governmental market deregulatory measures, moved the center of 705's political power into democracy-friendly UPS barns. Second, the painful deregulatory and corporate assault on unionized transportation workers ignited long-suppressed grievances among workers unwilling to tolerate corrupt and ineffective leadership. Third, Local 705 was placed into trusteeship by union president Ron Carey. Recall that Ligurotis had run in 1991 on a slate challenging for control of the international union. Fourth, the trusteeship at 705 was not only genuinely about governance, but it had a transformative purpose; both the union and the people who would govern it would be different from what came before.

Fifth, the governing reformers represented a rare mix of dissident "insiders" and progressive "outsiders," who, because they were detached from clannish union loyalties, could contrive radical political possibilities. Sixth, reformers like Zero and McCormick had been voices in the wilderness for many years. They were known entities, real Teamster drivers who did not bear the stain of "union bureaucrat" or "International lackey." Here were actual rank-and-file workers with a penchant and capacity for political change. Finally, Chicago Teamsters, and Local 705 in particular, have had a different historical trajectory from that of other unions. Leadership at 705 has been autonomous and even defiant of international-union power. In short, though doing things in Chicago often meant an all-too-typical Local 705 "working" with the mob, when the right moment arrived, operating there also—ironically—made possible a Local 705 that could be unlike any other group of Teamsters.

But for all of Local 705's democratic features, it still represents just one species of democratic unionism. Dramatic change has occurred at the local, but the exact placement of the union on a democratic continuum is imprecise. How then to situate Local 705? According to Dan Campbell, it is among "approximately twenty IBT reform locals." In so designating the union, Campbell takes great care to point out how distinct one reform local is from another. He stresses that a democratic union should "equip the stewards and members to do the work of the union." For Campbell, union bureaucracy is not objectively a detriment to democracy. Elected and appointed staff can serve rank-and-file control, as long as it "maintains the steward system." The ultimate test is whether the union structure enables the members and their stewards to "become autonomous" and to then "place demands" upon the institution.[25]

Achieving this end requires a synthesis between rank-and-file mobilization and the democratic process. Campbell makes the important point that one can exist without the other: "A local could be reform, but not mobilized or have mobilizing tendencies, yet is hostile to reform." In the former case, an elite cadre of union democrats might retain control by simply adopting honest and fair procedures; here, workers exercise their enfranchisement rights, but like civic voters, they simply select others to make decisions for them. In contrast, locals that selectively rally the ranks behind leader-directed actions, absent rank-and-file input, might effectively achieve their material objectives but do nothing to extend control to the membership. In this case, workers participate in collective actions as puppets on the end of a string.

Instead of a democracy-versus-mobilization dichotomy, Campbell's insights offer students of union governance a two-dimensional matrix for understanding the character of a particular union democracy. Reform and mobilization can be measured as separate variables on dual axes. Union locals can then be designated as "high," "medium," or "low" on each item. The ideal union, of course, would be highly democratic and highly mobilized. But as Campbell notes, "that would require a wide range of mobilization at the fullest discretion of the rank and file."

Although Local 705 has emerged as one of the most reformed within the Teamsters union, Joe Allen, interviewed in 2000, saw plenty of room for improvement. Allen is a steward of the Jefferson Street UPS facility. He has been a solid Zero supporter and is one of the editors of the rank-and-file newsletter, the *Brown Boxer*. Allen is also an active TDU member with an impressive grasp of labor history and politics. Union reform, Allen noted, has to be more than the machinations of a democratically inclined "ruling caucus." He admitted that Zero had been a democratic union leader but said, "We need to create a rank-and-file reform caucus within the local." The problem was that though IBT leaders like Carey and Zero certainly promoted membership involvement and mobilization, it was still too much like "turning on a faucet." Having a strong, visionary leadership responsive to the membership was essential for democracy to flourish, but Allen argued that "a culture of reform" had yet to take hold within the rank and file.[26]

Since the trusteeship, Local 705 had done a very good job of representing members' interests and providing workers with the means and opportunity to participate in the decision-making life of the union. These are impressive accomplishments, not to be minimized. But for Allen, they still represented a kind of "democratic rule on behalf of the membership and not by the membership." He endorsed and worked for the Zero slate but nonetheless believed that an independent union caucus was needed. Allen felt that the electoral process itself created the need for a watchdog group. "To get elected you have to embrace coalitional dynamics," and this means to some extent that a candidate, even a reform-minded one, has to "play both sides of the fence." But once the election is over, and the reformer wins, he or she "inherits" an opposing political philosophy and agenda that must be answered to. In the end, union politics creates a "truncated coalition" that may be necessary to govern in the name of the workers, but it waters down the principle of rank-and-file control. Allen was encouraged by the direction Local 705 had taken and recognized how the needs of workers had been defended by this species of democracy. He was now ready to push reform a little closer to the ideal.

By any conventional standard, Local 705 has implemented much of the machinery necessary for effective rank-and-file representation. In addition, the union has demonstrated a willingness and a sophistication to organize the membership to act collectively on behalf of worker interests. In short, members are well served and responsive to the leadership-identified need to mobilize for action. An integrated conception of reform and mobilization suggests that a fuller rank-and-file participation be pursued, but it is clear that democracy is being served at Local 705. More importantly, democracy has been good for union members. "When you dig beneath the political rhetoric," Gerald Zero claimed, "the facts speak for themselves—reform has made Local 705 and the IBT a better, stronger union."[27]

To students of union democracy, the significance of the union's transformation is that rank-and-file participation pays off. Local 705's experience gives credence to the idea that union democracy is more than rules and procedures. Democracy is the outcome of realigned power relationships. When workers can defend themselves against oppressive employers, they are operating within a more democratic relationship. The case of Local 705 demonstrates that democracy becomes real when workers come to have greater influence over how their shop-floor and their union are governed.

The struggles of Chicago Teamsters to gain a voice in their union, while also trying to negotiate a dignified and fair exchange of labor with their employers, relocates the union democracy debate. Instead of limiting the elements of democratization to the conditions in which union members interact, the focus shifts to the power relationship between management and workers. In the process of embodying the needs of the members, Local 705 and other democratic unions have influenced the balance of power between powerful corporations and working-class Americans. Workers within all unions, particularly democratic ones, are more likely to be safer at work, better compensated for their toil, less worn down by their working lives, and in control over the value of their hard labor.

Epilogue

Local 705's reform project has continued to evolve, and two years after the 2000 election of the Gerry Zero–led slate, the meaning of some of the changes is a matter of contested interpretations. Of course, much at 705 has held constant or improved. The local continues to represent members, file grievances, and negotiate contracts. It has implemented and distributed a written "Member's Bill of Rights" for processing grievances. Among other things, that document includes an assurance that "no grievance will be settled without the grievant being offered an opportunity to participate in the decision."[1] Behind the grievance machinery is a union still unafraid to confront the employer. In August of 2002, Kmart warehouse members in Kankakee defeated a company-inspired campaign to withdraw union recognition, and in the same month, Airborne package delivery workers staged a one-day walkout over health and safety issues.[2]

Michael Holland returned as local executive board counsel and has continued to monitor regular board sessions and the publishing of membership-meeting agendas. Membership meetings remain open, and attendance regularly exceeds three hundred. Floor microphones remain conspicuous in the union hall and are well used. Rank-and-filers still read the local newsletter, and business agents' phone numbers are still public information. The local has appointed additional business agents, and its newly elected stewards are invited to participate in local-sponsored training programs. And for workers interested in university-based education, the local continues to provide multiple opportunities.

Local 705 also continues to be a politically conscious union. In the summer and fall of 2002, the local set an impressive pace in registering union members to vote and was actively involved in statewide political elections. According to the Illinois Campaign for Political Reform, in the past ten years the democratized local has contributed over half a million dollars to a Teamster joint council political fund in support of statewide constitutional and legislative offices.[3] The local was also politically distinguished as being the first—and one of the few—unions to ultimately endorse pro-labor Nancy Kaszak in Illinois's 2002 fifth congressionl district primary race. Kaszak lost her bid against former Clinton administration insider and free-trade advocate Rahm Emanuel. One of the electoral races in which the local not only focused its energies, but demonstrated its progressive political ideology, was the Democratic primary contest for Chicago's heavily blue collar 5th Congressional District. While nearly all of the states' AFL-CIO labor unions endorsed Clinton-aide Rahm Emanuel, Local 705 worked on behalf of the more labor-friendly Nancy Kasak. Emanuel had earned 705's rebuff for his role as one of the architects of the North American Free Trade Agreement, which the Teamsters and AFL-CIO opposed. Local 705 official Paul Waterhouse defended the union's independent position in this race by noting that "Trade is an important election issue for working people in places where jobs are disappearing," and that labor leaders need "to be the ones standing strong on these issues."[4]

The local's political activism was also boldly and singularly displayed in its fall 2002 public declaration opposing the Congressional war resolution against Iraq. At a union general meeting in October, over 300 members overwhelmingly approved a "Resolution Against the War." The measure reads in part as follows:

> Whereas, we value the lives of our sons and daughters, of our brothers and sisters more than Bush's control of Middle East oil profits;
>
> Whereas, we have no quarrel with the ordinary working-class men, women, and children of Iraq who will suffer the most in any war;
>
> Whereas, the billions of dollars being spent to stage and execute this invasion, means of billions taken away from our schools, hospitals, housing, and social security;
>
> Whereas, Teamsters local 705 is known far and wide as fighters for justice;
>
> Be it resolved that Teamsters Local 705 stands firm against Bush's drive for war.[5]

As of mid-November, Local 705's declaration was the only one published by a Chicago area union.

Local 705 also kept up its exemplary record of showing support for the area labor movement. In late August of 2002, the Teamster local aided unionized hotel workers in their contract struggle with Chicago employers by contributing to the employees' Hungry for Justice Campaign.[6] Moreover, the union's organizing efforts have expanded with the appointment of two organizers assigned to the local from the IBT's national office, and by the end of 2002, 705 had signed up all the eligible area rail yards' employees.

Furthermore, a national and 705 Teamster contract with UPS was negotiated ahead of schedule in 2002 and included some impressive monetary improvements. Based in large part on the support of part-time workers, the local agreement was approved by 64 percent. Negotiation teams still make room for the rank and file, and crafts can be found holding prenegotiation proposal meetings. Most importantly, the local still involves reform activists and other leaders committed to rank-and-file unionism in policymaking. By standard accounts, Local 705's post-2000-election record appears consistent with the union's professed democratic principles.

But Local 705 is not a standard Teamster local, and questions have been raised about the union's direction. According to some 705ers, the post-2000 record reveals the local administration's troubling hesitation to fully practice what it preaches. Contrary voices charge that, while the local may not be rejecting wholesale the idea of union democracy, it has begun to practice a degree of retail extraction.

Critics have pointed to the fact that not quite as many dues-payers are sitting as consistently at the bargaining table or being invited as often to craft proposal meetings as before the 2000 election. They acknowledge that some new hires and job assignments have been made but believe that these moves have weakened the union's ability to represent the membership. And some prodemocracy advocates have complained about the unavailability of business agents at particular worksites or the lack of progress in processing grievances. Union reformers acknowledge that they have roles as business agents and stewards, but then they qualify their participation by stating that they are not as often counseled about local policy. One activist pointed out that, although the local is not formally in trusteeship, a Hoffa personal representative has been assigned to monitor the union's behavior. The implication was that the local had already been informally placed under Hoffa's control. Organizing is happening, detractors admit, but they state that fewer member volunteers are involved. In addition, though part-timers seemed pleased with the new local UPS labor agreement, there was considerable hostility to the deal on the part of many full-time hub drivers. Critics contend that this conflict was caused by the leadership's undemocratic disregard for the opinions of drivers.

Two major points of contention dividing pro-Zero and anti-Zero democrats are the dismissal of TDU activist and 705 business agent Richard DeVries and that recent labor agreement with UPS. Devries was fired by Zero in 2001 for his alleged failure to support administration policies, but DeVries's supporters believe he was jettisoned because of his uncompromising support for TDU-endorsed Tom Leedham in the Teamsters 2001 general election. Zero had backed Leedham in 1998 but shifted his allegiance to Hoffa three years later. And though these same union democrats admit that the UPS national and local contract has some real pluses for the members, they contend that it also includes a few major negatives and serious omissions. Critics argue that the single source of the local's major and minor problems was Zero's support for James P. Hoffa in the 2001 international officer election.

A number of union activists claim that Zero's past internal union political struggles forced him into an accommodation with the Teamster international president. For activists like DeVries and TDU 705 member Joe Allen, this was paramount to a surrender of the local's reform movement leadership. To these individuals, Hoffa represents, rightly or wrongly, everything the reformers have ever fought against at Local 705, and Zero's unwillingness to speak out strongly on behalf of Tom Leedham signaled that a democratic retrenchment had begun.

According to this perspective, Local 705 is not fulfilling its democratic potential because Hoffa is now influencing the local's behavior. To this charge, Zero defiantly declares, "Hoffa hasn't stopped me from doing anything."[7] He and other reformers acknowledge that the local did confront some financial and personnel problems that limited the local's expansion of rank-and-file-style unionism, but they insist that a temporary limit on the local's resources, and not political ideology, was to blame. The union leadership's defenders note that the problem of representation at some barns was caused not by dictatorial behavior but by the unexpected retirement and medical absence of business agents. Interestingly, even Zero's harshest reform-minded detractors admit that he is a unique, one-of-a-kind union leader who in principal remains deeply committed to union democracy. The problem, as his democratic opponents see it, is that Zero must now act cautiously and sometimes against his democratic nature because Hoffa is not friendly to reform. They contend that if Zero had backed Leedham or aggressively advanced reform measures too far, Hoffa would have acted punitively toward the local and might even have initiated another trusteeship.[8]

The result, according to Zero's one-time advocates, has not been a return to the old guard days nor a complete overhauling of the local's democratic procedures. Nevertheless, they insist that there is less rank-and-file activity and more top-down leadership. Reform critics have enunciated a list of ways that 705 has faltered, but their assessment can be summed up this way: although rank-and-file involvement programs still occur, the 705 leadership professes less enthusiasm for them. Thus, although the local may stage work stoppages and organize new members, the essence of reform has been frustrated. Zero and other local officers scoff at the idea that their commitment to rank-and-file unionism has waned. Most contend that even though it exposed a split in the local's political loyalties, Hoffa's election has not negatively influenced the governance of 705.

Despite the emerging internal debate, no one at Local 705 can credibly deny that the reformers (in any configuration) have maintained a higher performance and behavioral standard than the one in force before the trusteeship. While Zero may infuriate his democratic critics by acknowledging that Hoffa "has proven himself to be a great general president," he has also governed within a local democratic process—largely to his making—that continues to stress open debate and rank-and-file participation.[9] Reform may have settled into a plateau period, but regardless of what Zero and Hoffa's relationship is, Local 705 has not turned back the clock. What has developed in Chicago is the realization that local union reform requires a strong measure of institutional support from the international office.

It is apparent at 705, as at any other union local, that the international's union governance philosophy is of paramount importance to how the local is governed. Whatever particular influence Hoffa has had over Local 705, it will likely be different from that of the governing direction once provided by Ron Carey. This difference could have a substantial impact on the lives of 705 members, but there is no proof that Hoffa's influence is any more extraordinary or hegemonic than was Carey's. Although Carey's governing approach opened up possibilities for reform at 705, what ultimately developed in the local was a homegrown version of union democracy. Hoffa appears to govern with less opportunity for rank-and-file imprint, but what takes shape at 705 will probably not happen without contradiction. Put another way, Local 705's democratic birth was no more exactly in Carey's image than the present changes at 705 are in Hoffa's. Local 705's reform effort may sputter or speed up throughout the period in which Zero and Hoffa remain elected leaders, but it is certain that how the local is governed in the future will be linked to the political actions of Teamster members inside and outside of Chicago. If the post-2000 local election period has signified anything, it is that the fortunes of a democratic, independent Local 705 are now more dependent than ever before on Teamster politics.

Notes

Introduction

1. Kenneth C. Crowe, *Collision: How the Rank and File Took Back the Teamsters* (New York: Charles Scribner's, 1993), 91.

2. *Wall Street Journal*, 6 April 1998.

3. See Henry Faber, "Analysis of Union Behavior," in *Handbook of Labor Economics*, ed. Orley Ashenfelter and Richard Layard (Amsterdam: North Holland, 1986), 1031–90. Theoretical and empirical studies of local union restructuring and behavioral change have admirably addressed multiple subjects, and most have given some centrality to the importance of democratic unionism in achieving the goal of stronger unions. A few good and varied examples of the union-transformation literature include Paul Clark, *Building More Effective Unions* (Ithaca, N.Y.: ILR Press, 2000); Kim Voss and Rachel Sherman, "Breaking the Iron Law of Oligarchy: Union Revitalization in the American Labor Movement," *American Journal of Sociology* 106, no. 2 (September 2000): 303–49; Ray Tillman and Michael Cummings, eds., *The Transformation of U.S. Unions: Voices, Visions, and Strategies from the Grassroots* (Boulder: Lynne Rienner, 1999); Kate Bronfenbrenner, Sheldon Freidman, Richard Hurd, Rudolph Oswald, and Ronald Seebers, eds., *Organizing to Win: New Research on Union Strategies* (Ithaca, N.Y.: ILR Press, 1998); Tom McDonald and Peter Robson, *Unions 2001: A Blueprint for Trade Union Activism* (Sydney: Evatt Foundation, 1995); Paul Johnston, *Success While Others Fail: Social Movement Unionism and the Public Workplace* (Ithaca, N.Y.: ILR Press, 1994); Jane Jensen and Rianne Mahon, eds., *The Challenge of Restructuring; North American Labor Movements Respond* (Philadelphia: Temple University Press, 1992); Arthur Shostak, *Robust Unionism: Innovations in the Labor Movement* (Ithaca, N.Y.: ILR Press, 1991); Seymour Martin Lipset, *Unions in Transition* (San Francisco: Institute for Contemporary Studies, 1986); Thomas A. Kochan, ed., *Challenges and Choices Facing American Labor* (Cambridge, Mass.: MIT Press, 1985); Bruce Nissan, ed., *Which Direction for Labor? Essays in Organizing, Outreach, and International Transformation* (Detroit: Wayne State University Press, 1998); and Jo-Ann Mott, *Not Your Father's Labor Union: Inside the AFL-CIO* (New York: Verso Press, 1998).

4. "Teamsters Independent Review Board: Five Year Report 1992–1997, *United States v. IBT*, 88 Civil 4486 (DNE)," *Daily Labor Report* 218 (12 November 1997): E3–E17.

5. Dan E. Molden, *The Hoffa Wars: Teamsters, Rebels, Politicians, and the Mob* (New York: Paddington Press, 1978).

6. In Chicago, organized crime has been commonly referred to as the "Outfit" instead of the more East Coast referenced "La Costra Nostra" or "Mafia" (Chicago Crime Commission, *The New Faces of Organized Crime* (Chicago, 1997), 8.

7. Robert Kennedy, *The Enemy Within: The McClellan Committee's Crusade*

against Jimmy Hoffa and Corrupt Labor Unions (New York: Da Capo Press, 1964), 84–85. The quote appears in Michael Goldberg, "Cleaning Labor's House: Institutional Reform Litigation in the Labor Movement," *Duke Law Journal* 4 (1989): 944.

8. Kennedy, *The Enemy Within;* the quote comes from Crowe, *Collision,* 273. An excellent review of IBT reform efforts up to the 1989 Consent Order is Goldberg, "Cleaning Labor's House," 904–1011.

9. Crowe, *Collision,* 76. Kennedy, *The Enemy Within,* 161, quotes George Meany, ex-president of the AFL-CIO, who was speaking of Teamster president Jimmy Hoffa.

10. President's Commission on Crime, *The Edge: Organized Crime, Business, and Labor Unions: A Report to the President and the Attorney General* (Washington, D.C.: U.S. Government Printing Office, 1986); Crowe, *Collision;* Kenneth Conboy, Decision of Election Officer for the International Brotherhood of Teamsters, in "Cheatem, Spaerman, Hoffa Election Protests," 17 November 1997. The commentator is Goldberg, "Cleaning Labor's House," 904.

11. Paul Weinstein, "Racketeering and Labor: An Economic Analysis," *Industrial and Labor Relations Review* 19, no. 3 (1966): 402; Dan La Botz, "Teamsters and the Federal Government: Unhappy Marriage" (paper delivered at the Fifteenth Annual North American Labor History Conference, Wayne State University, Detroit, October 1993), 4–5.

12. Carey was later fully exonerated by a federal court (see Steven Greenhouse, "Former Teamster President Is Cleared of Lying Charges," *New York Times,* 13 October 2001, 8); "Teamsters Independent Review Board," E3–E17; Conboy, Decision of Election Officer; "Republican and Democratic Executive Summaries of House Subcommittee Report on Teamsters," *Daily Labor Report* 37 (25 February 1999): E39–E48; "Special Report: Teamsters Draft Plan for Reform Is Criticized and Defended," *Union Labor Report* 54, no. 16 (20 April 2000): 128. The quotation is from George Kannar, "Making the Teamsters Safe for Democracy," *Yale Law Review* 102 (1993): 1654–55.

13. The law is titled the Labor-Management Reporting and Disclosure Act, and a detailed description is provided by *The Labor Law Source Book,* (Cambridge, Mass.: Work Rights Press, 1999), 64–84.

14. Ligurotis had once before come very close to losing his union office. On the morning of August 21, 1991, local police arrested him for shooting in the back of the head and killing his adoptive son, Daniel C. Ligurotis Jr. Ligurotis junior was at the time on the staff of Local 705 and was killed during a dispute with his father in the basement of Teamster City. Ligurotis was eventually acquitted of the charge of second-degree murder (Leon Pitt, "Ligurotis Found Not Guilty; Judge Rules without Hearing Defense Case in Son's Killing," *Chicago Tribune,* 3 September 1992, News sec., 3).

15. A good overview of how unions benefit workers is provided in Richard Freeman and James Medorf's classic work *What Do Unions Do?* (New York: Basic Books, 1984) and in Toke Aidt and Zafiris Tzannatos's *Unions and Collective Bargaining: Economic Effects in a Global Enviroment* (Washington, D.C.: World Bank, 2002). Also the AFL-CIO has produced a curriculum titled "Common Sense Economics for Working Families" that provides a detailed comparison of union and nonunion workers. A few excellent accounts of organized labor's working-class political influence can be found in Daniel Cornfield, "The U.S. Labor Movement: Its Development and Impact on Social Inequality and Politics," *Annual Review of Sociology* 17 (1991): 27–49; Benjamin Radcliff and Patricia Davis, "Labor Organization and Electoral Participation in Industrial Democracies," *American Journal of Political Science Review* 44, no. 1 (January 2000): 132–41; Benjamin Radcliff, "Organized Labor and Electoral Participation in American National Elections," *Journal of Labor Research* 22, no. 2

(spring 2001): 405–14; and David Sousa, "Organized Labor in the Electorate, 1960–1988," *Political Research Quarterly* 46 (December 1993): 741–58.

16. Michael Belzer, *Sweatshops on Wheels: Winners and Losers in Trucking Deregulation* (New York: Oxford University Press, 2000), 21.

17. The quotation is in ibid., 223. Truckload carriers are "shipment[s] weighing more than 10,000 pounds"; the term also is used for "a carrier primarily hauling these large shipment[s]." *Less-than-truckload* means a "shipment weighing less than 10,000 pounds" or a "carrier hauling these small shipments" (201–4).

18. *American Trucking Trends, 1969* (Washington, D.C.: American Trucking Association, 1969); Tom Lewis, *Building Divided Highways: The Interstate Highways, Transforming American Life* (New York: Viking Press, 1997), 22.

19. Belzer, *Sweatshops on Wheels*, 28.

20. Ibid., 21.

21. Ibid., 38.

22. Freeman and Medoff, *What Do Unions Do?*

23. Karl Marx, letter to F. Bolte, "Economics and Politics in the Labor Movement," in *The Marx-Engels Reader*, 2d ed., ed. Robert Tucker (New York: W. W. Norton, 1978), 520.

24. Seymour Martin Lipset, Martin Trow, and James Coleman, *Union Democracy: What Makes Democracy Work in Labor Unions and Other Organizations?* (Garden City, N.Y.: Anchor Books, 1956). For works relating primarily to democracy, see Judith Stepan-Norris, "The Making of Union Democracy," *Social Forces* 76, no. 2 (December 1997): 475–510; Steven Fraser, "Is Democracy Good for Unions?" *Dissent* (summer 1998): 33–39; Stanley Aronowitz, "Union and Democracy," *Dissent* (winter 1999): 81–83; Michael Eisenscher, "Leadership Development and Organizing: For What Kind of Union?" *Labor Studies Journal* 24, no. 2 (summer 1999): 3–21; Paul Jarley, Sarosh Kuruvilla, and Douglas Casteel, "Member-Union Relations and Union Satisfaction," *Industrial Relations Journal* 29 (winter 1990): 128–34; and Jack Fiorito, Daniel G. Gallagher, and Cynthia V. Fukami, "Satisfaction with Union Representation," *Industrial and Labor Relations Review* 41 (January 1988): 294–307.

Organizational theory is dealt with in the following works: David J. Edelstein and Malcom Warner, *Comparative Union Democracy: Organization and Opposition in British and American Unions* (New Brunswick, N.J.: Transaction Books, 1979); Robert Michels, *Political Parties* (New York: Collier Books, 1962); Thomas P. Jenkin, "Oligarchy," in *International Encyclopedia of the Social Sciences*, ed. David L. Stills (New York: Free Press, 1968), 2:281–83; John D. May, "Democracy, Oligarchy, Michels," *American Political Science Review* 59 (June 1965): 417–29; G. Parry, *Political Elites* (London: George Allen and Unwin, 1969); and Lloyd Fisher and Grant McConnell, "Internal Conflict and Labor-Union Solidarity," in *Industrial Conflict*, ed. Arthur Kornhauser, Robert Dubin, and Arthur M. Ross (New York: McGraw Hill, 1954), 132–43.

25. Grant McConnell, *Private Power and American Democracy* (New York: Vintage, 1966); Samuel Estreicher, "Deregulating Union Democracy," in *The Internal Governance and Organizational Effectiveness of Labor Unions*, ed. Samuel Estreicher, Harry Katz, and Bruce Kaufman (New York: Kluwer Law International, 2001), 435–55; Seymour Martin Lipset, "The Political Process in Trade Unions: A Theoretical Statement," in *Labor and Trade Unionism*, ed. Walter Galenson and Seymour Martin Lipset (New York: John Wiley, 1960), 204.

26. Edelstein and Warner, *Comparative Union Democracy*.

27. Grant McConnell, "Factionalism and Union Democracy," *Labor Law Journal*

9 (1958): 635–40, and *Private Power and American Democracy;* Roderick Martin, "Union Democracy: An Explanatory Framework," *Sociology* 2 (May 1968): 205–20; Philip Nyden, *Steelworkers Rank-and-File: The Political Economy of a Union Reform Movement* (New York: Praeger Press, 1984); Judith Stepan-Norris and Maurice Zeitlin, "The Insurgent Origins of Union Democracy" in *Reexamining Democracy: Essays in Honor of Seymour Martin Lipset,* ed. Gary Marks and Larry Diamond (London: Sage, 1992); Ruth Needlemen, "Black Caucuses in Steel," *New Labor Forum* (fall–winter 1998): 41–56. On rank-and-file participation, see Bert Cochran, *Labor and Communism* (Princeton, N.J.: Princeton University Press, 1977); Mike Parker, "Appealing for Democracy," *New Labor Forum* (fall–winter 1998): 57–73; and Katherine Sciacchitano, "Unions, Organizing, and Democracy," *Dissent* (spring 2000): 75–81.

  28. William Leiserson, *American Trade Union Democracy* (New York: Columbia University Press, 1959); Judith Stepan-Norris and Maurice Zeitlin, "Union Democracy, Radical Leadership, and the Hegemony of Capital," *American Sociological Review* 60, no. 6 (December 1995): 829–50; George Strauss, "Union Democracy," in *The State of the Unions,* ed. George Strauss, Daniel Gallagher, and Jack Fiorito (Madison, Wis.: Industrial Relations Research Association, 1991); Robert Bruno, "Democratic Goods: Teamster Reform and Collective Bargaining Outcomes," *Journal of Labor Research* 21 (winter 2000): 83–102. For an empirical analysis of the effects of union democracy and bargaining outcomes, see Jack Fiorito and Wallace Henricks, "Union Characteristics and Bargaining Outcomes," *Industrial and Labor Relations Review* 40 (July 1987): 569. A case study approach was taken by Morris Kleiner and Adam Pilarski in "Does Internal Union Political Competition Enhance Its Effectiveness?" in *The Internal Governance and Organizational Effectiveness of Labor Unions,* ed. Samuel Estreicher, Harry Katz, and Bruce Kaufman (New York: Kluwer Law International, 2001), 75–101.

  29. The quotations are from Karl Marx, "Wages, Price and Profit," in *Karl Marx and Frederick Engels: Selected Works in Three Volumes* (Moscow: Progress Publishers, 1969–70), 31–76. On union governance, see Robert Taft, *The Structure and Government of Labor Unions* (Cambridge, Mass.: Harvard University Press, 1954); John Hemingway, *Conflict and Democracy: Studies in Trade Union Government* (New York: John Wiley, 1978); Jim Wallihan, *Union Government and Organization* (Washington, D.C.: Bureau of National Affairs, 1985); Morris Horowitz, *The Structure and Government of the Carpenters' Union* (New York: John Wiley, 1962); Lloyd Ulman, *The Government of the Steelworkers* (New York: John Wiley, 1962); Melvin Rothbaum, *The Government of the Oil, Chemical, and Atomic Workers Union* (New York: John Wiley, 1962); Sam Romer, *The International Brotherhood of Teamsters* (New York: John Wiley, 1962); Joel Isaac Seidman, *The Brotherhood of Railroad Trainmen: The Internal Political Life of a National Union* (New York: John Wiley, 1962); Leo Kramer, *Labor's Paradox: The American Federation of State, County, and Municipal Employees, AFL-CIO* (New York: John Wiley, 1962); Glenn Perusek, "Classical Political Sociology and Union Behavior," in *Trade Union Politics: American Unions and Economic Change, 1960s–1990s,* ed. Glenn Perusek and Kent Worcester (Atlantic Highlands, N.J.: Humanities Press, 1995), 57–76; Marick L. Masters, "AFSCME as a Political Union," *Journal of Labor Research* 19 (spring 1998): 313–49; Marten S. Estey, Philip Taft, and Martin Wagner, *Regulating Union Government* (New York: Harper and Row, 1964); Herman Benson, *How to Get an Honest Union Election* (New York: Association for Union Democracy, 1987); Clyde W. Summers, Joseph Rauh, and Herman Benson, *Union Democracy and Landrum-Griffin* (New York: Association for Union Democracy, 1986); and Arthur Z. Schwartz, "The Judicial Imperative—Court Intervention and the Protection of the

Right to Vote in Unions: A Case Study of *Fight Back Committee v. Gallagher*," *Hofstra Labor Law Journal* (spring 1987): 269–98.

On corruption and rank-and-file commitment, see Lester Velie, *Labor USA* (New York: Harper Brothers, 1959); Philip Taft, *Corruption and Racketeering in the Labor Movement*, ILR Bulletin 38 (Ithaca, N.Y.: Cornell University Press, 1970); John Hutchinson, *The Imperfect Union: A History of Corruption in American Trade Unions* (New York: E. P. Dutton, 1970); President's Commission on Crime, *The Edge: Organized Crime, Business, and Labor Unions: A Report to the President and the Attorney General* (Washington, D.C.: U.S. Government Printing Office, 1986); Allen Freidman and Ted Schwarz, *Power and Greed: Inside the Teamsters Empire of Corruption* (New York: Franklin Watts, 1989); Arthur Bowker, "Trust Violators in the Labor Movement: A Study of Union Embezzlement," *Journal of Labor Research* 19, no. 3 (summer 1998): 571–79; and Julian Barling, Clive Fullager, and Kevin E. Kelloway, *Union and Its Members: A Psychological Approach* (New York: Oxford University Press, 1992).

Dissenting caucuses are considered in James N. Edgar, "Union Democracy and the LMRDA: Autocracy and Insurgency in National Union Elections," *Harvard Civil Rights–Civil Liberties Law Review* (spring 1978): 247–356; and Nyden, *Steelworkers Rank-and-File;* and Crowe, *Collision.*

30. Paul F. Clark, Daniel G. Gallagher, and Thomas J. Pavlik, "Member Commitment in an American Union: The Role of the Grievance Procedure," *Industrial Relations Journal* 21 (summer 1990): 147–57; Fiorito, Gallagher, and Fukami, "Satisfaction with Union Representation," 294–307; Daniel Gallagher and Paul F. Clark, "Research on Union Commitment: Implications for Labor," *Labor Studies Journal* 14 (spring 1989): 213–27; Jarley, Kuruvilla, and Casteel, "Member-Union Relations and Union Satisfaction," 128–34; Lucy A. Newton and Lynn McFarland Shore, "Model of Union Membership: Instrumentality, Commitment, and Opposition," *Academy of Management Review* 17 (April 1992): 275–98.

1. Teamsters' Power and Politics

1. Robert Ziegler, *The CIO: 1935–1955* (Chapel Hill: University of North Carolina Press, 1995), 359.

2. Michael Belzer, *Sweatshops on Wheels: Winners and Losers in Trucking Deregulation* (New York: Oxford University Press, 2000), 24.

3. Dan La Botz, *Rank and File Rebellion* (New York: Verso Press, 1990), 120.

4. Belzer, *Sweatshops on Wheels,* 27.

5. Dane E. Moldea, *The Hoffa Wars: Teamsters, Rebels, Politicians, and The Mob* (New York: Paddington Press, 1978), 293–95. Unsealed documents later revealed that Presser was also an FBI agent (see Kenneth Crowe, *Collision: How The Rank and File Took Back the Teamsters* [New York: Charles Scribner's, 1993]).

6. Barbara Zack Quindel, Summary of Decision, Election Officer for the International Brotherhood of Teamsters, in "Cheatem, Spaerman, Hoffa Election Protests," 21 August 1997; Kenneth Conboy, Decision of Election Officer for the International Brotherhood of Teamsters, in "Cheatem, Spaerman, Hoffa Election Protests," 17 November 1997.

7. Motivated by intensifying Teamster organizing, Hobbs made it a felony to obstruct the movement of goods and services in interstate commerce by means of extortion. Despite Truman's claim that the law would not in any way "interfere with the rights of unions in carrying out their legitimate objectives," the act extended the

list of conventional actions that could be defined as criminal extortion and subsequently used against labor organizers (*Congress and the Nation*, vol. 1, *1945–1964* [Washington, D.C.: Congressional Quarterly, Inc., 1965], 565–657, quotation on 567).

8. The Landrum-Griffin Act (the Labor-Management Reporting and Disclosure Act) was passed in 1959 as a result of scandalous Senate hearings depicting, for the most part, corruption in the Teamsters union. For an account of the Senate hearings, see Robert Kennedy, *The Enemy Within: The McClellan Committee's Crusade against Jimmy Hoffa and Corrupt Labor Unions* (New York: Da Capo Press, 1994); and for a description of the law, see Bruce Feldacker, *Labor Guide to Labor Law*, 3d ed. (Englewood Cliffs, N.J.: Prentice Hall, 1990). The quotation is in Moldea, *The Hoffa Wars*, 147.

9. "The Daily Phone Diary of President Jimmy Carter," Jimmy Carter Library and Museum.

10. One last exception in the run of Republican endorsements was made for Hubert Humphrey in 1968. The new international union president, Frank Fitzsimmons, and the executive board unanimously endorsed the Democrat because they feared that Nixon would release Hoffa from prison. At the time it was widely believed, within Teamster circles, that Nixon had agreed to grant Hoffa a presidential pardon if elected. Hoffa's release would have set up a royal battle for control of IBT. As it happened, Nixon did pardon Hoffa in 1971, and then in 1975 the former union leader mysteriously "disappeared" (see Moldea, *The Hoffa Wars*, 293–95). The quotation is in Crowe, *Collision*, 26.

11. The quotation is in Crowe, *Collision*, 265.

12. The Teamsters, along with the Carpenters and the Building and Construction Trades Department of the AFL-CIO, endorsed Bush's plan to drill for oil in the Alaskan wildlife preserve (see Jim Larkin, "As Teamster-Turtle Ties Fray, Hoffa Faces Rematch with Leedham: Which Way for the Teamsters?" *Nation*, 8 October 2001).

13. Historically, two Chicago IBT locals, 705 and 710, have negotiated their own agreements with trucking companies. Neither local has ever been covered by the NMFA or any other national agreement. A third drivers' union, the non-IBT Independent Chicago Drivers Union (CDU), also negotiated contracts. In 2001 CDU merged with Local 710.

14. Jean Y. Tussey, ed., *Eugene V. Debs Speaks* (New York: Pathfinder Press, 1970), 71. The article was printed in the *Chicago Socialist*, 25 October 1902. The second quotation is from a Local 705 publication dated 12 February 1970.

15. Robert Spinney, *City of Big Shoulders: A History of Chicago* (DeKalb: Northern Illinois University Press, 2000), 43; Daphne Spain, *How Women Saved the City* (Minneapolis: University of Minnesota Press, 2001), 36.

16. Steven Pott, "The Chicago Teamsters' Strike of 1902: A Community Confronts the Beef Trust," *Labor History* 26, no. 2 (spring 1985): 250–67.

17. *Chicago Daily Tribune*, 30 December 1903.

18. "Employers Plan to Crush Union," *Chicago American*, 17 November 1904.

19. "War on Unions Believed Near," *Chicago Daily Tribune*, 3 December 1903. *Chicago Daily Tribune*, 6 April 1905.

20. "Employer Wants to Kill Union Workers," *New Majority*, 26 April 1919, 1.

21. "Asmus Jessen Shot by Strike Gunman," *New Majority*, 10 May 1919, 5.

22. Steven Brill, *The Teamsters* (New York: Simon and Schuster, 1978), 260.

23. Joseph Rasch dues book, 1911; "Labor Party Candidates for the Illinois State Constitutional Convention," *New Majority*, 25 October 1919.

24. Ezra Warner, owner representative, to Local 705, 4 August 1919.

25. The term *barn* obviously applied to a stable for horses, but Teamster drivers a hundred years later still refer to their work sites as barns. "Cartage Agreement with Local 705," 1934.

26. "Service Station Agreement with Local 705," 1939; "Contract Approved under General Order No. 40 of the National War Labor Board," 1945; "Master Cartage Agreement with Local 705," 1950.

27. Main Brief of Local 705, International Brotherhood of Teamsters and Independent 705 Chicago Truck Drivers, in the Matter of IBT 705 and Chicago Truck Drivers and the Cartage Exchange and Illinois Motor Truck Operators Association, National War Labor Board, Trucking Commission, 9 February 1943.

28. Program of 29th Annual Pension Meeting of Local Union 705 of IBT, 8 November 1985, Chicago; "Chicago Area Teamsters Win Increase, New Pact," *Chicago Federation of News*, 4 January 1958, 3; *Our First Century*, ed. Jeff Weiss and S. J. Peters for the Chicago Federation of Labor, special publication to honor the CFL's 100th anniversary (available at the CFL).

29. Arthur Sloan, *Hoffa* (Cambridge, Mass.: MIT Press, 1991), 278. IBT 705 Special Meeting Minutes, 1959.

30. Samuel Friedman, *Teamster Rank and File: Power, Bureaucracy, and Rebellion at Work and in a Union* (New York: Columbia University Press, 1980).

31. Information News Bank Abstract, *New York Times*, 9 April 1970, 37. "Fight for Wage Stability," *New York Times*, 7 May 1970, 42.

32. James Strong, "Two Drivers Unions Reject Terms for Their New Contract," *Chicago Tribune*, 25 March 1970, sec. 1, p. 7.

33. Friedman, *Teamster Rank and File*, 137.

34. Strong, "Two Drivers Unions Reject Terms."

35. A 1975 strike was mentioned in Weiss and Peters, *Our First Century*. Another in 1976 was reported in Information News Bank Abstracts, *New York Times*, 1 November 1976, 36. In 1979 there were nearly five thousand Local 705 UPS members. According to Belzer, a common carrier is a "carrier that offers its services to the public according to published rates" (*Sweatshop on Wheels*, glossary, 201). The data on UPS expansion in the 1960s is taken from a UPS special publication titled *50 Years Serving the Chicago Area*, from Metro Chicago *Big Idea* newsletter, June 1990, 2–6.

36. Local 705 organized the firm's workforce, except for the over-the-road drivers. The jurisdiction for over-the-road UPS drivers in Chicago belonged to Local 710. (Information about the merger is from retired UPS and Local 725 member Tony Bielick, interview by author, 4 October 2001.)

37. As of January 1999, Local 705's membership was distributed approximately as follows: UPS, 11,000; cartage, 1,200; air freight, 1,000; freight, 1,000; tankers, 600; liquor division, 300; movers, 200; municipalities, 150; and grocery houses, 100. There are also about 500 UPS long-haul drivers organized at Local 710.

38. File on IBT 705 picnic, 1963 and 1964.

39. For a good description of how the over-the-road trucking industry changed and its implications for unionization, see Belzer, *Sweatshops on Wheels*. Louis Peick, "Growing Duties of Labor Leadership, *Chicago Federation of News*, September 1976, 14.

40. F. C. Duke Zeller, *Devil's Pact: Inside the World of the Teamsters* (Secaucus, N.J.: Union Birch Lane Press, 1997), 267. McCarthy soon had a change of perspective and came to view Ligurotis as a usurper of power. McCarthy then unsuccessfully attempted to remove Ligurotis from his Central State Conference directorship (312).

2. Fighting Corruption

1. Phillip Dine, "James Hoffa Is Rekindling the Unity in the Teamsters That His Father Bred," *St. Louis Post-Dispatch*, 4 June 2000, A12. Joey Glimco, the head of Teamsters Cab Drivers Local 777, was a notorious member of the Capone gang; he was accused of the car-bombing of a rival union official. *Chicago Sun-Times*, 1 June 1950. In addition, the one-time "Chicago-Capo," Joe "The Clown" Lombardo, controlled the infamous Teamsters Central States Pension Fund. It was also in Chicago where in 1983 Allen Dorfman, allegedly a Teamster union bagman and connected with the crime syndicate, was gunned down in a suburban parking lot (*Chicago Crime Commission Annual Report*, Chicago, 1969). Jon Hahn, "Order Teamsters to Repay Millions," *Chicago News*, 6 July 1973.

2. *T.R.U.T.H.* (newsletter), vol. 1, no. 4, March 1974.

3. Minutes of Membership Meeting, 18 October 1973.

4. Robert Persak, interview by author, 7 September 2001, Chicago. Persak now serves as a Local 705 representative. Subsequent quotations in this chapter from Persak, unless cited otherwise, are also from this interview.

5. A harsh condition of the 705 plan required that there be no voluntary or involuntary "break-in-service" in accumulating the years necessary to be eligible for retirement pay. A survey of thirty-two pension plans representing more than half of the Teamster membership revealed that no other plan would have disqualified a worker under Daniel's circumstances. Daniel's case became a class action involving retirees at fifty other Teamster locals (*John Daniel v. International Brotherhood of Teamsters*, 76-1855, U.S. Court of Appeals, Seventh District, Lexis 11915, 20 August 1977).

6. "Internal Report," 12 February 1978, 2 April 1978.

7. TDU evolved out of Teamsters for a Democratic Contract. The story of TDU's origins and accomplishments is best told in Dan La Botz, *Rank and File Rebellion* (New York: Verso Press, 1990); and Kenneth Crowe, *Collision: How the Rank and File Took Back the Teamsters* (New York: Charles Scribner's, 1993). See p. 19 in the latter work for the account of incidents in Romulus.

8. Minutes of Membership Meeting, 15 March 1984.

9. La Botz, *Rank and File Rebellion*, 190.

10. Local 705 flyer, 18 May 1972; Minutes of Membership Meeting, 19 October 1978; John McCormick, interview by author, Chicago, 20 October 1998.

11. Crowe, *Collision;* Dan E. Moldea, *The Hoffa Wars: Teamsters, Rebels, Politicians, and the Mob* (New York: Paddington Press, 1978). See Phil Dine, "Teamster Revolution Has Diverse Leaders," *St. Louis Post-Dispatch*, 10 January 1992, 1B; Bob Herguth, "Leroy Ellis," *Chicago Sun-Times*, 14 September 1992, Chicago Profile sec., 12; and Peter Elstrom, "Teamster Leader Entering Rocky Ring," *Crain's Chicago Business*, 6 January 1992, 3. The quoted phrases are from Minutes of Membership Meeting, 20 November 1975.

12. Bill Kelly, phone interview by author, 10 March 2002.

13. John McCormick, Local 705 Grievance File, no. 00551, 30 October 1979.

14. Robert Maziarka, phone interview by author, 9 March 2002.

15. National Labor Relations Board, 13-CB-13080, 4 September 1990.

16. Minutes of Membership Meetings, 15 October 1981, 18 October 1994, 15 October 1987, 18 October 1990; Mike Belzer, interview by author, Chicago, 21 September 2001; Gerald Zero, interview by author, 26 September 2001, Chicago. Subsequent quotations in this chapter from Belzer, unless cited otherwise, are also from this interview.

17. Another bylaw change on the list required that all officer salaries be approved by the rank and file. It was recommended that elected membership committees be formed to internally audit all union funds and investments, to process grievances, and to negotiate contracts. Other measures required that strikes be called or ended only with a majority vote of the rank and file. Minutes of Membership Meetings, 18 May 1978, 20 October 1977, 18 April 1984; Bennie Jackson, interview by author, Chicago, 20 October 1998.

18. Ken Paff, TDU national organizer and chairman, is quoted from an issue of *Convoy*, TDU's paper, by La Botz, *Rank and File Rebellion*, 159.

19. Letter and report to Ron Carey, 25 May 1993.

20. *Teamster Local 705 News* 3, no. 1 (April 1996): 1.

21. Minutes of general executive board (GEB), 9 October 1992. The quoted protest is from two former secretary-treasurers, Daniel Ligurotis and Louis Peick (Minutes of Membership Meeting, Local 705, 20 January 1983).

22. Crowe, *Collision*, 120; Harold Burke to officers and members of Local 705, notice about a trusteeship hearing, 15 July 1993.

23. Harold Burke to Teamster Joint Council, letter and floor plan, 13 July 1993; Burke to all Local 705 representatives, agents, and staff, memorandum and attached copy of handbill from Committee to Defend Local 705.

24. Minutes of GEB, 11 November 1992.

25. Carey to Zero, letter and certificate of appointment, 18 July 1994; Zero to Carey, 22 December 1994.

26. Gerald Zero, interview by author, Chicago, 18 December 2000.

27. Dane Passo, interview by author, Rosemont, Ill., 22 December 2000. Subsequent quotations in this chapter from Passo, unless cited otherwise, are also from this interview.

28. Charges against Certain Members of Local 705, under the International Brotherhood of Teamsters Constitution, *Ron Carey v. Dane Passo et al.*, 12 April 1994; Ethical Practices Committee Hearing on Charges against Local 705 Members Dane Passo et al., 6 December 1994. Along with Passo, Ralph Mancini and presidential candidate James Colgan were also suspended. In response to their suspensions, Passo, Mancini, and Colgan filed a lawsuit against Carey and Zero. The three sought an injunction to overturn the suspension and to stop Zero from conducting the officer election (*Colgan et al. v. Carey and Zero*, 94-C-5685, U.S. District Court for the Northern District of Illinois, Eastern Division, 1995). Interestingly, Colgan was the father of union representative Mike Colgan and a key Breakfast Club participant.

29. Dennis M. Sarsany, election officer, to Zero, "IBT Local 705 Office Election Results," 11 April 1995; Carey to Zero, 13 April 1995; Gerald Zero, interview by author, Chicago, 7 December 1998.

30. Much of the opposition was constituted within those constituencies represented by the competing 1995 election slates ("Decision on Protest to 1995 Election of Officers and Business Agents of Local 705," IBT Joint Council No. 25, 1 November 1995) and from members antagonistic to the very idea of a trusteeship.

31. Zero interview, 26 September 2001.

32. Local 705's 1997 summer strike paralleled the national walkout called by the international IBT. But because Local 705 negotiates a separate stand-alone agreement with UPS, it stayed on the picket line for one week after the international union agreed to settle with the company.

33. It was common in past 705 officer elections for 400 to 500 ballots never to

be removed from their mailing envelopes. These were ballots submitted by workers who were later determined to be ineligible voters. Members' ballots were typically ruled ineligible on the grounds that the person had not paid his or her dues in full prior to the month of the election. This time an inordinately large volume of part-time UPS workers had cast nearly all of the ballots checked for eligibility. Passo rightly believed that if eligible members cast these ballots, his chances of being elected were substantially improved. But the election officer, Dennis Sarsany, ruled that hundreds of the ballots were invalid.

34. "Teamster Local 705 Officer Election, Announcement of Results," from Election Officer Dennis Sarsany, 17 December 1997. Paff's statement is recorded in Diane Lewis, "Reform Candidates Take Teamsters Election in Chicago," *Boston Globe,* 9 December 1997, Economy sec., 2. Michael Holland, interview by author, Chicago, 15 January 1999; Holland is a Chicago-based labor attorney who has represented Local 705 since the trusteeship and was also the election officer for the first IBT referendum election in 1991.

35. Peggy Hillman, interview by author, Chicago, 21 March 2000.

3. Democratic Governance

1. The quotation is from Michael Matejka, *Fiery Struggle: Illinois Fire Fighters Build a Union, 1901–1985* (Chicago: Illinois Labor History Society, 2002), 61. Lass's firefighter career is described there also.

2. Gerald Zero, interview by author, Chicago, 7 December 1998.

3. Minutes of a Special GEB Meeting, 21 September 1976.

4. *Clarence Campbell et al. v. Local Union 705,* 76-C-4240, Memorandum Opinion and Order, U.S. District Court, 8 May 1978.

5. Campbell et al., Supplement to Complaint, Count II, 19 March 1978.

6. Minutes of Membership Meetings, January 1972–May 1993.

7. Elroy W. Heniff, Joint Area Tank Truck Association employer, to Louis Peick, IBT Local 705 secretary-treasurer, 7 September 1983; Minutes of Membership Meeting, 15 April 1982.

8. Minutes of GEB Meeting, 25 April 1995. Every officer and representative whom I interviewed recounted examples of temporary "power outages."

9. The total is from meetings held between January 1997 and December 1998. Meetings were not held from April to December 1995, and records from January to December 1996 were unavailable.

10. From Charles Fuller Voices, 29 June 1987, treatment outline of video titled "The Spirit, the Pride, the Teamsters of 705."

11. Michael Holland, interview by author, Chicago, 15 January 1999. Subsequent quotations in this chapter from Holland, unless cited otherwise, are also from this interview.

12. Minutes of GEB, January 1996–December 1998.

13. Michael Colgan, interview by author, Chicago, 11 January 1999.

14. Mark Postilion, interview by author, Chicago, 11 January 1999. The Brotherhood of Loyal Americans and Strong Teamsters was formed in the 1970s to terrorize TDU supporters (See Kenneth C. Crowe, *Collision: How the Rank and File Took Back the Teamsters* [New York: Charles Scribner's, 1993], 178).

15. Gerald Zero, interview by author, Chicago, 7 December 1998.

16. Charlie Teas, interview by author, Chicago, 14 December 1998.

17. "Local 705 Craft Meeting Schedule," 1997; Craft Meeting Agendas, 23 March 1997–24 November 1998; Jim Lyons, interview by author, Chicago, 12 December 1998. Subsequent quotations in this chapter from Lyons, unless cited otherwise, are also from this interview.

18. Seminars have been taught by the author, and DePaul University in Chicago offers labor education classes. *705 Update* 2, no. 2 (March 1998): 3.

19. One exception to this was a conference on organizing in the transportation industry (Minutes of GEB, 18 January 1978).

20. *705 Update* 1, no. 4 (May 1997): 15

21. Paul Waterhouse, interview by author, Chicago, 10 December 1998. The survey was conducted by the author, and the results were published in Robert Bruno, "Consenting to be Governed: Union Transformation and Teamster Democracy," *Advances in Industrial and Labor Relations* (2002).

22. *705 CACH-Update,* 11 June 1990.

23. In responses to a set of court interrogatories, the defendants (i.e., the deposed Local 705 officers) revealed that no more that 130 "Officers, etc." attended membership meetings from 1974 to 1978. In addition, membership meeting minutes indicated that from 1987 until 1993, no more than 89 stewards ($X = 58$) were ever in attendance (*Campbell v. Local Union 705,* 1978).

24. James Harris, interview by author, Chicago, 6 March 1999.

25. Benjamin Barber, *Strong Democracy: Participatory Politics for a New Age* (Berkeley: University of California Press, 1984), 3.

26. See assorted announcements, agendas, and enrollment reports, January–December 1998, and materials from Pocztowski files. The Trakys quotation is in *705 Update* 1, no. 2 (January 1997): 3.

27. Nick Slusher, Robert Coleman, Jim McKee, and Rick Carlucci, interviews by author, Chicago, 6 March 1999.

28. *Convoy Dispatch,* no. 172, October–November 1998, 7.

29. Election results taken from Local 705 voting records, May 2002.

30. UPS charged that in 1997 the local had violated the law by staging an illegal seven-hour strike. The company contended that the union had breached the collective bargaining "no-strike" provision by not arbitrating deadlocked grievances. Teamster attorneys countered that the agreement permitted a work stoppage where UPS fails "to comply with any final decisions." The court agreed with the local's interpretation and concluded "that Local 705 could initiate a strike because the language of the collective bargaining agreement permits this action for violation of a previous settlement" (*UPS v. IBT et al.,* U.S. District Court, Northern District of Illinois, 95-C-6304, 29 September 1998). Minutes of Membership Meeting, 18 October 1998; *Chicago Tribune,* 19 December 1998.

4. Democracy Brings Results

1. J. G. A. Pocock, "The Idea of Citizenship since Classical Times," in *Theorizing Citizenship,* ed. Ronald Beiner (Albany: State University of New York Press, 1995), 35.

2. Minutes of GEB Meetings, 20 September, 19 January 1996.

3. Ibid., 28 April, 16 July, 11 August 1995.

4. Ibid., 11 August 1995. The quotations are in ibid., 14 November 1997 and 15 May 1998.

5. Ibid., 17 June, 28 April 1998.

6. Ibid., 15 March 1996.

7. "Results of UPS Grievance Meetings," 1995–1998.

8. "Chicago Area Consolidation Hub (CACH)," news release from United Parcel Service, n.d.

9. Ledger numbers 27-353 (1980), 36-693 (1982), 1193 (1979), 26-088 (1979). These quotations make up a tiny representative sample from a very large correspondence file.

10. Ibid.

11. J. Jeffrey Zimmerman, Esq., to IBT 705 business agent Frank Snow, 17 June 1992.

12. Only 85 cases were "settled" prior to the trusteeship.

13. *705 Update* 1, no. 4 (May 1997): 16.

14. "Local 705 Arbitration Files."

15. An accurate accounting of board charges filed by the local's pretrusteeship legal representatives was impossible to compile from available records. It is unlikely, however, given the previous comparisons of grievances and arbitrations, that the old regime was a stronger advocate of members' rights than their more recent counterparts ("Local 705 Weekly Status Report on National Labor Relations Board Cases"). *705 Update* 2, no. 5 (September 1995): 1.

16. *705 Update* 2, no. 4 (July 1998): 8.

17. "705 Membership of T.S.C" to Dan Ligurotis, letter and petition, 10 July 1991; "Security Lumber and Supply Company Workforce" to Peick, 10 April 1979.

18. See, for example, Minutes of Special Meetings, July–September 1973; and "Local 705 Notice," 22 October 1991. The quotations are from Minutes of Membership Meeting, 3 September 1973, and Tom Nightwine, interview by author, Chicago, 7 January 1999. Subsequent quotations in this chapter from Nightwine, unless cited otherwise, are also from this interview.

19. *705 Update* 1, no. 1 (October 1996).

20. "UPS-705 Negotiating Committee Rank-and-File Notes," May–August 1997, emphasis added.

21. "Local 705 Contract Files," 1994–1998, 1971–1985. Local 705 Trial Committee Hearing transcripts, 31 March 1974.

22. Gerald Zero, interview by author, Chicago, 7 December 1998.

23. Local 705 has always negotiated completely separate agreements with UPS, freight, and cartage employers. Over the years, this practice has allowed it to win contractual gains that exceeded the benefits negotiated under national agreements.

24. Richard DeVries, interview by author, Chicago, 14 December 1998; Local 705–Chicago Movers agreements, 1987 and 1990. Subsequent quotations in this chapter from DeVries, unless cited otherwise, are also from this interview.

25. Movers' Association of Greater Chicago, Individual Employers in the Moving Industry, 1987 and 1990 Labor Agreements.

26. IBT attorney Peggy Hillman to Elizabeth Kinney, regional director, Region 13, NLRB, 2 May 1994.

27. Paul DiGrazia, interview by author, Chicago, 3 December 1998.

28. Minutes of Membership Meetings, 16 February, 18 May 1989. Quotation from Gregory Foster, interview by author, Chicago, 7 December 1998. Fosco generated some unwanted publicity for the local when he was charged with "aggravated battery" for beating up a nonunion truck driver who attempted to cross a strike picket line. The charges were eventually dropped (Tim Gerber, "Teamsters Member

Charged in Beating," *Chicago Sun-Times,* 27 April 1994, 11).

29. Minutes of GEB Meetings, 17 January 1997; 15 February, 19 April 1998.

30. *705 Update* 2, no. 4 (July 1998): 4; 1, no. 2 (January 1997): 11. In one case, local members established that UPS management was using the "wrong people to do two jobs," and consequently the company was required to create new positions (*705 Update* 1, no. 2 [January 1997]: 6).

31. *705 Update* 1, no. 6 (September 1997): 10.

32. Ibid., 2, no. 1 (January 1998): 10.

33. Financial figures taken from Local Union 705 Political Contributions from 1994 to 2002. *705 Update* 1, no. 4 (May 1997): 3.

34. *705 Update* 1, no. 3 (March–April 1997): 14.

35. Michael Matejka, *Fiery Struggle: Illinois Fire Fighters Build a Union, 1901–1985* (Chicago: Illinois Labor History Society, 2002).

36. Michael Flannery and Alan Mutter, "Firefighters Reach Accord with Byrne," *Chicago Sun-Times,* 23 February 1980.

37. The story of the confrontation and the quote came from Dale Berry, who during the work stoppage was Firefighters Local 2's attorney and a key union strategist. Dale Berry, interview by author, Chicago, 17 October 2002.

38. The quotation from letters of appreciation is in ibid., 1, no. 6 (September 1997): 11. For an account of the Decatur labor disputes, see Steve Franklin, *Three Strikes: Labor's Heartland Losses and What They Mean for Working Americans* (New York: Guilford Press, 2001). "Chicago Teamsters Help End Actors' Strike," *705 Update* 4, no. 6 (December 2000): 3.

39. From the text of edited remarks delivered by artist Mike Alewitz at the mural dedication, September 1997.

40. Foster interview.

5. The Reformers Split

1. Van Barns, interview by author, Chicago, 8 January 2001.

2. *The People of the State of Illinois v. Gerald Zero,* Appellate Court of Illinois, First District, 96-MC1-25404, 2 June 1998, 4, 6, quotations on 3 and 4. A second defendant, Nick Petrecca, claimed that Zero grabbed him "in a bear hug and rammed him down the stairs into a steel girder" (3).

3. The quotations are from the appeal's court order, ibid., 9. Zero's defense cited four different arguments. He argued, first, that his affirmative defense was not properly considered at trial and, second, that the trial court had erred in excluding evidence establishing the tendency of Passo to "forcibly disrupt union meetings." Counsel further added that the evidence failed to sustain a verdict of guilty beyond a reasonable doubt. Finally, Zero maintained that the court had prejudiced the evidence against him, "thus violating his right to a fair and impartial trial" (ibid., 1).

4. Report from Independent Review Board to Local 705 Executive Board in the matter of "Proposed Charges against Local 705 Member Gerald Zero," 13 November 1996, 1.

5. Ibid.

6. Ibid.

7. His candidacy for a third term would have been destroyed because according to the IBT constitution, "a member must be in continuous good standing in the Local Union in which he is a member . . . for a period of twenty-four (24) consecutive

months prior to the month of nominations" for the office the individual is seeking (*Constitution of the International Brotherhood of Teamsters*, adopted 24th International Convention, sec. 4 [a] [1], 24–28 June 1991, 9–10).

8. Minutes of GEB Meeting, 14 January 2000.

9. The actual vote to file charges was five to one with one trustee joining the majority, one opposing, and one abstaining (ibid.).

10. Gerald Zero, lecture at CWS on 15 January, Chicago.

11. Michael Holland to John McCormick, subject: "Withdrawal from Representation, Local 705 Executive Board," 20 January 2000.

12. According to McCormick, organized representatives would constitute a form of "dual unionism" and would be in violation of the IBT's constitution. "Who are you loyal to?" McCormick asked, in explaining the problem he had with unionized representatives. "Do you promote the Teamsters' agenda or the mineworkers?" McCormick expressed no opposition to entering into a labor agreement with the half-dozen or so clerical employees. He pointed out that the secretaries "aren't responsible for filing grievances or conducting the union's business." The representatives, in contrast, must enforce the union's program and "can't have contrary interests" (interview by author, Chicago, 28 September 1999).

13. Gerald Zero, interview by author, Chicago, 18 December 2000.

14. Katina Barnett, interview by author, Chicago, 21 November 2000.

15. John McCormick, interview by author, Chicago, 28 September 2000.

16. John B. McCormick to Tom Nightwine, 29 June 1999; John B. McCormick to Ron Damerjian, memo, subject: Tom Nightwine, 29 June 1999.

17. "Notice to Employees," Teamster Local Union 705, Case 13-CA-38198-2, 25 July 2000.

18. McCormick interview, 28 September 2000.

19. *Sam Lodovico v. Gerald Zero*, internal union charge, 10 February 2000.

20. IBT Local 705, Executive Board Meeting Minutes, 1 September 2000. A third charge was also brought against Zero by dismissed representative William Blake. Blake had also voted against the mineworkers, but apparently without conviction. In a bizarre turn of attitude, Blake later accepted a nomination to run for the staff's new union executive board. As in the Lodovico case, a McCormick-appointed local union panel dismissed Blake's charges by a two-to-one vote. The fourth representative discharged did not bring charges. He not only opposed the organizing drive but also was a McCormick-recommended UPS representative. There is one last ironic twist to the coal miners' saga. Three of the four fired employees who rejected mineworker protection during the certification vote contacted UMW regional director Jerry Cross about appealing their discharge. He offered to defend them and requested additional information from each representative. None responded. See *William Blake v. Gerald Zero*, internal union charges, in Minutes of GEB Meeting, 11 May 2000.

21. This quotation and all accompanying quotations about the "Accord" are taken directly from Leedham's handwritten settlement dated 26 January 2000.

22. Charge one accused Zero of threatening to fire a union representative for "non job related activities." Charge two alleged that Zero had offered to remove Ed Bensech from the Health and Welfare and Pension Fund and appoint Jackson if he would "support Brother Zero in his union activities to regain his position as Principal Officer." The third charge was that Zero had "made claims to Brother Jackson that Brothers John McCormick and Ed Benesch were racist." In charge four the secretary-treasurer was accused of contravening a directive of the local board in negotiating a

"Tentative Agreement with the UMWA [United Mine Workers of America], who was representing Local 705 Staff." Charge five reported that Zero had given "pre-approval" to two staff employees for "12 weeks leave, with full pay and benefits for Disability, without any prior medical documentation." Charge six accused Zero of "knowingly and without Local 705 executive board approval provid[ing] raises for Elected Business Agents" ("A Notice of Filing," in a letter from John McCormick to Robert Barnes, secretary of IBT Joint Council 25, subject: "Charges against Gerald Zero," 7 February 2000).

23. John McCormick, interview by author, Chicago, 17 May 2000.

24. Gerald Zero, "An Open Letter to Local 705 Members." Zero actually mentioned "Gang of Four" four times.

25. Ibid.

26. In 1977 Harold Leu defeated Omar Brown for the presidency of an IBT local. During the campaign appointed business agents had publicly supported Brown for reelection. Upon taking office, Leu fired the business agents who had backed the incumbent, claiming that they would be unable to follow and implement the new president's policies and programs. The appointed agents then brought a lawsuit under the 1959 Labor-Management Reporting and Disclosure Act, alleging that as union members they had been fired for their protected political activities. But since the agents working for Leu's opponent did not have their union membership negatively impacted, they suffered no unwarranted "discipline" for acting politically. The Supreme Court established "that a union president should be able to work with those who will cooperate with his program and carry out his directives" (*Finnegan v. Leu*, 456 U.S. 431; 102 Supreme Court 1867; 1982, Lexis-Nexis Legal Texts, 1–9). In a footnote explaining the law's legislative history, the decision pointed out that as originally passed by the Senate, Title I of the LMRDA protected "any member *or officer* [emphasis in original] of a labor organization." However, in conference the words "or officer" were deleted from the final bill (H.R. 8400) (6).

27. *John McCormick et al. v. Gerald Zero*, 00-C-2750, U.S. District Court, Northern District of Illinois, Eastern Division, Temporary Restraining Order, 24 May 2000.

28. *Sheet Metal Workers' International v. Lynn*, 488 U.S. 347; 109 Supreme Court 639; 1989 in Lexis-Nexis Legal Text 432. The opinion for a unanimous court was written by Justice Thurgood Marshall. Labor organizations are required to annually submit a detailed set of Labor-Management Reporting and Disclosure (L-M), statements. L-M 2 reports include a list of the names of all union employees, their positions, and the salaries paid to them.

29. *John McCormick et al. v. Gerald Zero*, 00-C-2750, U.S. District Court, Northern District of Illinois, Eastern Division, Finding of Facts and Conclusion of Law, 23 August 2000.

30. Zero interview, 18 December 2000.

31. *McCormick et al. v. Zero*, 23 August 2000.

32. The quotations are from IBT 705 Membership Meeting, 21 May 2000, Chicago. Subsequent quotations in the following paragraphs are also from this meeting.

6. The Nomination of Political Parties

1. Roderick Martin, "Union Democracy: An Explanatory Framework." *Sociology* 2 (May 1968): 207.

2. *705 Update* 4, no. 4 (October–November 2000): 8.

3. United Slate 2000 campaign flyer. When he ran for recording secretary,

Cook came up short by less than three hundred votes. All vote figures are taken from Dennis Sarsany, election officer, "Announcement of IBT Local 705 Results," 11 April 1995, 17 December 1997.

4. Steve Franklin, "Fight Helps Right Teamsters Local's Wrongs," *Chicago Tribune,* 13 March 1996, sec. 1.

5. Michael Holland, interview by author, Chicago, 2 November 2000. See Francine Knowles, "Lawsuit Settled, Teamsters Say," *Chicago Sun-Times,* 13 March 1996, 58; Steve Franklin, *Chicago Tribune,* 13 March, 1996; and Brendan Stephens, "7th Circuit Holds Line on Fee Award in Pension Class Action," *Chicago Daily Law Bulletin,* 27 April 1998, 1.

6. Stephen Franklin, "Fight Helps Right Teamsters Local's Wrongs," *Chicago Tribune,* 13 March 1996, Metro Chicago, sec. 1.

7. Archie Cook, interview by author, Chicago, 12 June 1999.

8. Michael Deane, interview by author, Burbank, Ill., 28 July 1999.

9. Michael Deane, interview by author, Chicago, 13 November 2000.

10. Deane interview, 28 July 1999.

11. IBT 705 Officer Election Protest Case P-0024, 16 October 2000.

12. See Sandra Livingston, "Hoffa Backers Halt Teamster Convention with Raucous," *Philadelphia Plain Dealer,* 16 July 1996, 1C, "Bickering Stymies Teamster Convention," 19 July 1996, 1C; and Phil Dine, "Teamster Behavior Strangely Parallels That of Former Soviet Union," *St. Louis Post-Dispatch,* 19 July 1996, 1C.

13. Eugene Phillips, interview by author, Chicago, 17 October 2000. Subsequent quotations in this chapter from Phillips, unless cited otherwise, are also from this interview.

14. Michael Husar, interview by author, Chicago, 27 July 2000.

15. The IBT organizational structure had once included regional bodies, known as conferences. But one of Ron Carey's early actions was to eliminate the conferences on the grounds that they were inefficient and undemocratic and served as excuses for union officials to draw additional salaries.

16. Husar interview, 27 July 2000.

17. Local 705 Resolution, 18 May 1972.

18. Husar interview, 27 July 2000.

19. Ibid.

20. Michael Husar, interview by author, Chicago, 7 November 2000.

21. Ibid.

22. Dane Passo, interview by author, Rosemont, Ill., 22 December 2000. Subsequent quotations in this chapter from Passo, unless cited otherwise, are also from this interview.

23. Hoffa's desire to rid the union from government oversight included funding a $2 million report analyzing past and present organized crime-union ties. The 526-page study titled *The Teamsters: Perception and Reality, An Investigative Study of Organized Crime Influence in the Union* (prepared by Stier, Anderson and Malone, LLC) concluded that while vestiges of organized crime influences continue, "they are no longer symptoms of fundamental defects in the union culture" (2002, 33). The report was primarily based on a national field study of 80 IBT locals, including Local 705, which had demonstrated a historical connection to organized crime.

24. Dan Campbell, interview by author, Chicago, 14 December 2000. Passo's plum appointment was apparently too ripe not to exploit. He and fellow Chicago

Teamster William Hogan Jr. were charged by the IRB with concocting a scheme to divert Teamster jobs into a nonunion firm. The two men were suspended from their union positions (see "Feds Charge Hoffa Associates in Vegas Scam," *Labor Notes* 268 (July 2001): 13–15.

25. Philip Dine, "James Hoffa Is Rekindling the Unity in the Teamsters That His Father Bred," *St. Louis Post-Dispatch*, 4 June 2000, A12.

26. Campbell interview.

27. Zero had also included three on his slate. The one-time RTSers now on the Zero slate were Otis Cross, Mark Postilion, and Jim Sylvester. Mike Colgan, Paul Di-Grazia, and Mike Bolvenizer were also union representatives.

28. An excellent account of the kind of union democracy that TDU promotes can be found in Mike Parker and Martha Gruelle, *Democracy Is Power: Rebuilding Unions from the Bottom Up* (Detroit: Labor Notes Book, 1999).

29. John McCormick, interview by author, Chicago, 28 September 2000.

30. John McCormick, interview by author, Chicago, 17 May 2000.

7. The Campaign Begins

1. The vote total is taken from *1998 IBT Election Vote Totals,* at http://members.aol.com/ibtvote/index.htm, last accessed 7 December 1998.

2. Campaign literature, 1978; The breakaway group actually drew slightly more votes (17,978 compared to the loyalists' 17,969).

3. The best example of campaign literature depicting the threesome was the teal and black, hard-stock, multipaneled brochure titled *Re-Elect the Zero-McCormick Reform Slate.*

4. Pat Floyd, *Putting Faith to Work: A Study of James* (Nashville: Abingdon Press, 1996).

5. James 2:24 New International Version.

6. Dan Campbell, interview by author, Chicago, 19 April 2000.

7. Breakfast Club Meeting, Chicago, March 2000.

8. *T-Shirts and Televisions,* www.teamster.net, 3 September 2000.

9. Archie Cook, interview by author, Orland Park, Ill., 23 September 2000. Subsequent quotations in this chapter from Cook, unless cited otherwise, are also from this interview.

10. Breakfast Club Meeting, Chicago, July 2000.

11. *Passo/Zero Shirts Half Off,* www.teamster.net, 7 September 2000.

12. Paul Waterhouse quoted at Zero campaign meeting, 1 November 2000.

13. www.Teamstersforunity.com, 13 November 2000.

14. Michael Husar, interview by author, Chicago, 27 July 2000.

15. Peter D. Hart Research Associates, "International Teamster Union Public Opinion Poll," December 1994.

16. http://www.igc.org/tdu/, last accessed 1 December 2000.

8. Campaign Platforms and Rank-and-File Votes

1. http://www.Teamstersforunity.com/pledge.htm, last accessed 13 November 2000.

2. The quotations are from a True Reform Party campaign flyer titled *Protection for Working Families.*

3. Selected campaign flyers from the Membership Slate.

4. Selected campaign flyers from Continued Reform Party.

5. Allen and other TDU members also printed a Jefferson Street newsletter called the *Brown Boxer,* which endorsed Zero.

6. Lee Dembart, *New York Times,* 19 January 1976, 1; Michael Deane, interview by author, Chicago, 13 November 2000. Deane's anger may have grown out of his knowledge that Peick had on two occasions refused to accept a national freight agreement, thereby embarrassing Frank Fitzsimmons, who was then international president.

7. Mark Postilion, quoted at Zero campaign meeting, 1 November 2000, Chicago.

8. Paul Waterhouse quoted at Zero campaign meeting, 17 May 2000, Chicago.

9. *Constitution of the International Brotherhood of Teamsters,* adopted by the 24th International Convention, 24–28 June 1991, Art. IV, Secs. 1–2, 32–40.

10. Under the union's constitution, each local could run the delegate election either separately within six months of the July convention or during the fall of a preceding year if a local officer contest was held (see ibid., Art. III, Secs. 3–5, 16–17). See Bruce Boyens, independent election officer, Local 705, to IBT 705 General Executive Board, 14 April 2000 (Minutes of GEB Meeting, 14 April 2000). The board voted four to three in favor of separate elections.

11. Notes from Zero campaign meeting, 16 August 2000, Racine Café, Chicago.

12. Gerald Zero, interview by author, Chicago, 16 August 2000.

13. Gerald Zero, interview by author, Chicago, 26 February 2000.

14. Andrew Speck, interview by author, Chicago, 17 November 2000.

15. *705 Update,* July 1997, 2.

16. "Cleanup of Teamsters Shows Some Results," *Wall Street Journal,* 6 April 1998, 1.

17. Chicago Jobs with Justice was started in 1993 by Zero and fellow city union leaders Tom Balanoff (Service Employees International Union Local 1) and Carl Rosen (United Electrical Workers District 11). Since its inception JwJ has received financial or in-kind support from Local 705, as well as from other local unions. JwJ is a coalition of labor unions and community, faith-based, and student organizations organizing for worker justice. The national JwJ organization was founded in 1987 and has chapters in more than forty cities and approximately thirty states.

18. Speck interview.

19. Francine Knowles, "Union Members Claim Official Misused Dues," *Chicago Sun-Times,* 17 October 2000.

20. Ibid. See Christopher Kania, assistant vice president of Amalgamated Bank of Chicago, to IBT 705 attorney Michael Holland, about revolving line of credit, including copy of original (18 September 1997) promissory note, 27 June 2000.

21. The quotation is from Knowles, "Union Members Claim Official Misused Dues." At the end of 1999, the surplus was $86,988 (Form LM-2, Labor Organization Annual Report, 24 March 2000), and at the end of 1998, when McCormick took over, it was $253,149 (Form LM-2, Labor Organization Annual Report, 30 March 1999).

22. Gerald Zero, interview by author, Chicago, 18 December 2000.

23. See "Local 705 Trustee Reports," 1 January to 1 October 2000. The quotation is from Zero interview, 18 December 2000.

24. "Local 705 Launches New 'Members Power' Program in UPS," *705 Update* 4, no. 2 (May 2000): 4.

25. Comments like the following quickly came to the secretary-treasurer's defense: "If stewards are calling other stewards and telling them NOT to go to stewards meetings they SHOULD be removed. If stewards are telling members NOT to go the membership meetings they are NOT representing the members and SHOULD be removed" (www.teamster.net, postings dated 3 and 4 September).

26. "IBT 705 Record of Steward Appointments and Removals," 1 April 2000–30 August 2000.

27. For example, at K&R Trucking he appointed a single steward to cover one of a number of shifts that occurred between 5:00 A.M. and 9:00 P.M. and consequently lowered the worker-to-representative ratio to 31 to 1. The local chief executive also placed three additional stewards at two separate Airborne Express locations. One took the job about two months before the election, bringing the worker-steward ratio at that location down to 70 to 1. A second appointee at a different barn was asked to serve after a resignation created a vacancy. The final new steward was appointed within a month of Zero's return to office and was given the responsibility to cover night-shift workers (the data on K&R and Airborne and the quotation are taken from an election protest (P-0003) filed by United candidate Richard Scrima against Continued Reform slate, 14 September 2000. The protest was denied).

28. John Boettinger, interview by author, Hodgkins, Ill., 28 September 2000.

29. Gerald Zero to John Boettinger, 25 September 2000. Two other Membership candidates and supporters were dropped during the campaign season in similar fashion. One of them, Kathy Gideon, had once been selected as the local's Steward of the Year. She was removed for "conveying to members a negative view of the Union" and because she "need[ed] some work on [her] grievance writing and understanding of the contract" (Gerald Zero to Kathy Gideon, IBT 705 file, September 8, 2000). She had served as a steward for eight years and a few months before being unceremoniously dumped and had been approached about being a business agent (Kathy Gideon, interview by author, Chicago, 15 October 2000).

30. Boettinger interview.

9. Campaign Issues

1. *Harry R. Gorge, III, et al. v. Ronald Carey et al.*, U.S. Court of Appeals, Fourth Circuit, Record 98-1022, Brief of Appellants, 16 March 1998, 7; press release, "Arkansas Best Corporation and WorldWay Corporation Agree to Merger," Fort Smith, Ark., 10 July 1995.

2. *Harry R. Gorge, III, et al. v. Ronald Carey et al.*, 2.

3. ABF corporate origins went back to 1923, but the corporation had purchased thirty small to medium regional motor carriers since 1935, before acquiring Carolina and Red Arrow Freight in 1995 (data on ABF from general information provided by the company).

4. Carey is quoted in Daniel P. Bearth, "Former ABF Workers Fight Union," n.d. Mike Sweeney, interview by author, Orland Park, Ill., 23 September 2000.

5. Transcripts of "ABF Freight System-Multi-Change of Operations, Carolina Freight and Red Arrow Freight," 14 September 1995, Rosemont, Ill., 271.

6. Tom Nightwine, interview by author, Forest Park, Ill., 15 October 2000. Subsequent quotations in this chapter from Nightwine, unless cited otherwise, are also from this interview.

7. Transcripts of *ABF Freight System-Multi-Change of Operations, Carolina Freight and Red Arrow Freight*, 270.

8. Letters dated 23 October 1995 and 11 November 1995, respectively, in Askin's personal records.

9. Mike Sweeney to Law Offices of Jeffry Knuckles and Peter Jagel, 29 March 1999. Itemized compilation of financial contributions, kept in Jim Askin's records as of 12 December 1998. See those records also for the legal counsel's letter.

10. Sweeney interview.

11. Glenn Pomonis, interview by author, Chicago, 17 May 2000.

12. Otis Cross, interview by author, Chicago, 16 August 2000.

13. Ralph M. List, vice president and general manager of Rail Terminal Services, to Otis Cross, subject: "Understanding Productivity Incentive Plan, BNSF-Corwith Intermodal Facility," 1 May 2000.

14. Cross interview, 16 August 2000.

15. Otis Cross, interview by author, Chicago, 1 November 2000.

16. Just one example of how the UPS contract was defined was the prominent postsettlement headline "Union Label for Deal: Victory" on the front page of the *Chicago Tribune*, 7 August 1997.

17. The arbitration ruling was based on a case brought by the international union, but it was applicable to Local 705's struggle with UPS (Teamsters United Parcel Service National Negotiating Committee and United Parcel Service, American Arbitration Association Inc., Opinion and Award, 13-300-1908-98, 11 February 2000). Paul Waterhouse, interview by author, Chicago, 27 July 2000.

18. Membership Slate campaign flyer.

19. Michael Husar, interview by author, Chicago, 7 November 2000.

20. Dan Shaughnessy, interview by author, Wheeling, Ill., 21 October 2000.

21. Eugene Phillips, interview by author, Chicago, 17 October 2000.

22. Michael Deane, interview by author, Burbank, Ill., 28 July 2000. Subsequent quotations in this chapter from Deane, unless cited otherwise, are also from this interview. "Memorandum of Understanding," signed by Ed Burke, 17 December 1993.

23. True Reform campaign flyer titled *Protection for Working Families*. McCormick accused Zero of negotiating a deal with UPS that produced an "inferior" agreement (see *The True Reform Times*, True Reform campaign flyer, October 2000).

24. For example, see *The Jerry Zero Record On Organizing*, Continued Reform campaign flyer. The quotation is from *McCormick Forgets about Part Timers Slate*, Continued Reform campaign flyer. Executive board positions include president, vice president, recording secretary, and the three trustees.

25. *John McCormick And The Truth—Have They Ever Met?* Continued Reform campaign flyer; *United Parcel Service, Inc. v. International Brotherhood of Teamster Local 705*, Judgment in a Civil Case, 95-C-6304, U.S. District Court, Northern District of Illinois, 29 September 1998, 2–3.

26. Francine Knowles, "Brief Teamster Strike Slows UPS Operations," *Chicago Sun-Times*, 10 December 1998, 62.

27. Settlement Agreement, United Parcel Service, Inc. and International Brotherhood of Teamster, Local 705, U.S. District Court, Northern District of Illinois, 98-C-7872, 15 December 1999, 2.

28. Michael Holland, interview by author, Chicago, 2 November 2000.

29. Minutes of GEB Meeting, and Board Resolution, "Local 705 Executive Board Approval, Union Funds for Litigation against Individuals for Union Related Issue," approved 17 March 2000. Out of 15 pending lawsuits against the local, 9 were

filed by employers, 4 by individual members, and 1 by an insurance company. *Jerry Zero Rolled Up His Sleeves and Fixed the Mess in the Funds,* Continued Reform campaign flyer. McCormick supported a successful strike fund referendum calling for a $5.00-a-month surcharge for two years. Zero proposed a bylaw amendment to establish a permanent fund at $2.00 per month ("Strike Fund Referendum Results," Local 705, 30 July 2000). The United Slate's platform was called "Rebuilding a Strike Fund to Give Local 705 Credibility in Negotiations" (*Here Are Some of the Issues We Stand For,* United 2000 campaign flyer).

30. See Phillips's position in *Teamsters for Unity Pledge* and Zero's record in *The Jerry Zero Record On Membership Rights,* Continued Reform campaign flyer. McCormick followed suit with his own different proposal for elected stewards. Neither was approved. McCormick's amendment failed to get 50 percent of the vote. Although the Zero proposal received 62 percent of the vote, the measure failed because there was not at least two-thirds of the membership (as required by local bylaws) attending the bylaw meeting. See the United position in *Here Are Some of the Issues We Stand For;* Husar quoted at Membership campaign rally, 18 October 2000, Wheeling, Ill.; Zero and McCormick's bylaws amendments are in *Brown Boxer,* March 2000.

31. Tony Gatson, interview by author, Hodgkins, Ill., 28 September 2000.

32. Quotes were taken from the actual tape recording, emphasis added.

33. Dan Cassidy, interview by author, Wheeling, Ill., 21 October 2000.

34. Gerald Zero to Dan Cassidy, 8 September 2000.

35. *What Is Going On with the Membership Slate?* and *A Special Message to 705 Freight Teamsters,* Continued Reform campaign flyers.

36. *Racist Threat Made by the Membership Slate,* Continued Reform campaign flyer.

37. Dan Campbell, interview by author, Hodgkins, Ill., 25 September 2000.

38. The Zero team believed that Cassidy had a third and consequential reason for leaving the slate: he knew it could not win and he wanted to cut himself loose from a failed effort.

39. Michael Husar, interviews by author, Chicago, 18, 30 October 2000.

10. The 705 Vote

1. Richard DeVries, speaking at a Breakfast Club meeting on 1 November 2000 at Racine Café in Chicago.

2. Breakfast Club Meeting, Chicago, 6 November 2000.

3. Michael Husar, interview by author, Chicago, 4 October 2000.

4. Michael Deane, interview by author, Chicago, 13 November 2000.

5. Mark Postilion, speaking at a Breakfast Club meeting on 1 November 2000 at Racine Café, Chicago.

6. This was not the cheapest way to elect union officers. Since 1995 the local had chosen to hire a neutral agent to conduct their officer elections. But designating an outside third party went beyond the requirements of the law or the IBT constitution. For example, the executive board could have selected three members or appointed an election committee to count ballots. Instead the fractious board agreed to hire Chicago attorney Bruce Boyens, who was an assistant to election officer Michael Holland during the 1991 IBT referendum election.

7. In most union elections, slate voting represents nearly 90 percent of the votes cast.

8. As a result of a lottery that occurred during a meeting in Boyens's office to establish rules for conducting the election, the Continued Reform Party was awarded the top line on the ballot.

9. Mark Postilion, interview by author, Chicago, 21 February 2001. Subsequent quotations in this chapter from Postilion, unless otherwise cited, are also from this interview. Protest by Richard Scrima, United Slate 2000, to Bruce Boyens, Office of the Independent Election Officer, IBT Local 705, P-0064, 4 December 2000. "Rules for the IBT Local 705 Officer Election," submitted by Bruce Boyens, Office of the Independent Election Officer IBT Local 705.

10. Francine Knowles, "Court: Kmart Must Bargain with Union," *Chicago Sun-Times,* 19 September 1997, Financial sec., 54.

11. A pretty solid estimate of where the vote was coming from could be made, because the returned carrying envelope had an employer code printed on the back.

12. Ironically, Passo helped to prevent this scenario from unfolding by testifying before the House Oversight and Investigations Subcommittee, which was looking into the allegations of fraud during the 1996 IBT election. Passo charged that Carey had received "suspicious financial contributions." It was also his findings in a review of Carey's campaign records that prompted the Hoffa election protest that ultimately led to the voiding of the election (Francine Knowles, "Hoffa's Chicago Election Chief to Testify Today," *Chicago Sun-Times,* 14 October 1997, 50).

13. Michael Holland, interview by author, Chicago, 21 December 2000.

14. Paul Clark, *The Miners Fight for Democracy: Arnold Miller and the United Mine Workers* (Ithaca, N.Y.: Cornell University Press, 1981).

15. For an example of political upheaval in the autoworkers' union, see Dan Georgakas and Marvin Surkin, *Detroit: I Do Mind Dying* (Cambridge, Mass.: South End Press, 1998); for an account in the steelworkers' union, see Phillip Nyden, *Steelworkers Rank and File: The Political Economy of a Union Movement* (New York: Praeger Press, 1984).

16. James Jacobs and David Santore, "The Liberation of Local 506," New York Law School, *Criminal Law Bulletin* 37, no. 2 (March–April 2001): 125–58.

17. "Crime Commission Reports Organized Crime Continues to Influence Some Labor Unions," *Daily Labor Report,* 10 October 1997, A-10–11; *Union Democracy Review* 133 (December 2000): 4.

18. "Crime Commission Reports Organized Crime Continues to Influence Some Labor Unions," A-10-11.

19. Andy Piascik, "SEIU Roundup: 'Bevona of Boston' Ousted," *Union Democracy Review* 136 (June–July 2001): 3; "Crime Commission Reports Organized Crime Continues to Influence Some Labor Unions," A-10-11; "Contested Election in SEIU Local 32B–32J," *Union Democracy Review* 132 (October–November 2000): 6; "32B–32J: From a Shadowy Past," *Union Democracy Review* 131 (August–September 2000): 4; "SEIU Moves to Clean Up Local 144," *Union Democracy Review* 120 (November 1997): 5.

20. "Insurgents Win in Troubled NYC AFSCME Local," and "Democracy in the Musicians Union," *Union Democracy Review* 120 (September 1998): 4–5; Carl Biers, "Maneuvering in District Council 37," *Union Democracy Review* 131 (August–September 2000): 2–3.

21. Carl Biers, "Carpenters Reformers Win in New England," *Union Democracy Review* (December–January 2002).

22. "Democracy Runs Express in NYC Transit Election," *Union Democracy Review* (February–March 2001).

23. For information on REAP, see http://www.reapinc.org.

24. Bill Fletcher Jr., "Whose Democracy? Organized Labor and Member Control," in *A New Labor Movement for the New Century,* ed. Gregory Mantsios (New York: Monthly Review Press, 1998), 20.

25. Dan Campbell, interview by author, Chicago, 7 January 1999. Subsequent quotations in this chapter from Campbell, unless cited otherwise, are also from this interview.

26. Joseph Allen, interview by author, Chicago, 11 September 2000.

27. *705 Update* 2, no. 3 (June 1998).

Epilogue

1. *Member's Bill of Rights for Grievance Processing,* current Local 705 flyer.

2. "K-Mart Teamsters Local 705," 22 August 2002, and "Local 705 Trustee and REP Mark Postilion Terminated!" 15 August 2002, at www.teamster.net.

3. "Career Patron Profiles," *Illinois Campaign for Political Reform,* 9 January 2003.

4. John Nichols, "Trade Fights," *The Nation,* 1 April 2002.

5. www.teamsterslocal705.org

6. The Hotel Employees and Restaurant Employees (HERE) Local 1 established the Hungry for Justice Campaign as a food donation drive for members in case a strike was called against the hotel employers. Local 705's support was acknowledged in a letter from HERE President Henry Tamarin to Zero on 9 September 2002.

7. Gerald Zero, interview by author, Chicago, 9 September 2002.

8. Reformers pointed to Hoffa's imposition of a trusteeship over Northwest Airlines flight attendants Local 2000 as evidence of the potential for retribution. Local 2000 had a well-earned reputation for rank-and-file democracy, militancy, and anti-Hoffa sentiment ("Hoffa Seizes Flight Attendants Local 2000," at www.tdu.org, 30 September 2002).

9. *705 Update* 6, no. 4 (September 2002): 2.

Bibliography

Teamsters Local Union 705 Files and Documents

Member's Bill of Rights for Grievance Processing, current Local 705 flyer.

"Local 705 Trustee Reports," 1 January–1 October 2000.

Henry Tamarin to Gerald Zero, 9 September 2002.

Gerald Zero to John Boettinger, 25 September 2000.

Gerald Zero to Dan Cassidy, 8 September 2000.

Gerald Zero to Kathy Gideon, IBT 705 file, 8 September 2000.

Gerald Zero, "An Open Letter to Local 705 Members," n.d.

"IBT 705 Record of Steward Appointments and Removals," 1 April 2000–30 August 2000.

"Strike Fund Referendum Results," Local 705, 30 July 2000.

"Notice to Employees," Teamster Local Union 705, Case 13-CA-38198-2, 25 July 2000.

Christopher Kania, assistant vice president of Amalgamated Bank of Chicago, to IBT 705 attorney Michael Holland, 18 September 1997, 27 June 2000.

Ralph M. List, vice president and general manager of Rail Terminal Services, to Otis Cross, subject: "Understanding Productivity Incentive Plan, BNSF-Corwith Intermodal Facility," 1 May 2000.

"Local 705 Executive Board Approval, Union Funds for Litigation against Individuals for Union Related Issue," General Executive Board resolution, 17 March 2000.

Tom Leedham, handwritten settlement, 26 January 2000.

Michael Holland to John McCormick, subject: "Withdrawal from Representation, Local 705 Executive Board," 20 January 2000.

John B. McCormick to Ron Damerjian, memo, subject: Tom Nightwine, 29 June 1999.

John B. McCormick to Tom Nightwine, 29 June 1999.

"Local 705 Arbitration Files," 1970–1999.

"Local 705 Weekly Status Report on National Labor Relations Board Cases."

"Labor Organization Annual Report," Local 705, Department of Labor, Labor Management Form, No. 2, 30 March 1999.

Assorted announcements, agendas, and enrollment reports, January–December 1998.

"Craft Meeting Agendas," 23 March 1997–24 November 24, 1998.

"Results of Local 705–UPS Grievance Meetings," 1995–1998.

"Local 705 Contract File," 1994–1998, 1971–1985.

"UPS-705 Negotiating Committee Rank-and-File Notes," May–August 1997.

"Local 705 Craft Meeting Schedule," 1997.

Independent Review Board to Local 705 Executive Board, report in the matter of

"Proposed Charges against Local 705 Member Gerald Zero," 13 November 1996.

Transcripts of "ABF Freight System-Multi-Change of Operations, Carolina Freight and Red Arrow Freight," 14 September 1995, Rosemont, Ill.

Ron Carey to Gerald Zero, 13 April 1995.

Gerald Zero to Ron Carey, 22 December 1994.

Ron Carey to Gerald Zero, letter and certificate of appointment, 18 July 1994.

"Chicago Area Consolidation Hub (CACH)," news release from United Parcel Service, n.d.

IBT Attorney Peggy Hillman to Elizabeth Kinney, regional director, Region 13, NLRB, 2 May 1994.

Harold Burke to all Local 705 representatives, agents, and staff, memorandum and attached copy of handbill from Committee to Defend Local 705, 1994.

"Memorandum of Understanding," signed by Ed Burke, 17 December 1993.

Harold Burke to officers and members of Local 705, notice about a trusteeship hearing, 15 July 1993.

Harold Burke to Teamster Joint Council, letter and floor plan, 13 July 1993.

Letter and report to Ron Carey, 25 May 1993.

J. Jeffrey Zimmerman, Esq., to IBT 705 business agent Frank Snow, 17 June 1992.

"Local 705 Notice," 22 October 1991.

"705 Membership of T.S.C" to Dan Ligurotis, letter and petition, 10 July 1991.

Constitution of the International Brotherhood of Teamsters, 1991.

"50 Years Serving the Chicago Area," from UPS Metro Chicago *Big Idea* (newsletter), June 1990, 2–6.

Local 705–Chicago Movers agreements, 1987 and 1990.

Program of 29th Annual Pension Meeting of Local Union 705 of IBT, 8 November 1985, Chicago.

Elroy W. Heniff, Joint Area Tank Truck Association employer, to Louis Peick, IBT Local 705 secretary-treasurer, 7 September 1983.

Ledger numbers 36-693 (1982), 27-353 (1980), 1193 (1979), 26-088 (1979).

John McCormick, Local 705 Grievance File, no. 00551, 30 October 1979.

"Security Lumber and Supply Company Workforce" to Louis Peick, 10 April 1979.

"Internal Report," 2 April 1978.

"Internal Report," 12 February 1978.

Local 705 Trial Committee Hearing transcripts, 31 March 1974.

T.R.U.T.H. (newsletter) 1, no. 4 (March 1974).

Local 705 flyer, 18 May 1972.

"Local 705 Resolution," 18 May 1972.

Local 705 publication, untitled, 12 February 1970.

File on IBT 705 picnic, 1963 and 1964.

"Master Cartage Agreement with Local 705," 1950.

"Contract Approved under General Order No. 40 of the National War Labor Board," 1945.

"Service Station Agreement with Local 705," 1939.

"Cartage Agreement with Local 705," 1934.

Ezra Warner, owner representative, to Local 705, 4 August 1919.

Joseph Rasch dues book, 1911.

Materials from Steve Pocztowski files, various years.

Local 705 Court and Internal Hearing Proceedings

John McCormick et al. v. Gerald Zero, 00-C-2750, U.S. District Court, Northern District of Illinois, Eastern Division, Finding of Facts and Conclusion of Law, 23 August 2000.

John McCormick et al. v. Gerald Zero, 00-C-2750, U.S. District Court, Northern District of Illinois, Eastern Division, Temporary Restraining Order, 24 May 2000.

William Blake v. Gerald Zero, internal union charges, in Local 705 General Executive Board Meeting Minutes, 11 May 2000.

Teamsters United Parcel Service National Negotiating Committee and United Parcel Service, American Arbitration Association Inc., Opinion and Award, 13-300-1908-98, 11 February 2000.

Sam Lodovico v. Gerald Zero, internal union charge, 10 February 2000.

"A Notice of Filing," in a letter from John McCormick to Robert Barnes, secretary of IBT Joint Council 25, subject: "Charges against Gerald Zero," 7 February 2000.

Settlement Agreement, United Parcel Service, Inc., and International Brotherhood of Teamsters, Local 705, U.S. District Court, Northern District of Illinois, 98-C-7872, 15 December 1999, 2.

United Parcel Service, Inc. v. International Brotherhood of Teamsters Local 705, Judgment in a Civil Case, 95-C-6304, U.S. District Court, Northern District of Illinois, 29 September 1998, 2-3.

The People of the State of Illinois v. Gerald Zero, Appellate Court of Illinois, First District, 96-MC1-25404, 2 June 1998.

Harry R. Gorge, III, et al. v. Ronald Carey et al., U.S. Court of Appeals, Fourth Circuit, Record 98-1022, Brief of Appellants, 16 March 1998.

Conboy, Kenneth. Decision of Election Officer for the International Brotherhood of Teamsters, in "Cheatem, Spaerman, Hoffa Election Protests," 17 November 1997.

Quindel, Barbara Zack. Summary of Decision, Election Officer for the International Brotherhood of Teamsters, in "Cheatem, Spaerman, Hoffa Election Protests," 21 August 1997.

Colgan et al. v. Carey and Zero, 94-C-5685, U.S. District Court for the Northern District of Illinois, Eastern Division, 1995.

Ethical Practices Committee Hearing on Charges against Local 705 Members Dane Passo et al., 6 December 1994.

National Labor Relations Board, 13-CB-13080, 4 September 1990.

Sheet Metal Workers' International v. Lynn, 488 U.S. 347; 109 Supreme Court 639; 1989 in Lexis-Nexis Legal Text 432.

Finnegan v. Leu, 456 U.S. 431; 102 Supreme Court 1867; 1982, Lexis-Nexis Legal Texts.

Clarence Campbell et al. v. Local Union 705, 76-C-4240, Memorandum Opinion and Order, U.S. District Court, 8 May 1978.

Campbell et al., Supplement to Complaint, Count II, 19 March 1978.

John Daniel v. International Brotherhood of Teamsters, 76-1855, U.S. Court of Appeals, Seventh District, Lexis 11915, 20 August 1977.

Main Brief of Local 705, International Brotherhood of Teamsters and Independent 705 Chicago Truck Drivers, in the Matter of IBT 705 and Chicago Truck Drivers and the Cartage Exchange and Illinois Motor Truck Operators Association, National War Labor Board, Trucking Commission, 9 February 1943.

International Teamster and Local 705 Election and Campaign Material

2000 Local Election

Breakfast Club Meetings, March–November 2000.

Bruce Boyens, independent election officer, Local 705, to IBT 705 General Executive Board, 14 April 2000.

IBT 705 Officer Election Protest Case P-0024, 16 October 2000.

The Jerry Zero Record on Membership Rights, Continued Reform campaign flyer.

The Jerry Zero Record on Organizing, Continued Reform campaign flyer.

Jerry Zero Rolled Up His Sleeves and Fixed the Mess in the Funds, Continued Reform campaign flyer.

John McCormick and the Truth—Have They Ever Met? Continued Reform campaign flyer.

K&R and Airborne election protest (P-0003) filed by United candidate Richard Scrima against Continued Reform Slate, 14 September 2000.

McCormick Forgets about Part Timers Slate, Continued Reform campaign flyer.

Membership Slate campaign flyer.

Passo/Zero Shirts Half Off, www.Teamster.net, 7 September 2000.

Protection for Working Families, True Reform campaign flyer.

Protest by Richard Scrima, United Slate 2000, to Bruce Boyens, Office of the Independent Election Officer, IBT Local 705, P-0064, 4 December 2000.

Racist Threat Made by the Membership Slate, Continued Reform campaign flyer.

"Rebuilding a Strike Fund to Give Local 705 Credibility in Negotiations," *Here Are Some of the Issues We Stand For,* United 2000 campaign flyer.

Re-Elect the Zero-McCormick Reform Slate, brochure.

"Rules for the IBT Local 705 Officer Election," submitted by Bruce Boyens, Office of the Independent Election Officer, IBT Local 705.

Selected campaign flyers from Continued Reform Party.

Selected campaign flyers from the Membership Slate.

A Special Message to 705 Freight Teamsters, Continued Reform campaign flyer.

Teamsters for Unity Pledge, Teamsters for Unity Campaign flyer.

The True Reform Times, True Reform campaign flyer.

T-Shirts and Televisions, www.Teamster.net, 3 September 2000.

United Slate 2000 campaign flyer.

What Is Going On with the Membership Slate? Continued Reform campaign flyer.

www.igc.org/tdu/, last accessed 1 December 2000.

www.teamster.net, 3 and 4 September 2002.

www.Teamstersforunity.com, 13 November 2000.

1998 International Election

1998 IBT Election Vote Totals, http://members.aol.com/ibtvote/index.htm, last accessed 7 December 1998.

1997 and 1995 Local Elections

Dennis Sarsany, election officer, "Announcement of IBT Local 705 Results," 11 April 1995, 17 December 1997.

Dennis Sarsany, election officer, "Teamster Local 705 Officer Election, Announcement of Results," 17 December 1997.

"Decision on Protest to 1995 Election of Officers and Business Agents of Local 705," IBT Joint Council No. 25, 1 November 1995.

"IBT Local 705 Office Election Results," from Election Officer Dennis M. Sarsany to Gerald Zero, 11 April 1995.

Personal Records of Local 705 Members

Askin, Jim

Deane, Mike

Sweeney, Mike

Interviews (all by the author)

Notes on the interviews are in the author's files.

Allen, Joseph. Chicago, 11 September 2000.

Barnett, Don. Chicago, 14 November 2000.

Barnett, Katina. Chicago, 21 November 2000.

Barns, Van. Chicago, 8 January 2001.

Belzer, Mike. Chicago, 21 September 2001.

Benesch, Edward. Chicago, 20 October 1998.

Berry, Dale. Chicago, 17 October 2002.

Bielick, Tony. Chicago, 4 October 2001.

Boettinger, John. Hodgkins, Ill., 28 September 2000.

Campbell, Dan. Chicago, 19 April, 14 December 2000; 7 January 1999; Hodgkins, Ill., 25 September 2000.

Carlucci, Rick. Chicago, 6 March 1999.

Cassidy, Dan. Wheeling, Ill., 21 October 2000.

Coleman, Robert. Chicago, 6 March 1999.

Colgan, Michael. Chicago, 11 January 1999.

Cook, Archie. Orland Park, Ill., 23 September 2000; Chicago, 12 June 1999.

Cross, Otis. Chicago, 16 August, 1 November 2000.

Deane, Michael. Chicago, 13 November 2000; Burbank, Ill., 28 July 1999.

DeVries, Richard. Chicago, 14 December 1998.

DiGrazia, Paul. Chicago, 3 December 1998.

Foster, Gregory. Chicago, 7 December 1998.

Gatson, Tony. Hodgkins, Ill., 28 September 2000.

Gideon, Kathy. Chicago, 15 October 2000.

Harris, James. Chicago, 6 March 1999.

Hillman, Peggy. Chicago, 21 March 2000.

Holland, Michael. Chicago, 2 November, 21 December 2000; 15 January 1999; 20 October 1998.

Husar, Michael. Chicago, 27 July, 4, 18, 30 October, 7 November 2000.

Jackson, Bennie. Chicago, 20 October 1998.

Kelly, Bill. Chicago, 10 March 2002.

Lyons, Jim. Chicago, 12 December 1998.

Maziarka, Robert. Chicago, 9 March 2002.

McCormick, John. Chicago, 17 May 2000; 28 September 2000; 28 September 1999; 20 October, 7 December 1998.

McKee, Jim. Chicago, 6 March 1999.

Nightwine, Tom. Forest Park, Ill., 15 October 2000; Chicago, 7 January 1999.
Passo, Dane. Rosemont, Ill., 22 December 2000.
Persak, Robert. Chicago, 7 September 2001.
Phillips, Eugene. Chicago, 17 October 2000.
Pomonis, Glenn. Chicago, 17 May 2000.
Postilion, Mark. Chicago, 21 February 2001; 11 January 1999.
Shaughnessy, Dan. Wheeling, Ill., 21 October 2000.
Slusher, Nick. Chicago, 6 March 1999.
Speck, Andrew. Chicago, 17 November 2000.
Sweeney, Mike. Orland Park, Ill., 23 September 2000.
Teas, Charley. Chicago, 14 December 1998.
Waterhouse, Paul. Chicago, 28 September 2001; 27 July 2000; 10 December 1998.
Zero, Gerald. Chicago, 9 September 2002; 26 September 2001; 27 July, 16 August, 14 November, 18 December 2000; 26 February, 7 December 1998.

Reports and Papers

"32B–32J: From a Shadowy Past." *Union Democracy Review* 131 (August–September 2000): 4.
American Trucking Trends, 1969. Washington, D.C.: American Trucking Association, 1969.
"Arkansas Best Corporation and WorldWay Corporation Agree to Merger." Press release, Fort Smith, Ark., July 10, 1995.
Biers, Carl. "Carpenters Reformers Win in New England." *Union Democracy Review* 139 (December–January 2002): 1.
———. "Maneuvering in District Council 37." *Union Democracy Review* 131 (August–September 2000): 2–3.
"Career Patron Profiles." *Illinois Campaign for Political Reform,* 9 January 2003.
Chicago Crime Commission Annual Report. Chicago, 1969.
Congress and the Nation. Vol. 1, *1945–1964.* Washington, D.C.: Congressional Quarterly, Inc., 1965.
"Contested Election in SEIU Local 32B–32J." *Union Democracy Review* 132 (October–November 2000): 6.
"Crime Commission Reports Organized Crime Continues to Influence Some Labor Unions." *Daily Labor Report,* 10 October 1997, A-10–11.
"The Daily Phone Diary of President Jimmy Carter." Jimmy Carter Library and Museum, Online Archive at jimmycarterlibrary.org, 2 December 1979.
"Democracy in the Musicians Union." *Union Democracy Review* 120 (September 1998): 4–5.
"Democracy Runs Express in NYC Transit Election." *Union Democracy Review* 134 (February–March 2001): 1.
"Hotel Workers Local 1 in Chicago." *Union Democracy Review* 133 (December 2000): 4.
"Insurgents Win in Troubled NYC AFSCME Local." *Union Democracy Review* 120 (September 1998): 4–5.
Peter D. Hart Research Associates. "International Teamster Union Public Opinion Poll." December 1994.
Piascik, Andy. "SEIU Roundup: 'Bevona of Boston' Ousted." *Union Democracy Review* 136 (June–July 2001): 3.
President's Commission on Crime. *The Edge: Organized Crime, Business, and Labor*

Unions: A Report to the President and the Attorney General. Washington, D.C.: U.S. Government Printing Office, 1986.

"Republican and Democratic Executive Summaries of House Subcommittee Report on Teamsters." *Daily Labor Report* 37 (25 February 1999): E39–E48.

"SEIU Moves to Clean Up Local 144." *Union Democracy Review* 120 (November 1997): 5.

"Special Report: Teamsters Draft Plan for Reform Is Criticized and Defended." Bureau of National Affairs, Washington, D.C. *Union Labor Report* 54, no. 16 (20 April 2000).

"Teamsters Independent Review Board: Five Year Report 1992–1997, *United States v. IBT,* 88 Civil 4486 (DNE)." *Daily Labor Report* 218 (12 November 1997).

The Teamsters: Perception and Reality, An Investigative Study of Organized Crime Influence in the Union. Prepared by Stier, Anderson and Malone, LLC, September 2002.

Commercial and Labor Papers

Commercial

Boston Globe, 9 December 1997.

Chicago American, 17 November 1904.

Chicago Daily Tribune, 6 April 1905; 3 December 1903.

Chicago News, 6 July 1973.

Chicago Sun-Times, 17 October 2000; 10 December 1998; 19 September, 14 October 1997; 13 March 1996; 11 April 1994; 14 September 1992.

Chicago Tribune, 19 December 1998; 7 August 1997; 13 March 1996; 1 November 1976; 25 March, 9 April, 7 May 1970.

Crain's Chicago Business, 6 January 1992.

New York Times, 13 October 2001; 19 January 1976.

Philadelphia Plain Dealer, 16, 19 July 1996.

St. Louis Post-Dispatch, 4 June 2000; 19 July 1996; 10 January 1992.

Wall Street Journal, 6 April 1998.

Labor

705 CACH-Update, 11 June 1990.

705 Update, May, October–November, December 2000; January, March, June, July 1998; January, March–April, May, July, September 1997; October 1996; September 1995.

Chicago Federation of News, 14 September 1976; 4 January 1958.

Convoy Dispatch, October–November 1998.

Labor Notes, July 2001.

New Majority, 26 April, 10 May, 25 October 1919.

Teamster Local 705 News 3, no. 1 (April 1996).

UPS Brown Boxer, March 2000.

Weiss, Jeff, and S. J. Peters, eds. *Our First Century.* Chicago Federation of Labor booklet, 1999.

Books and Articles

Aidt, Toke, and Zafaris Tzannatos. *Unions and Collective Bargaining: Economic Effects in a Global Environment.* Washington, D.C.: World Bank, 2002.

Aronowitz, Stanley. "Union and Democracy." *Dissent* (winter 1999): 81–83.

Barber, Benjamin. *Strong Democracy: Participatory Politics for a New Age.* Berkeley: University of California Press, 1984.

Barling, Julian, Clive Fullager, and Kevin E. Kelloway. *Union and Its Members: A Psychological Approach*. New York: Oxford University Press, 1992.

Belzer, Michael. *Sweatshops on Wheels: Winners and Losers in Trucking Deregulation*. New York: Oxford University Press, 2000.

Benson, Herman. *How to Get an Honest Union Election*. New York: Association for Union Democracy, 1987.

Bowker, Arthur. "Trust Violators in the Labor Movement: A Study of Union Embezzlement." *Journal of Labor Research* 19, no. 3 (summer 1998): 571–79.

Brendan, Stephens. "7th Circuit Holds Line on Fee Award in Pension Class Action." *Chicago Daily Law Bulletin*, 27 April 1998, 1.

Brill, Steven. *The Teamsters*. New York: Simon and Schuster, 1978.

Bronfenbrenner, Kate, Sheldon Freidman, Richard Hurd, Rudolph Oswald, and Ronald Seebers, eds. *Organizing to Win: New Research on Union Strategies*. Ithaca, N.Y.: ILR Press, 1998.

Bruno, Robert. "Consenting to be Governed: Union Transformation and Teamster Democracy." *Advances in Industrial and Labor Relations* (2002).

———. "Democratic Goods: Teamster Reform and Collective Bargaining Outcomes." *Journal of Labor Research* 21 (winter 2000): 83–102.

Clark, Paul. *Building More Effective Unions*. Ithaca, N.Y.: ILR Press, 2000.

———. *The Miners Fight for Democracy: Arnold Miller and the United Mine Workers*. Ithaca, N.Y.: Cornell University Press, 1981.

Clark, Paul F., Daniel G. Gallagher, and Thomas J. Pavlik. "Member Commitment in an American Union: The Role of the Grievance Procedure." *Industrial Relations Journal* 21 (summer 1990): 147–57.

Cochran, Bert. *Labor and Communism*. Princeton, N.J.: Princeton University Press, 1977.

Cornfield, Daniel. "The U.S. Labor Movement: Its Development and Impact on Social Inequality and Politics." *Annual Review of Sociology* 17 (1991): 27–49.

Crowe, Kenneth. *Collision: How the Rank and File Took Back the Teamsters*. New York: Charles Scribner's, 1993.

Edelstein, David J., and Malcom Warner. *Comparative Union Democracy: Organization and Opposition in British and American Unions*. New Brunswick, N.J.: Transaction Books, 1979.

Edgar, James N. "Union Democracy and the LMRDA: Autocracy and Insurgency in National Union Elections." *Harvard Civil Rights–Civil Liberties Law Review* (spring 1978): 247–356.

Eisenscher, Michael. "Leadership Development and Organizing: For What Kind of Union?" *Labor Studies Journal* 24, no. 2 (summer 1999): 3–21.

Estey, Marten S., Philip Taft, and Martin Wagner. *Regulating Union Government*. New York: Harper and Row, 1964.

Estreicher, Samuel. "Deregulating Union Democracy." In *The Internal Governance and Organizational Effectiveness of Labor Unions*, ed. Samuel Estreicher, Harry Katz, and Bruce Kaufman, 435–55. New York: Kluwer Law International, 2001.

Faber, Henry. "Analysis of Union Behavior." In *Handbook of Labor Economics*, ed. Orley Ashenfelter and Richard Layard, 1031–90. Amsterdam: North Holland, 1986.

Feldacker, Bruce. *Labor Guide to Labor Law*. 3d ed. Englewood Cliffs, N.J.: Prentice Hall, 1990.

Fiorito, Jack, Daniel G. Gallagher, and Cynthia V. Fukami. "Satisfaction with Union

Representation." *Industrial and Labor Relations Review* 41 (January 1988): 294–307.

Fiorito, Jack, and Wallace Henricks. "Union Characteristics and Bargaining Outcomes." *Industrial and Labor Relations Review* 40 (July 1987): 569–84.

Fisher, Lloyd, and Grant McConnell. "Internal Conflict and Labor-Union Solidarity." In *Industrial Conflict*, ed. Arthur Kornhauser, Robert Dubin, and Arthur M. Ross, 132–43. New York: McGraw Hill, 1954.

Flannery, Michael, and Alan Mutter. "Firefighters Reach Accord with Byrne," *Chicago Sun-Times*, 23 February 1980.

Fletcher, Bill, Jr. "Whose Democracy? Organized Labor and Member Control." In *A New Labor Movement for the New Century*, ed. Gregory Mantsios, 16–23. New York: Monthly Review Press, 1998.

Franklin, Steve. *Three Strikes: Labor's Heartland Losses and What They Mean for Working Americans*. New York: Guilford Press, 2001.

Fraser, Steven. "Is Democracy Good for Unions?" *Dissent* (summer 1998): 33–39.

Freeman, Richard, and James Medorf. *What Do Unions Do?* New York: Basic Books, 1984.

Freidman, Allen, and Ted Schwarz. *Power and Greed: Inside the Teamsters Empire of Corruption*. New York: Franklin Watts, 1989.

Friedman, Samuel. *Teamster Rank and File: Power, Bureaucracy, and Rebellion at Work and in a Union*. New York: Columbia University Press, 1980.

Gallagher, Daniel, and Paul F. Clark. "Research on Union Commitment: Implications for Labor." *Labor Studies Journal* 14 (spring 1989): 213–27.

Georgakas, Dan, and Marvin Surkin. *Detroit: I Do Mind Dying*. Cambridge, Mass.: South End Press, 1998.

Goldberg, Michael J. "Cleaning Labor's House: Institutional Reform Litigation in the Labor Movement." *Duke Law Journal* 4 (1989): 904–1011.

Hemingway, John. *Conflict and Democracy: Studies in Trade Union Government*. New York: John Wiley, 1978.

Horowitz, Morris. *The Structure and Government of the Carpenters' Union*. New York: John Wiley, 1962.

Hutchinson, John. *The Imperfect Union: A History of Corruption in American Trade Unions*. New York: E. P. Dutton, 1970.

Jacobs, James, and David Santore. "The Liberation of Local 506." New York Law School. *Criminal Law Bulletin* 37, no. 2 (March–April 2001): 125–58.

Jarley, Paul, Sarosh Kuruvilla, and Douglas Casteel. "Member-Union Relations and Union Satisfaction." *Industrial Relations Journal* 29 (winter 1990): 128–34.

Jenkin, Thomas P. "Oligarchy." In *International Encyclopedia of the Social Sciences*, vol. 2, ed. David L. Stills. New York: Free Press, 1968.

Jensen, Jane, and Rianne Mahon, eds. *The Challenge of Restructuring; North American Labor Movements Respond*. Philadelphia: Temple University Press, 1992.

Johnston, Paul. *Success While Others Fail: Social Movement Unionism and the Public Workplace*. Ithaca, N.Y.: ILR Press, 1994.

Kannar, George. "Making the Teamsters Safe for Democracy." *Yale Law Review* 102 (1993): 1654–55.

Kennedy, Robert. *The Enemy Within: The McClellan Committee's Crusade against Jimmy Hoffa and Corrupt Labor Unions*. New York: Da Capo Press, 1994.

Kleiner, Morris, and Adam Pilarski. "Does Internal Union Political Competition Enhance Its Effectiveness?" In *The Internal Governance and Organizational Effectiveness of Labor*

Unions, ed. Samuel Estreicher, Harry Katz, and Bruce Kaufman, 75–101. New York: Kluwer Law International, 2001.

Kochan, Thomas A., ed. *Challenges and Choices Facing American Labor.* Cambridge, Mass.: MIT Press, 1985.

Kramer, Leo. *Labor's Paradox: The American Federation of State, County, and Municipal Employees, AFL-CIO.* New York: John Wiley, 1962.

The Labor Law Source Book. Cambridge, Mass.: Work Rights Press, 1999.

La Botz, Dan. "Teamsters and the Federal Government: Unhappy Marriage." Paper delivered at the Fifteenth Annual North American Labor History Conference, Wayne State University, Detroit, October 1993.

———. *Rank and File Rebellion.* New York: Verso Press, 1990.

Larkin, Jim. "As Teamster-Turtle Ties Fray, Hoffa Faces Rematch with Leedham: Which Way for the Teamsters?" *Nation,* 8 October 2001, 20–24.

Leiserson, William. *American Trade Union Democracy.* New York: Columbia University Press, 1959.

Lewis, Tom. *Building Divided Highways: The Interstate Highways, Transforming American Life.* New York: Viking Press, 1997.

Lipset, Seymour Martin. *Unions in Transition.* San Francisco: Institute for Contemporary Studies, 1986.

———. "The Political Process in Trade Unions: A Theoretical Statement." In *Labor and Trade Unionism,* ed. Walter Galenson and Seymour Martin Lipset, 339–60. New York: John Wiley, 1960.

Lipset, Seymour Martin, Martin Trow, and James Coleman. *Union Democracy: What Makes Democracy Work in Labor Unions and Other Organizations?* Garden City, N.Y: Anchor Books, 1956.

Martin, Roderick. "Union Democracy: An Explanatory Framework." *Sociology* 2 (May 1968): 205–20.

Marx, Karl. "Economics and Politics in the Labor Movement." In *The Marx-Engels Reader,* 2d ed., ed. Robert Tucker. New York: W. W. Norton, 1978.

———. "Wages, Price, and Profit." In *Karl Marx and Frederick Engels: Selected Works in Three Volumes,* 31–76. Moscow: Progress Publishers, 1969–70.

Masters, Marick L. "AFSCME as a Political Union." *Journal of Labor Research* 19 (spring 1998): 313–49.

May, John D. "Democracy, Oligarchy, Michels." *American Political Science Review* 59 (June 1965): 417–29.

McConnell, Grant. *Private Power and American Democracy.* New York: Vintage, 1966.

———. "Factionalism and Union Democracy." *Labor Law Journal* 9 (1958): 635–40.

McDonald, Tom, and Peter Robson. *Unions 2001: A Blueprint for Trade Union Activism.* Sydney: Evatt Foundation, 1995.

Michels, Robert. *Political Parties.* New York: Collier Books, 1962.

Moldea, Dan E. *The Hoffa Wars: Teamsters, Rebels, Politicians, and the Mob.* New York: Paddington Press, 1978.

Mott, Jo-Ann, ed. *Not Your Father's Union: Inside the AFL-CIO.* New York: Verso Press, 1998.

Needlemen, Ruth. "Black Caucuses in Steel." *New Labor Forum* (fall–winter 1998): 41–56.

Newton, Lucy A., and Lynn McFarlane Shore. "Model of Union Membership: Instrumentality, Commitment, and Opposition." *Academy of Management Review* 17 (April 1992): 275–98.

Nissan, Bruce, ed. *Which Direction for Labor? Essays in Organizing, Outreach, and International Transformation.* Detroit: Wayne State University Press, 1998.

Nyden, Philip. *Steelworkers Rank-and-File: The Political Economy of a Union Reform Movement.* New York: Praeger Press, 1984.

Parker, Mike. "Appealing for Democracy." *New Labor Forum* (fall–winter 1998): 57–73.

Parker, Mike, and Martha Gruelle. *Democracy Is Power: Rebuilding Unions from the Bottom Up.* Detroit: Labor Notes Book, 1999.

Parry, G. *Political Elites.* London: George Allen and Unwin, 1969.

Perusek, Glenn. "Classical Political Sociology and Union Behavior." In *Trade Union Politics: American Unions and Economic Change, 1960s–1990s,* ed. Glenn Perusek and Kent Worcester, 57–76. Atlantic Highlands, N.J.: Humanities Press, 1995.

Pott, Steven. "The Chicago Teamsters' Strike of 1902: A Community Confronts the Beef Trust." *Labor History* 26, no. 2 (spring 1985): 250–67.

Pocock, J. G. A. "The Idea of Citizenship since Classical Times." In *Theorizing Citizenship,* ed. Ronald Beiner, 29–52. Albany: State University of New York Press, 1995.

Radcliff, Benjamin. "Organized Labor and Electoral Participation in American National Elections." *Journal of Labor Research* 22, no. 2 (spring 2001): 405–14.

Radcliff, Benjamin, and Patricia Davis. "Labor Organization and Electoral Participation in Industrial Democracies." *American Journal of Political Science Review* 44, no. 1 (January 2000): 132–41.

Romer, Sam. *The International Brotherhood of Teamsters.* New York: John Wiley, 1962.

Rothbaum, Melvin. *The Government of the Oil, Chemical, and Atomic Workers Union.* New York: John Wiley, 1962.

Schwartz, Arthur Z. "The Judicial Imperative—Court Intervention and the Protection of the Right to Vote in Unions: A Case Study of *Fight Back Committee v. Gallagher.*" *Hofstra Labor Law Journal* (spring 1987): 269–98.

Sciacchitano, Katherine. "Unions, Organizing, and Democracy." *Dissent* (spring 2000): 75–81.

Seidman, Joel Isaac. *The Brotherhood of Railroad Trainmen: The Internal Political Life of a National Union.* New York: John Wiley, 1962.

Shostak, Arthur. *Robust Unionism: Innovations in the Labor Movement.* Ithaca, N.Y.: ILR Press, 1991.

Sloan, Arthur. *Hoffa.* Cambridge, Mass.: MIT Press, 1991.

Sousa, David. "Organized Labor in the Electorate, 1960–1988." *Political Research Quarterly* 46 (December 1993): 741–58.

Spain, Daphne. *How Women Saved the City.* Minneapolis: University of Minnesota Press, 2001.

Spinney, Robert. *City of Big Shoulders: A History of Chicago.* DeKalb: Northern Illinois University Press, 2000.

Stepan-Norris, Judith. "The Making of Union Democracy." *Social Forces* 76, no. 2 (December 1997): 475–510.

Stepan-Norris, Judith, and Maurice Zeitlin. "Union Democracy, Radical Leadership, and the Hegemony of Capital." *American Sociological Review* 60, no. 6 (December 1995): 829–50.

———. "The Insurgent Origins of Union Democracy." In *Reexamining Democracy: Essays in Honor of Seymour Martin Lipset,* ed. Gary Marks and Larry Diamond, 250–73. London: Sage, 1992.

Strauss, George. "Union Democracy." In *The State of the Unions*, ed. George Strauss, Daniel Gallagher, and Jack Fiorito, 310–18. Madison, Wis.: Industrial Relations Research Association, 1991.

Summers, Clyde W., Joseph Rauh, and Herman Benson. *Union Democracy and Landrum-Griffin*. New York: Association for Union Democracy, 1986.

Taft, Philip. *Corruption and Racketeering in the Labor Movement*. ILR Bulletin 38. Ithaca, N.Y.: Cornell University Press, 1970.

Taft, Robert. *The Structure and Government of Labor Unions*. Cambridge, Mass.: Harvard University Press, 1954.

Tillman, Ray, and Michael Cummings, eds. *The Transformation of U.S. Unions: Voices, Visions, and Strategies from the Grassroots*. Boulder: Lynne Rienner, 1999.

Tussey, Jean Y., ed. *Eugene V. Debs Speaks*. New York: Pathfinder Press, 1970.

Ulman, Lloyd. *The Government of the Steelworkers*. New York: John Wiley, 1962.

Velie, Lester. *Labor USA*. New York: Harper Brothers, 1959.

Voss, Kim, and Rachel Sherman. "Breaking the Iron Law of Oligarchy: Union Revitalization in the American Labor Movement." *American Journal of Sociology* 106, no. 2 (September 2000): 303–49

Wallihan, Jim. *Union Government and Organization*. Washington, D.C.: Bureau of National Affairs, 1985.

Weinstein, Paul. "Racketeering and Labor: An Economic Analysis." *Industrial and Labor Relations Review* 19, no. 3 (1966): 402–13.

Zeller, F. C. Duke. *Devil's Pact: Inside the World of the Teamsters*. Secaucus, N.J.: Union Birch Lane Press, 1997.

Ziegler, Robert. *The CIO: 1935–1955*. Chapel Hill: University of North Carolina Press, 1995.

Index

Lightning Source UK Ltd.
Milton Keynes UK
UKHW011251050520
362554UK00010B/189

9 780875 805962